KU-721-854

DESIGN
FOR A
COMPLEX
WORLD

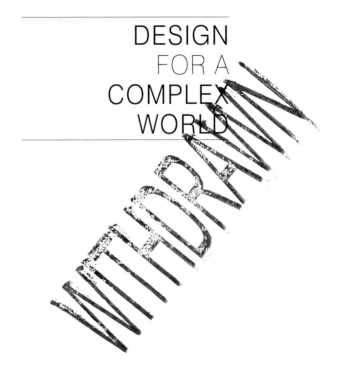

LIVERPOOL JMU LIBRARY

3 1111 01446 3507

DESIGN
FOR A
COMPLEX
WORLD

First published in 2014 by Libri Publishing

Copyright © Libri Publishing Ltd.

Authors retain the rights to individual chapters.

ISBN 978 1 907471 74 2

The right of Graham Cairns to be identified as the editor of this work has been asserted in accordance with the Copyright, Designs and Patents Act, 1988. All rights reserved. No part of this publication may be reproduced, stored in any retrieval system or transmitted in any form or by any means, electronic, mechanical, photocopying, recording or otherwise, without the prior written permission of the copyright holder for which application should be addressed in the first instance to the publishers. No liability shall be attached to the author, the copyright holder or the publishers for loss or damage of any nature suffered as a result of reliance on the reproduction of any of the contents of this publication or any errors or omissions in its contents.

The Principal Research Consultant on this book was Rachel Isaac-Menard. Additional support was provided by various members of the Information Services committee of the scholarly journal Architecture_MPS.

A CIP catalogue record for this book is available from The British Library

Book and cover design by Carnegie Publishing

Printed in the UK by CPI Books UK

Libri Publishing
Brunel House
Volunteer Way
Faringdon
Oxfordshire
SN7 7YR

Tel: +44 (0)845 873 3837

www.libripublishing.co.uk

CONTENTS

Rob MacDONALD

FOREWORD

Design for a Complex World concerns architecture and cities and takes a social and political perspective. As we engage with the twenty-first century, it concerns itself with the challenges we all face – global forces. To take a global view we need to address radical design, architecture, art and politics in diverse locations. This book does that through the cases of Australia, East Germany, the UK, the US, Mexico, Hong Kong, Finland, Central India, Greece and South Africa. These featured countries are of great contradiction, change and contrast.

In *Design for a Complex World* the construction of the built environment is sometimes viewed as a new vehicle for capitalist enclosure – not only of raw materials, resources, markets and ways of life, but also of cognitive forms of linguistic and analytic affective labour. By taking a global perspective the built environment is tied to the constant modulations of capitalism and global political forces. We have of course seen the development of world-wide counter cultures in response to these global forces, starting in revolutionary Paris in 1968 and in the West Coast USA of the 1970s and continuing up to the present day. From the utopian political ideals of these movements, economic determinations and disciplinary fetishes developed in response to seemingly irreconcilable social values, and an intellectual struggle to redefine architectural relationships with society ensued.

In that context, and in practice, the process of individual creativity was imbued with a certain utopian potential and intrinsic positive value and universal social dimensions. Today however, that 'creativity' is reduced to a caricature of aesthetic forms, expressionistic objects or sculpture – and is mobilised in the service of dominant power structures. The issues that concern us, however, are more than just aesthetic.

LIVERPOOL JOHN MOORES UNIVERSITY
LEARNING SERVICES

As the crisis of global environmental change unfolds we are becoming increasingly aware of the difficult and continuing historical legacy of indigenous societies in post-colonial regions such as Africa, Australia and India. Two hundred years after the height of the colonial age, we still struggle to understand the unique ecology and complex diverse cultures of these places.

Across the globe, many universities offer important avenues for exploring new models of urbanism and place-making which encompass local perspectives and knowledge in response to this. Architectural, urban and landscape design education is now perceived as a desirable activity for previously excluded indigenous populations. In line with social principles and based on local community studies, many projects have emerged in 'place-making'. As mentioned in this book, these involve anthropological 'deep listening', cultural mapping and 'ways of knowing and seeing'. Mapping and creative walking have become urban research methods based on these ideas and, in the Western tradition, call upon the Situationists and the dérive. There is a rediscovery of the importance of landscape and place-making that will be central to the future.

Of all the global phenomena covered in this book, the notion of 'the shrinking city' is the most socially, economically and politically challenging. Every sixth city in the world is thought to be shrinking, as in the case of Magdeburg, Halle and Dessau in East Germany covered in these pages. In the cities of the future we need to foster human welfare and more socially relevant architectural/urban design and planning. We need to develop new jobs of worth in a more global and meaningful way. We can contribute to this by focusing on issues of social justice such as low-cost housing, medical clinics and urban schools. There are many issues concerning deprived communities in which problems of space allocation and energy conservation are important factors. In addressing these issues, we need more global comparisons because architecture, landscape and urban planning are diverse disciplines that need collaborative design teams. Architectural design, for example, is no longer linear: it jumps and skips and involves human welfare, building users, occupants and public health.

From a landscape architecture perspective, cities can be seen as interlocking ecological systems. In a fragile world, global cities are influenced by climate change, technological change, diminishing resources, pollution, water quality, energy sources and population dynamics. In addition, some places, such as the Mexico City Region, have been subject to various forms of government and levels of external interference in domestic affairs – all having a dramatic effect on their architecture and urban environment. Understanding these extrinsic factors is essential, moving forward.

In the Pacific Rim, cities are expanding, progressing and urbanising at an unprescented rate. Such rapid growth has created a host of issues for architects and urban planners and their sustainable development cannot but involve government agencies and local communities. This can also be said to apply to South and Central India where, as this book points out, we find some of the world's most sophisticated historic cultures. Their monuments and buildings continue to be reinterpreted today and the design of their cities was not only celebrated but reflected the changing conditions of political and cultural forces. They still offer us lessons today.

In current political terms, South Africa is a young democracy that in 1994 saw its first fully democratic election, with the ANC coming into power. However, the vast majority of the population is still in poverty and living in townships with major issues of poor education. This is a major concern – and one addressed in this book that documents projects in Soweto that could be applied to other locations.

European and North American countries are not immune from issues and problems raised by current global social and economic structures. Athens, a city covered in this book, is presented as suffering from traffic deadlock, neglect, a deteriorating city centre, immigrant ghettos, the severing of the social fabric, the decomposition of the middle class, breaches of security and increasing homelessness. Addressing such issues will need various responses, amongst which we can count more flexible design studios, partnerships and bigger consortia. Increasingly, residents, public bodies, national architectural institutes and schools of architecture and urban planning will need to compile development plans to resolve such complex issues.

What can we learn from all these global sites of contradiction, for design education?

How should design education respond to the new economic conditions and changing realities of these places? The development of fee-paying schools and more independent institutions are taboo in many countries and are feared as potentially producing a market-oriented education. What will be needed is a broader interdisciplinary curriculum that includes the humanities, social and natural sciences, technology and the arts.

It is the general view that design education in the future should have a holistic approach and be diverse. It should aim to develop aesthetic and compositional ability with the acquisition of technical and design knowledge. In addition, combined courses in town and country planning, urban design, architecture, interior design, landscape and environmental design will be required. The most radical schools will include courses in sociology and psychology.

To be socially relevant, design education needs to engage with global community politics and urban regeneration. Ultimately, it needs to address questions of urban and rural poverty, immigration and homelessness. In the complex and integrated modern world it seems fair to ask: are these the real issues involved in **design for a complex world**?

Dr Robert MacDonald, RIBA, Reader in Architecture LJMU,
Emeritus President Liverpool Architectural Society,
WAN World Architecture News Judge, Author/Editor *DIY City*

INTRODUCTION

Design for a Complex World – Challenges in Practice and Education is a book conceived in the ever-widening realm of design practice and education. It is premised on the belief that the forces of globalisation that have affected design practice for decades have, in recent years, manifest themselves in design education as well. Despite this trend often being associated with the homogenisation of the built environment as per the argument of Saskia Sassen, this book offers a different perspective. Drawing on the notions of critical regionalism popularised through the writings of Kenneth Frampton, it seeks to illustrate how these general global forces have manifest themselves in different and distinct ways depending on specific regional contexts.

Consequently, it brings authors, practitioners and educators together from ten countries across six continents. They each offer an overview of the socio-cultural and economic factors that effect the built environment in their particular region of the world. They discuss how the practices of architecture, interior design, planning and landscape architecture interact with those forces but, equally as importantly, they discuss how design education does the same.

This book, then, is written by and for practitioners, educators and students of the built environment whose critical eye is prepared to scan the globe for lessons that are applicable both universally and specifically to their own geographical and discipline context. It is more specifically geared to those who see the built environment through a socio-political prism – as a phenomenon shaped by this broader non-design context – but also as a model through which we can better understand that external context.

It is thus a book that conflates the differences that often separate standard distinctions between practice and pedagogy on the one hand, and the activity of design and social reality on the other. In line with an analogy to critical regionalism, however, it does this in a particularly heterogeneous way. Each chapter takes its particular region of the world as its starting point. They seek to identify a particular social, economic, political or cultural set of issues that are of specific relevance in that region and then lay out their response to it.

These responses range from calls for changes to local, regional and national planning policy; the proposal of new methodologies for design pedagogy; arguments for the explicit politicisation of design practice; proposals for developing new design curricula; and suggestions on how to align cutting-edge technologies with traditional belief systems and knowledge forms. In each case, the authors offer critical appraisals of the current situation specific to their region but inevitably raise issues and questions that have global resonance. It is thus a book written in the age of global cities, but one that seeks to disseminate ideas from local regions.

DESIGN IN A SOCIO-POLITICAL WORLD – AN OVERVIEW

Design is a multifaceted subject. It ranges from the smallest manufactured objects to the planning of cities, regions and entire countries. In today's world it is not only local but, inevitably, global. It plays a key part in the development of the most intricate and technically complicated items and the barest and simplest hand-made implements. Its origins reach back millennia – to the moments when the first humans found and modified stones for the chopping or grinding of foodstuffs. It is all around us – in the clothes we wear, the cars we drive, the offices we work in and the houses we occupy. It improves lives and can, if done badly, ruin them.

Given this context, it is perhaps inevitable that it is a multi-disciplined field which includes product design, fashion, graphics, textiles and numerous other areas of endeavour. It has manifested itself in material disciplines such as interior design, architecture, landscape design and urban planning. However, its thought processes and schemata are at work in both the physical and non-physical realms – they are not only operative in the design of physical objects and spaces, but are fundamental to computer programming, time scheduling, transport policy, economic planning and military strategy, to name but a few of its more ethereal arenas. It is omnipresent.

Despite its manifest importance and influence, however, design is not a field that is universally accepted or understood. It is certainly not subject to any sort of consensus about how it operates or, indeed, how it should operate. The concepts and theories that have developed around it have been legion. For some, it is an abstract concept, for others a very real activity with specific and concrete effects. To some minds it borders on being an art, for others it is purely a question of function. In some eyes, it is an almost spiritual experience – for both the designer and the public that engage with the object designed.

Beyond this, some say it affects the heart. In other perspectives, however, it is purely cerebral – a question of the mind. According to alternative discourses it is about the body. It affects human health, well being and overall happiness. It is a complex, multifaceted and, at times, polemic field. In terms of its definition, contradiction is as common place as criticism and consensus is nothing but a chimera. It defies imposed distinctions.

The fluxus of this scenario applies not only to the world of design practice – in which the conceiving, planning and manufacture of objects and systems of all sorts directly and indirectly affects the lives of people – it is evident in the education of designers themselves. In this realm too, there are multiple competing ideas about what design 'is', should and could be. It is also a debate fractured into the physical and the functional, the spiritual and the mental, the conceptual and the 'real'.

Once more, the terrain of this specific debate is littered with contrasting arguments, polemical treatises, manifestos and explanations. It is another tapestry of conflict. There are those that focus on 'art for art's sake' and, by extension, 'education for the sake of education'. In this regard, the creative process of the young designer should not be stymied by questions of function or practicality – it should not be hampered by particular societal needs. Education is seen as having to be free of intellectual restraint and culturally imposed frameworks.

On the flip side, there is the view of education as vocational – as training and preparation. In the light shone by those of this ilk, education has to 'be real'. 'Live projects' become key, applicable knowledge becomes a God. The musings of the 'free thinkers' get interpreted as the whims of fantasists, and education embedded in the workplace becomes a framework without which nothing makes sense.

Running across the landscape found between these two poles are numerous other perspectives: education as social engagement, learning as spiritual understanding, teaching as nurturing activity. In the worst cases, it degenerates into indoctrination; in the best it becomes about the critical and active engagement of the young mind in the problems of the world around them. For some, the holding of the hand is a metaphor to be cherished whilst, for others, it is a habit to be discarded in a view of learning that seeks to break down conventions already imposed.

From within this menagerie of conflicting perspectives on our understanding of design and its education, this book draws together the strands of four perspectives. The first is *disciplinary*, the second *thematic*, the third is *practice* based, and the fourth is *pedagogical*. In terms of *discipline*, it focuses on the design of the built environment and thus deals primarily with landscape architecture, urban planning, architecture and interior design. However, it views these disciplines from a view point of social responsibility. It thus presents a *theme* that, in general terms, we may define as the socio-political.

From this dual perspective it intends to examine the role the *practice* of design plays in the world around us. Is it in part responsible for social problems, can it offer answers to political questions, or does it have to be an apolitical exercise operating on its own terms? This interest is specifically linked to questions of education and *pedagogy* that are framed in similar terms. Can the design curriculum help prepare designers capable of addressing societal issues, is it part of the problem – whatever that may be? Can it be, and should it be, deliberately apolitical – or explicitly political in focus and intent?

These questions are asked from a global perspective by drawing in authors from ten countries spread across the world. They each offer overviews of some of the broad socio-political and cultural factors that, in their particular region, are shaping design practice and the built environment – for better or for worse. They also ask how education is and should respond. The diverse contexts of each author inevitably raise and produce a diverse range of issues and ideas. However, their geographical diversity is only one of the things that distinguishes their work. Their particular sensibilities, knowledge areas and specific design disciplines all contribute to the wide range of overviews, proposals and opinions that their chapters offer.

The book begins in the United States with a chapter by Manuel Shvartzberg, 'The L.A. School – "Radical" Architecture between Art and Politics'. This text presents two opposed views of design and its education through the prism of two avant-garde design schools in the US: SCI-Arc and CalArts. Focusing on these two schools in the highly charged political environment and overly supplied consumer culture of 1970s California, Shvartzberg plays off a view of architectural practice and education that, on the one hand, viewed the intrusion of social thinking into the mindset of the designer as an anathema and, on the other, saw it as a bedrock – the designer's raison d'être.

His arguments draw on the work of the French philosopher and social critic Jacques Rancière; the German philosopher, sociologist and political theorist Herbert Marcuse; and the architects of the Los Angeles baby boomers: Robert Owen Moss, Thom Mayne and Frank Gehry, to name but a few. It is a chapter that contrasts architecture and its education as merely a part of the industry of cultural capital, with an ideal of architecture and its education as a form of political activism.

The second chapter is 'Designing Australia – Critical Engagement with Indigenous Place Making'. Its authors, Jefa Greenaway, Janet McGaw and Jillian Walliss, take on the politically delicate issue of aboriginal politics, identity and land rights. Offering an overview of colonial practices of land appropriation in the nineteenth century, they sketch out a view of the current social and political situation in which indigenous and 'settled' Australians are beginning, albeit tentatively, to garner some consensus – an agreement on how to design and understand the built environment of this ancient and, for the Aboriginal inhabitants, spiritually laden land.

The authors identify shifts at the political and institutional levels in Australia that are facilitating these reappraisals of the meaning and use of land and appropriate design practices for it. They highlight the establishment of the Aboriginal design unit by the

State Public Works department in New South Wales and the Institute for Indigenous Development at the University of Melbourne as examples. From this, they offer case studies for practice carried out at the University of Melbourne in which architecture students apply what the authors term 'creative research methods' intrinsically woven through with Aboriginal practices and ways of thinking.

The clearly socio-political perspective running through this chapter morphs in the following one by Mary Dellenbaugh and Andrea Haase: 'Designing in Shrinking Cities – The Case of Eastern Germany'. Focusing on the phenomenon of shrinking cities in the former East Germany, the authors set the framework for current practice and research-led education in this part of Europe with an overview of the effects of German reunification in the early 1990s – effects they suggest continue to resonate today. They focus on three case-study cities that they have examined through the prism of design projects: Magdeburg, Dessau & Halle. Through documenting student design projects run at the Applied University [Hochschule] Saxony-Anhalt, they propose a five-point framework for successful redevelopment in cities such as these.

In examining each of these cities the authors not only identify issues specific to these examples, they outline a number of general trends and factors that are of relevance in understanding the development of eastern German cities in the past three decades. In addition, however, they also underline a number of broader issues of importance to our more general comprehension of the shrinking city phenomenon in other potentially global contexts.

In Chapter 4 we return to the United States with a text written by Yelena McLane and Lisa Waxman from Florida State University. Entitled 'Designing for Good', their work calls for a reconsideration of project typology – from within and without the interior-design profession. Critical of the type of high-end commercial and private projects traditionally featured in glossy magazines or celebrity-led TV shows, they reframe interior design as a social practice.

Drawing on both primary and secondary sources and research, they set out arguments that are framed by the current financial situation in western economies. Highlighting the dichotomy between expectations of super-rich interiors and the reality of what most clients can afford today, they suggest a more sustainable – and socially responsible – future for interior-design practice. Integrating this research into their work as educators, they also describe how the preconceptions and eventual professional objectives of interior-design students can be reoriented in this direction through appropriate project-led pedagogy and training.

Chapter 5 returns to Europe and shifts disciplines once more. Examining the role landscape architecture practice and education can play in the future of the south east of England, Jeff Logsdon offers an explanation of what he calls a theory-to-practice methodology. Applicable to both practice and education, it is a holistic perspective on design that sees not only theory and practice as mutually influencing, but also practice and education.

This linkage of theory, practice and education becomes literal in Logsdon's text through an examination of Writtle School of Design and projects carried out on its Landscape Design Masters programme – an educational programme in which regional environmental issues, local-government policy, the surrounding city infrastructures and the school grounds themselves all entwine through design projects. Entitled 'Design Theory to Practice and the Design School Collective' this chapter also argues that the theory-to-practice ethos it expounds is one in which the local scale and the global issue come together. As such, its regionally focused arguments are seen as having implications that are universal.

A related focus on design methodology is evident in 'New Challenges for the Education of Architecture in Mexico', written by Joel Olivares Ruiz. In this text, the author outlines some issues of the general history of design trends in Mexico over the past three centuries, and describes the emergence of formalised architectural education. Suggesting that the current architectural educational system has numerous shortcomings that limit creativity, he expands on the problems this induces by arguing that a 'creative mind' is a necessary attribute for solving the very real and practical problems of Mexico's built environment today. In this regard, he reframes a conventional view of creativity as art practice and places it on the same terrain as engineering.

Through this placement of creativity in a more practical and problem-solving context, Joel Olivares Ruiz outlines the educational ethos of the Universidad Gestalt de Diseño in Xalapa, Mexico. This ethos is premised on arguments found in both psychology and design, and manifests itself through what he calls analytical and synthetic methods. These approaches to design thinking are explored in detail through what the tutors at the school define as an iconographic models methodology. Arguing, through both student projects and constructed buildings, that these approaches facilitate creative responses to practical issues, he concludes by suggesting that they are key if the next generation of designers in Mexico is to deal successfully with the problems facing the country's built environment.

The following chapter continues the more exclusively educational focus of this part of the book but turns its attention to Asia for the first time. Centred on Hong Kong, a city that has been at the heart of the Asian economy for decades and more, Puay-peng Ho of the Chinese University of Hong Kong identifies many issues of the utmost importance to established economic centres across the developed world. Drawing out Hong Kong's special relationship with China, he also focuses on issues of relevance to emerging economies and developing cities such as those found across the landscape of the Chinese mainland.

Of specific interest in this chapter, 'Walking the Tight Rope of Architectural Education in Hong Kong – Balancing Pedagogy and Practice', is how the educational system of Asia can, and has, responded to the issues of sustainability, urban population explosion and the preservation of architectural heritage. Outlining in detail the formula applied in the Chinese University of Hong Kong, the author suggests that, at times, practice and education become a mirror image of each other – the one responding to and informing the other. However, he also underlines the importance of experimentation in the educational context and leaves space for a view of education as a place for creative reinterpretations of standard solutions to the problems of the built environment in ways that should be unhindered by specific projects or conditions.

Following on from this, Helka-Liisa Hentilä from the University of Oulu moves right away from the densely populated environments of commercial cities and focuses her attention on land use and land-use planning in Finland's suburbs and rural communities. Outlining the peculiar demographic and geographic characteristics of Finland, she focuses on two issues: suburban sprawl and rural development. With regard to suburban sprawl, she gives an introduction to the emergence of Finland's suburbs and proposes the technique of complimentary building as an ameliorative planning measure.

In the context of rural development she centres on the possible opportunities and challenges facing planners in the region by linking the role of design to the emerging industries and economies of the country. Setting this context in a chapter entitled 'A Good Living Environment and Sustainable Communities as Goals – Challenges and Trends in Finnish Land-use Planning', she outlines student projects as a tool for developing the responses of practice. In these projects, the issues of suburban and rural development are addressed and an approach to design and planning applicable as a sort of model at national government level is proposed.

In Chapter 9, 'The Architectural Heritage of South and Central India – A Study of Environmental Design', authors Siddhartha Mukherjee, Sat Ghosh and Shreyas Panambur examine one very specific issue in the Indian context – sustainability. The projects they examine and lay out in detail represent a high-tech approach to the question of energy efficiency and resource appropriation in India that forms part of a government-led plan to turn the country into a world leader in environmental technologies by 2020. In this light, they reference a number of government and privately funded research and education programmes aimed at positioning Indian Universities at the forefront of these emerging industries.

Interestingly however, these authors also stress the use of low technologies and the lessons that can be learnt from the 'environmental heritage' of the architecture and planning systems of ancient Indian civilizations in the Indus Valley. Many of the projects they describe are examples of this dual approach towards contemporary technology and traditional eco construction and design, and underline a third argument in their text – the lessons to be learnt from an understanding of traditional cultural and religious beliefs. Stressing the contemporary relevance of these traditions, they suggest that as India continues to develop and its cities continue to grow, there is an ever more important role for traditional beliefs and ways of living – something they see now being accepted, and indeed reflected, by a growing interest in architectural heritage and preservation in India – both in practice and in education.

In the following chapter, authors Des Laubscher and Ingrid Leujes from South Africa offer a text entitled 'Design Intervention for Social Upliftment'. Directors of the innovative Greenside Design Centre in Johannesburg, these authors outline attempts they have made in their design school to integrate design education into a country-wide social agenda for improving the lives of people and communities in urban Johannesburg. Setting the scene by discussing the early initiatives of the post-apartheid government to promote design on the one hand, and ensure Higher Education engages socially on the other, they introduce their educational curriculum initiative: 10%.

10% represents a series of projects run across the Greenside Design Centre in which all staff and students engage in community projects for approximately four weeks – a time period that amounts to 10 per cent of the academic calendar. They outline one particular project in detail and, by explaining this scheme, give a clear indication of how education can respond to the socio-political needs and requirements of contemporary South Africa. Indeed, they identify how design education and design practice become one. Their inspirational projects illustrate a power of design as a social and economic driver in one of the more disadvantaged and politically fraught areas of the world.

The final chapter of the book picks up the more overtly political implications found in the previous chapter and, in a sense, returns to the beginning of the book through an explicit call for an active political role for design and education. In this case, it is done through the prism of urban design at the National Technical University of Athens in a text entitled 'Economic Crisis and Reform – Consequences in Planning, Architectural Practice and Education'. Authors Georgios Karatzas and Nikos Belavilas describe the process of neoliberal deregulation that the Greek planning system has been through in the past 10 to 20 years. Highly critical of the effects of this process on the social fabric of the city, they suggest that the political forces that pushed Greece down the neoliberal road are, today, evident in the arena of education and its funding.

Connecting the worlds of practice and education through the prism of neoliberal economic pressures, the authors of this final chapter outline how both educators and some practitioners have 'resisted' commercial forces – forces that they argue have, in some cases, threatened the sustainability of both the educational model of the country and some of the city's most impoverished residential areas. Using a combination of real examples and student projects, they argue for more state involvement in the preservation and socially beneficial development of the city fabric of the Greek capital.

As with the other chapters in this book then, what this final chapter offers is an essay focusing on the built environment that centres our attention on a pressing issue in its specific geographical location. In addition, it does so through examples of both practice and education. In this regard, it is typical of this book whose primary goal may be defined as an examination of the socio-political context in which the design of the built environment occurs in today's ever more globalised and connected world.

However, these essays do more than outline a passive response from design to the socio-political and cultural context in which it functions globally today. In many cases, they offer very specific arguments for how design can actively and positively work with or, when necessary, counter these trends and forces. As such, some of them operate as calls to action. These 'calls' are not only made in the context of practice, they are also made in the context of education and, as such, they oblige us to consider the training of the next generation of designers – they oblige us to consider the future of design in socio-political terms.

Manuel SHVARTZBERG

CHAPTER 1

THE L.A. SCHOOL – 'RADICAL' ARCHITECTURE BETWEEN ART AND POLITICS

Originally a self-proclaimed rarefied collection of outsiders, the architects of the 'L.A. School' have long synthesised their focus on an 'artistic' process into a fully professionalised and superbly managed profit machine.[1] This apparent shift from the margin to the centre is not just the personal victory of Los Angeles's global architects like Morphosis or Frank Gehry (whose concept of the 'Organisation of the Artist' so well emblematises the condition[2]), but is more broadly symptomatic of the centrality of so-called 'cultural capital' in contemporary 'cognitive capitalism' whereby *immaterial* productive processes such as design work or creativity have become highly prized commodities in themselves.[3]

Today, a certain kind of 'radicality', metonymical with the dominant global economic discourse – creativity, innovation, progress, understood in strictly free-market terms – has become hegemonic. As Eric Owen Moss, director of the L.A. School's *alma mater*, the Southern California Institute of Architecture's SCI-Arc since 2002, candidly put it: 'Go to Shanghai or any other world city: we won.'[4] This means that the radically aesthetic impulse originally championed by the L.A. School – as 1970s *L.A. Times* architecture critic John Dreyfuss put it, 'architecture as an art form'[5] – has become a new vehicle for capitalist enclosure not only of raw materials, resources, markets, and ways of life, but of cognitive forms of labour – affective, linguistic and analytic. To a

Figure 1: The Walt Disney Concert Hall, by Frank O. Gehry. Photograph by Carol M. Highsmith

certain degree, this is inevitable due to architecture's status as a service profession that is therefore intrinsically tied to the constant modulations of capitalism and global political forces, and in this sense it is unsurprising that 'creativity', reduced to the caricature of über-aestheticised forms – what some call radically expressionistic or sculptural architecture – is mobilised in the service of dominant power structures.[6] But the emergence of a (self-proclaimed) avant-garde with an explicitly de-politicised, if not directly anti-political, agenda for architecture is an intriguing twist of history given the highly politicised milieu in which it was born – California's countercultural movements of the 1960s and '70s. Why was the L.A. School so estranged from architecture's political questions, and how does that legacy play out today in practice and pedagogy?

A Brief History of American Architectural Counterculture

In the 1970s, the American architectural avant-gardes were undergoing a moment of redefinition after the crumbling of the modernist canons. The rise of postmodernist sensibilities, together with the pervasive economic instabilities of the 1970s, challenged modernist assumptions of progress and modern architecture's social and political 'universal mission'. In post-war Southern California, architects were instrumental in developing and marketing the vision for a specific type of American modernism: the dream of a hyper-consumerist way of life which was intimately tied to the post-war baby boom, the myth of California as the quintessential place for individual self-realisation, and the perception of America's 'golden age of prosperity' in the context of the ideological battle of the Cold War.[7] In reaction to this technocratically institutionalised semblance of stability,[8] the 1960s social and political upheavals (including the Berkeley Free Speech Movements, the L.A. riots in 1965, civil rights, anti-war, ecological and Feminist protests, and the rise of a general countercultural sensibility) thoroughly destabilised that vision. The consequences of these social, cultural and political turbulences were also dramatic for architectural practice and academia. Schools, universities, museums and leading institutions across America, infected by the anti-bureaucratic, de-structuring ethos of progressive students and cultural elites, began to challenge the very foundations of what, until that moment, had been the unquestionable tenets of architecture under the rubrics of modernism.[9]

With the 1960s' eclectic blend of anti-consumerist and ecological consciousness, psychic liberation and anti-authoritarianism, architecture became impregnated with (and helped to propel) many different discourses, each with their own contrasting methods and values. In one direction, design became associated and broadened with 'environmentalism', a current itself diversely imbibed with distinct forms of 'holistic' thinking: from narratives and practices as disparate as Eastern philosophies, psychotropic drug use or psycho-social liberation, to cybernetic, systems, information and communication theories. In another direction, parallel to the environmentalist currents, design was addressed structurally and semantically as pure deconstructed text, sign, aesthetic event or particularity.

In the wake of these momentous ruptures in the cultural fabric of architecture – emblematised in the epochal publications of, on the one hand, the *Whole Earth Catalogue* (Stuart Brand, 1969–1972) and, on the other, *Complexity and Contradiction in Architecture* (Robert Venturi, 1966) – design underwent a critical redefinition with huge consequences for discussions and values of technology, art/creativity and politics. Just a few years earlier, John Entenza's *Arts and Architecture* magazine's 'Case Study House' projects in Southern California had captured the design establishment's imagination (as well as the popular media's) with their utopian use of industrialised technology (i.e. the Eames house as a universal kit-of-parts providing infinite variability within rationalised repetition).[10] Now there emerged a conception of architecture based on post-industrial paradigms of 'network' thinking, 'artistic' (expressive) individualism or ecological culture, which dispersed the until-then hegemonic modernist notions of elitist professionalism, the centrality of the design object, and medium-specific boundaries between disciplines. [11] In this context, diverse understandings of architecture as well as new political configurations took shape and became instrumentalised in a number of ways – not least in the emerging discourses of post-modernity and post-industrial society themselves.

The founding of different design schools in the early 1970s in Los Angeles is a crucial aspect of this discursive battlefield mobilised around multiple political and

Figure 2: Students of the New School, currently the Southern California Institute of Architecture (SCI-Arc), on 12 December 1972. © SCI-Arc

cultural vectors competing to fill the rhetorical vacuum of architecture at the end of modernism. From utopian political ideals to pragmatic economic determinations, from disciplinary fetishes to irreconcilable social values, an intellectual struggle to redefine architecture's relationship with society ensued. As such, new schools such as SCI-Arc may be seen as prototypical case studies of pedagogies articulating different, and often contradictory, aesthetico-political theories and values.[12]

According to founder Ray Kappe, SCI-Arc was born in 1972 as a school 'that offered a new alternative, a very different alternative, than some of the other educational facilities within the Los Angeles area.'[13] Ray Kappe was an avowed modernist with an interest in architecture's political and social responsibility, but also an open-minded administrator who encouraged plurality and eclecticism – with many of the nascent L.A. School 'stars' among the faculty.[14] Thus, during Kappe's tenure as director, SCI-Arc remained in dialogue (however ambivalently) with social questions. As Kappe noted in early SCI-Arc conversations:

> six years ago, or seven years ago... we were very much involved at that time in issues of housing, transportation, grey areas, that whole thing. And of course, the

social aspects were particularly key at that time, how does one solve housing, and social needs, and all these problems, for minority groups throughout the city and all the problems that were going on, and so forth. Through the last six years of dealing with that in the office we found that it has become more and more difficult to get into that whole area. So gradually, one starts to wonder what is the role in the city of Los Angeles, particularly as an architect–planner; what role can you play, what can you do, what can you do in terms of the political process, what can you do in terms of the transportation systems, mass-transit nets, and so forth. And now I feel less able to grab hold of those issues than I once felt about it. Again, I think the architect has to be out there, concerned, but I'm not sure we can make the inroads that we think should be made. ... I've come to the point of accepting what *is*, and dealing within the terms of what *is*.[15]

Throughout the 1970s, Kappe continued to refer to this intellectual tension regarding architecture's relation to society: a discourse marked by a deep ambivalence between the poles of pragmatism (accepting the realities of the market) and modernist idealism (striving for a socially responsible practice).[16] But by the 1980s, however, SCI-Arc's new director (Morphosis co-founder Michael Rotondi) effected a 'house cleaning' to get rid of 'some of the social thinkers' at the school.[17] The L.A. School's radical agenda of aesthetics *without* politics, today hegemonic in terms of 'global' architecture's alliance with dominant power structures, was by this point officially institutionalised.

Despite its avant-gardish rhetoric, the L.A. School's idea of radicality was always predicated on a rather classical notion of 'the aesthetic.' Referred to as a sphere of individual play for the free engagement with form and sensual experience, the L.A. School's notions of aesthetics connected with eighteenth-century – Enlightenment, modernist – discourses of art, such as that of Friedrich Schiller in his *Letters Upon the Aesthetic Education of Man* (1794). In this work, Schiller attempted to reconcile the French Revolution's high ideals and his disenchantment with its dramatic episodes of violence, posing that an aesthetic education involving creative contemplation (the withdrawal from political and other constraints) might have a civilising effect by forming more discerning individuals and thus potentially leading to the making of a better world. Schiller's idea of the aesthetic – in practice, the process of individual creativity – is imbued with a certain utopian potential, an intrinsically positive value and universal social dimension, at the same time as enshrining creativity within the tradition of Western liberal individualism.[18]

The L.A. School replicated this idea of the aesthetic in its privileging of individual free play with form, materials and sensuality, but purged it of any kind of political signification beyond the reification of liberal individualism. As architect Thom Mayne has noted, his development of an 'artistic' approach involved the marginalisation of larger social issues, such as one encounters in urbanism: 'I soon realised policy and planning were not going to work for me... I needed more tangible resolution.'[19] And in similar fashion, Frank O. Gehry also abandoned the murky arenas of spatial politics early on in his career: 'I went to city planning school at Harvard and I discovered that you never got to change a fucking thing or do anything. Urban planning is dead in the US.'[20]

As a result of this privileging of form, sensuality and expression, galvanised by Southern California's care-free, frontier and outsider *mythos*, today's architectural radicality – that one boldly professed at SCI-Arc – projects an idea of the architect as a part-artist, part-techno-inventor; an image widely identified in the media with Gehry as an 'architect–sculptor' who is able to deliver fantastical structures thanks to his artistic genius and the creative utilisation of the latest digital design and fabrication technology. [21] This type of radicality thus effects two separate but inter-related types of fetishisation that together displace social and political questions from architectural discourse: 'Art' and 'technology', understood as tools for handling materiality and moulding sensual experience (*not* political or social relations), become the unique focus of architectural education. The most radical and 'free' creativity, plugged into by techno-artistic architects, develops new products, new fabrication processes and new visuals worthy of the most entertaining TED talks. But, as architectural critic Reinhold Martin says:

> little, if anything, is actually being produced that is new. Instead, in perfect postmodern acquiescence, too much of the rhetoric surrounding the new machines, new forms of teamwork, and new professional arrangements misrecognizes reproduction for production. That is, rather than producing a new, postconsumerist world inaccessible within the horizon of our television screens... these arrangements seem all too often dedicated to reproducing the world as it already exists: a world inhabited by consumer–subjects who imagine themselves as mass-customized 'persons' on a parametric sliding scale, each thinking (or really, not thinking) a little differently.[22]

Martin cautions on the loss, or seizure, of political subjectivity by the paradigms of new (re)productive and creative processes in architecture.[23] In contrast with this critical view of contemporary architectural techno-invention, Eric Moss explicitly rejects the question of political subjectivisation in architectural education, claiming that SCI-Arc's pedagogy is based exclusively on 'creating the conditions for individuality', where idiosyncratic, personal talent may thrive, because 'you can't make great designers, just let them emerge' – a limited, if not cynical, view of aesthetic education in relation to architecture's wider social and political stakes. Still anchored around the ideals of the 1970s L.A. School, SCI-Arc's pedagogy tends to approach design as a hyperindividual, purely formalistic, pursuit – an avowedly anti-political perspective that echoes neoconservative opinions on history and society. As Moss affirms: '*Individuals* make history, *not ideas*.'

This problematic stance was recently dramatised through a polemic between SCI-Arc and French 'radical' architect, Francois Roche, who accused the school of a 'lack of interest for politics and attitude'[24] wherein '[t]he interest of the school in scripting, computation and tooling is purely for the purpose of one end goal: cool-looking shit.'[25] Writing in defence of the school and also as a rhetorical counter-attack, Archigram founder and frequent SCI-Arc collaborator Peter Cook rebutted:

Figure 3: © '1979 Frankenboyz', L.A. School architects in Venice, L-R, Fred Fisher, Robert Mangurian, Eric Moss, Coy Howard, Craig Hodgetts, Thom Mayne, Frank Gehry (© Ave Pildas)

Figure 4: Frank Gehry's seminal Santa Monica house (1978) (© IK's World Trip)

'[L]ack of interest for politics and attitudes.' Now where do I remember hearing such phrases? Surely around 1968, when the young sparks of French architecture would march and shout plenty of politics and attitude, and insist on 'reform'. But what followed was 20 years in which those same revolutionaries bedded themselves surprisingly comfortably with Paris's fat-cat developers, and many of them became the most narrow-minded generation of inept professors that Europe has ever known. … The trouble is that the polemic, and this curious Gallic insistence on politics, gets to be a bore. … Maybe [SCI-Arc is] low on rhetoric, but – hey – it's certainly high on 'stuff'.[26]

Cook thus acknowledged and defended an anti-political stance, at the same time as painting any kind of political ambitions for architecture as 'boring', debased and hypocritical – employing a generic critique of May 1968's aftermath to de-legitimise any kind of political questioning in architectural discourse whatsoever.

Architecture and 'the Political'

But how, in fact, are we to understand 'the political' in architecture? The L.A. School's general ideology and pedagogy enshrines a hyper-individualistic *ethos* even more radical than classical liberalism's belief in the primacy of individual self-interest as the motor of society.[27] As such, it is consistent with neoliberal discourses of de-regulation and privatisation, while also, as illustrated by Cook, purging the discipline of any kind of political dissent in the name of a disingenuous or cynical reality principle.

French philosopher Jacques Rancière refers to this state of affairs as a kind of enforced 'consensus' that is the opposite of democracy – the reification and fortification of an order rather than a plural, polemic and indeterminate 'space of appearance'.[28] According to Rancière, there is not always (democratic) politics, even though there are always power relations and prescriptive forms of social administration – what Rancière calls 'the police'. Democracy is rather understood as the particular instance where the consensus 'police' system is disturbed by the spontaneous appearance of previously unaccounted subjects enacting principles of equality: what Rancière defines as processes of subjectivisation or dis-identification. These demonstrations of equality (i.e. the performative denouncement of a wrong within a normative order, such as marginalised 'workers', 'women' or 'slaves' directly acting as actual 'citizens') cause ruptures in the police order and effectively reconfigure the 'distribution of the sensible'. As a result, they materially and cognitively re-map the nature, roles, places and positions of subjects within a social system.[29] It is this performative re-mapping that makes processes of subjectivisation political, and not essentialised notions of 'man', 'citizen', 'community' or equality itself.[30]

The L.A. School's essentialisation of aesthetics in terms of individualism, creativity and technology is a very different *appearance of radicality* – a 'coolness' fetish – than Rancière's theories on the *radicality of appearance* – aesthetic ruptures in the socio-political fabric. SCI-Arc's appearance of radicality obscures the implicit ideology of a pedagogy that overdetermines and disenfranchises architecture of democratic potential through its alignment with the neoliberal technocratic consensus, which is presented by its proponents as the only possible political model in which to think space and architectural education. So while the L.A. School promotes an architecture predicated on 'infinite' aesthetic variability (in the digital–expressive–formal sense), the discussion surrounding architectural pedagogy and practice is in fact circumscribed to a single political, social and economic framework – the dominant status quo.[31]

This fusion of an ideological representation of reality with reality itself – the lack of a gap which defines a lack of critical distance – has been epitomised by critic Mark Fisher as a form 'capitalist realism'.[32] Rancière also characterises the totality of a vision which collapses representation onto itself as one of the singular attributes of 'consensus'. According to Rancière, '[r]ealism claims to be that sane attitude of mind that sticks to observable realities. It is in fact something quite different: it is the police logic of order, which asserts, in all circumstances, that it is only doing the only thing possible to do'. [33] In such a regime of total accountability and total visibility – the perennial fantasy of positivism – 'the people' are 'entirely caught in a structure of the visible where everything is on show and where there is thus no longer any place for appearance.'[34]

Rancière argues that the substitution of the public sphere by a technocratic regime of total visibility is governed by representation itself. Thus, the shrinking of the public sphere (and with it, the disappearance of the space of appearance) resulting from its privatisation is the replacement of political stages by intermediaries (i.e. representatives) who claim to speak on behalf of 'reality' – this being the interpretation of the social as a purely economic affair, guided by the principle of the free market and thus governed by the dominant institutional complex. This logic of privatisation and managerialism/expertism (which, for Rancière, is nothing but a contemporary form of aristocracy) impregnates all discourses and materialisations of society, policing the political itself by domesticating and recuperating conflict to the acceptable forms of consensus.[35]

The ideal neoliberal city is precisely this: an aggregation of private interests where space is privatised for the chief enjoyment and protection of the oligarchic or aristocratic few. The proliferation of gated communities, shopping malls, privatised leisure spaces, all manner of prisons, and the denial of basic public services linked to the city (housing, transport, schools, etc.), is correlative to the shrinking of the public sphere as the space of appearance where conflicts may be staged. Neoliberal discourses often employ the language of 'urbanisation' instead of 'the city', as if to prevent public discourse around space as an object of common concern.[36] Urbanisation replaces the critical negativity of the city – a space of diversity and equality, of conflict and potential – with the instrumental logic of capital surplus opportunity, when not with outright ethnic or class discriminations. Thus, the public sphere of the city is reduced to either 'police' infrastructure or productive capital machine.

As social geographer David Harvey has persuasively argued, the city should be one of the first sites of political struggle. Harvey identifies an integral connection between capital surplus and urbanisation, a relation which under capitalism's logic generates and accentuates dispossession and inequality, at the same time as turning quality of urban life into a commodity and an agent of social exclusion. In Harvey's words:

> This is a world in which the neoliberal ethic of intense possessive individualism, and its cognate of political withdrawal from collective forms of action, becomes the template for human socialisation. ... The results are indelibly etched on the spatial forms of our cities, which increasingly consist of fortified fragments, gated communities and privatised public spaces kept under constant surveillance.[37]

Thus, cities are privatised and become prime instruments in the exacerbation of inequalities. This privatisation is a direct result of the shrinking of the public sphere, whereby the space of appearance of the political disappears. Architecture, as a social 'technology', is one of the instruments used in this re-presentation of the city as sheer urbanisation. The professionalisation of architecture in the terms traditionally professed by the L.A. School accentuates this condition, as it fundamentally de-politicises the thinking and practice of city-making, purging the activity from its political content by regimenting subjects to conform with the status quo's demand for spectacularised buildings under the guise of a 'radical' aesthetic.

In this situation, which we could describe as an 'architectural pornography' totalising collective imagination and desire,[38] the very idea of an architectural egalitarianism is almost by definition an experimental and transgressive vector towards democracy. But this type of imagination is contained *from within* (as in Cook's anti-political remarks) by expertist, 'artistic' and managerial ways of thinking which anaesthetise architecture as a potentially democratic tool; a condition that is naturalised by an elitist architectural discourse denying the city its fundamentally polyphonic and agonistic character – flattening it out from its potential as political site. The political, as event of rupture, is hindered and contained in the architect's established mode of agency through contracts, laws, regulations, or in the refuge of 'pure aesthetics', inhibiting the emergence of public, collective and experimental forms of practice and ways of thinking that may have the potential to constitute new political subjectivities in non-policed public spaces. Cook's anti-political remarks perform this police function, which more broadly through *professionalisation* – from standardised pedagogies to protectionist trade bodies – effectively impede political subjectivisation by ensuring that no other form of practice appears or is recognised outside its sanctioned topographies of action. Following Rancière:

> The police is thus first an order of bodies that defines the allocation of ways of doing, ways of being, and ways of saying, and sees that those bodies are assigned by name of a particular place and task; it is an order of the visible and of the sayable that sees that a particular activity is visible and another is not, that this speech is understood as discourse and another as noise. It is police law, for example, that traditionally turns the workplace into a private space not regulated by the ways of seeing and saying proper to what is called the public domain, where the worker's *having a part* is strictly defined by the remuneration of his work. Policing is not so much the 'disciplining' of bodies as

a rule governing their appearing, a configuration of *occupations* and the properties of spaces where these occupations are distributed.[39]

Developing intervals of architectural subjectivisation (the social meaning and consequences of architecture as an *occupation*, a particular identity) through platforms like education is thus where the political meets the discipline of architecture. In other words, the relation between architecture and politics involves designing and understanding *processes of subjectivisation*, rather than simply material forms or organisational paradigms. In this sense, the L.A. School's foundational neglect of politics (its reclusion within the purely 'aesthetic' since the 1970s) could be read as a form of either political naiveté or sheer cynicism normalising the political, social and economic status quo.

Ironically, as noted earlier, the philosophical (and perhaps also institutional) freedom the L.A. School was initially afforded to focus on architecture's 'artistic' dimensions came about through a highly politicised historical context.[40] And in fact, other emerging architecture schools in Los Angeles at that time, such as the California Institute of the Arts' (CalArts) School of Design (opened 1970), were explicitly involved in developing a political agenda for design. Inspired by critical theorist Herbert Marcuse's rhetoric of the 'Great Refusal' towards all capitalist forms and relations,[41] CalArts's attempt to institutionalise an explicitly political type of radicality, however, eventually proved too coarse and utopian – too ideological – within the *realpolitik* of a school governed by an ultra-conservative showbiz family – the Disneys. Eventually, the efforts of CalArts Design School's radical founders vaporised with the cancellation of the program in 1975, as they failed to arrive at an institutional pact with the school's conservative funders and trustees.[42]

By contrast, SCI-Arc was founded by architects and remains architect-run, if today many non-architects as well as seminal L.A. School figures sit on the board of trustees, in what constitutes a veritable power diagram of the agents shaping contemporary Los Angeles.[43] It is this realisation that SCI-Arc has *de facto* opened up – if still rather cynically – to its own socio-economic context that disjoints Cook's argument for an anti-political exceptionalism in contemporary architectural education.[44]

Caught between these two kinds of 'radicality', one purely aesthetic (the cynical and disenchanted politics of the early L.A. School) and the other politically deterministic (the Great – self-destructive – Refusal of CalArts' Design School), the legacy of 1970s Los Angeles experimental architecture continues to haunt contemporary practice and pedagogy.[45] As architectural historian Felicity D. Scott put it, reflecting on the period's influence and meaning for us today:

> How can the discipline not only figure a moment of assimilation to or withdrawal from the forces of late capitalism – whether they be economic, administrative, social, or informatic – but also take account of those contingencies in a manner that is less cynical than contestatory? What space is there, in other words, for political work?[46]

Architecture and Contemporary Aesthetic Discourses – Towards a New L.A. School?

The idea of architectural 'radicality' seen in the context of the L.A. School reveals not a universal object or condition to be attained, but rather very particular, and very heterogeneous, historical processes of subjectivisation mobilised in its name. Even when reified as immaterial processes rather than products (such as in contemporary architecture's fascination with CAD/CAM techniques and 'new' paradigms of production), 'radicality' effects a symbolic totalisation in the subjects upholding it, becoming a transcendental, legitimating source from which practices, codes and visualities are judged. The corollary is that a totalising mode of subjectivity is produced: chiefly the self-mastered, sovereign, heroic, artistic or technological individual 'genius'; whereby a more problematised subjectivity in which other collective, diverse, critical, contradictory, empathetic and contingent processes of (re-)subjectivisation are suppressed.

This is what the recuperation of radicality (and any other interested fetishisation of the 'avant-garde') entails: its domestication, commodification and instrumentalisation; not only of its products, processes and images, but of a heroicised mode of hyper-individualistic subjectivity that tends to atomise and isolate rather than generate critical linkages with the world at large. What we need, then, is a turn from an external radicality totalising subjectivity, to an internal one disrupting its own foundations – in other words, a practice that focuses on their inextricable and multiple relations.[47]

The continuously mystified redemptive qualities of art and technology amount to a theological technocratisation of politics – its replacement by 'automatic' (mystic or deterministic) processes of control and execution, rather than the uncertainty and unpredictability characteristic of democratic politics.[48] In this way, a too-narrow focus on instrumental skills in architectural pedagogy – a blinding obsession with their acquisition, management, perfectibility, especially when couched in the language of radical experimentation – evacuates the potentiality implicit in processes of subjectivisation that may lead to other political realities.

Interestingly in regards to the L.A. School's historical insistence on 'artistic' architectural processes, certain contemporary aesthetic discourses engage these issues from a more critical, experimental and explicitly political point of view – a very different idea of 'aesthetics' than the one promulgated by Southern California's dominant architectural avant-garde. These different avenues of inquiry for architecture's relation to the aesthetic and the political may give us an opportunity to re-think the discipline along other principles and thus towards a new 'radicality' – one that does not systematically eschew the social, political and ethical questions of any aesthetic endeavour.

If the original L.A. School was inspired by the informality and methodological freedom of Venice's (California) art community of the 1960s and '70s – their modernist will to be irreverent with tradition and to play with forms and codes, a 'game of self-consciously organised tat', as Cook put it[49] – many other L.A. artists since that time have worked with a very different idea of aesthetics: not necessarily making 'political art', but

Figure 5: Suzanne Lacy, Three Weeks in May (1977)

Figure 6: Michael Asher's exhibition at Claire Copley Gallery (1974)

rather 'making art politically'. While Gehry was inspired by Los Angeles's 'freeways, the industrial aesthetic, cheap not precious materials, quick turn-over, fast food syndrome, throw-away, instant architecture',[50] and explicitly aimed at reflecting this urban condition rather than changing it,[51] a wide range of contemporary artists, critics and cultural producers working in the Los Angeles area today have a less-naturalistic understanding of art. And crucially, many of these practitioners locate politics and pedagogy squarely *within* their aesthetic project, rather than as ancillary interests.[52] The result is a broad output of aesthetic experimentation that involves engaging the world through modes of seeing, learning and speaking – that is, focusing on intervals of subjectivisation – the key between aesthetics and politics.

In other words, the L.A. School, originally inspired by the minimalist, phenomenological (Light and Space), and pop art of Ed Ruscha, Robert Irwin, Larry Bell, James Turrell[53] and many others, would have probably followed a very different path if it had taken inspiration from other Southern California artists developing critical practices in the 1970s. An alternative L.A. School genealogy (in fact, the one influencing a number of critical artists today) would have to consider other L.A. artists who in fact developed their practices through urban and architectural space to understand, engage and deconstruct institutions and entrenched behaviours. Among them, Michael Asher was erasing the walls between exhibition and sales spaces in art galleries, Suzanne Lacy was mapping and exposing the horrors of rape in a quasi-militarised city, Asco were denouncing the racially coded, exclusionary effects of modernist city planning and the media through collective urban performances, and John Baldessari was taking art out of the privatised creative realm with his 'post-studio' conceptualism. These artists, and many others, developed aesthetico-pedagogical projects which were inextricable from their socio-political context and which were also, importantly for architects, all predicated on using and re-interpreting 'space' differently.[54]

All these practices engaged, to different degrees, an idea of art that was non-object based ('de-materialised', as critic Lucy R. Lippard would famously write[55]) and intrinsically political (in their generating new intervals of subjectivisation) rather than merely sensual or semantic. They didn't just develop instrumental forms of inter-disciplinarity,[56] but nurtured an art culture that had positive elements of indistinction with activism, social movements and experimental, contingent models of collectivity. In this, they opposed the dominant (neo)liberal individualism upheld by the L.A. School, and opened the idea of art (and aesthetics) to more nuanced or problematised forms of authorship, participation and collaboration.[57]

Since then, one can trace the massive influence these early experimental practices have had at a variety of scales in the art world. Globally, it can be seen in the rubrics of 'relational' and 'dialogical' aesthetics that have exerted a considerable pressure in the last ten years of contemporary art discourses.[58] It is also evident in a 'pedagogical turn' that has mobilised ideas of art, education and politics.[59] Furthermore, in the context of Southern California, it is manifest in the way that the legacy of the 1970s is constantly being engaged, negotiated and expanded, in the highly influential work

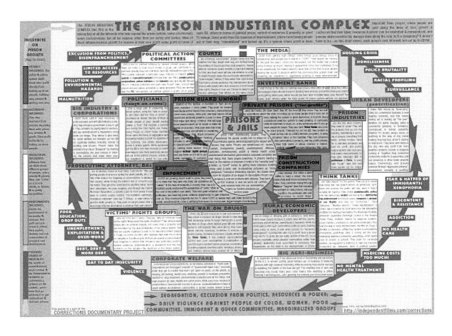

Figure 7: Ashley Hunt. *Prison Map 1*, from the Popular Education Poster Series (ca. 2003)

Figure 8: *Real Estate As Art: New Architecture in Venice* (1984), with works by the 'LA School'. Courtesy of the Sewell Archive, tomsewell. com

of a number of contemporary artists, critics and designers.[60] In other words, there is another kind of L.A. School developing a critical 'architecture as an art form', and engaging another kind of aesthetic discourse than the one upheld by the established architectural avant-garde of Gehry, Morphosis, Moss and their younger followers.

Far from the golden cage of aesthetics without politics, the architecture profession needs to re-address its critical engagement with the aesthetics of space *including* issues of urban social justice, rights, accessibility, ecology, the war economy, political representation, inequality, fair collaborative modes of working, post-humanism, and other discourses mobilising the aesthetic in an intrinsically political way.[61] The challenge for a renewed L.A. School (and any school) today and in the future is how, through pedagogy and practice, to address these questions as an integral part of the definitions of architectural quality, innovation, progress or *radicality*, and not in spite of them.

As has been argued here, it is not enough to declare 'real estate as architecture as an art form' like the L.A. School so enthusiastically did with their gentrification of Venice in the roaring 1980s.[62] The challenge is no longer how to generate a cultural opening for the free-form exploration of space, tools and materials – no matter how 'everyday', 'high-tech' or simply 'cool' they may be – as this today is already the language of an oppressive radical neoliberal establishment. The challenge today is how architects should engage with processes like gentrification, which are at once aesthetic and political. The challenge is how to engage political subjectivisation *within* technological advances blurring and reconfiguring the once-distinctive lines between disciplines, work and leisure; such as those implicit in BIM (Building Information Modelling) and novel procurement practices.[63]

If the original L.A. School managed to institutionalise architecture as a particular kind of 'art', today we need to critically re-engage with contemporary artists' and activists' developments of new modes of authorship – moving away from the master-artist/ architect predicated by the L.A. School (a model which was, as Cook recognised, fully continuing 'the inheritance from the École des Beaux-Arts'[64]) and into modes of production centred on the egalitarian contestation of social wrongs and modes of collective or common ownership and organisation.

Increased capabilities, whether through new digital design and fabrication technologies or through a renewed interest in collaborative paradigms of production, can, as Mayne recently noted, 'radically expand the nature of tasks that we can undertake'.[65] However, it is important to ask what we mean by this expanded 'nature of tasks' – for who, under what circumstances, in what contexts and with what consequences.[66] 'Collaboration and specialisation'[67] can't be divorced from larger processes of so-called 'cognitive' or 'affective' labour, leading to various psychopathological conditions related to the post-Fordist production paradigm – the paranoiac sublimation of 'life' and 'work',[68] the phenomena of mass-depression,[69] or the sheer expropriation of capital from our shared 'general intellect'.[70] Furthermore, it can't be divorced from the larger urban questions, despite their apparent lack of scalar correspondence: expanded 'collaboration and specialisation' cannot just mean, as they often do, more profitable privatised land speculation deals and faster processes of gentrification; they need to be employed *within and against* these aspects of our contemporary urban political life.

How to turn these capabilities born in our late capitalist world into weapons against its own shortcomings is the great challenge before us. Radicalising 'productivity', 'creativity', 'aesthetics', 'innovation' – and 'radicality' itself – to align them with non-commercial values and a critical engagement with the social wrongs around us is the purview of an experimental, progressive practice and pedagogy today. And as the L.A. School (then and now) shows us, we are not alone: 'art' can provide processes and models of experimentation for architecture, as long as we understand it within an ever-shifting, interrelated continuum of aesthetics and politics.

Notes

This essay is a version of a chapter from the author's thesis for the MA in Aesthetics and Politics at CalArts. The author would particularly like to thank faculty members Arne De Boever and Martin Plot for their guidance throughout the course of the program.

[1] See for instance: Jencks, C. (1993) *Heteropolis: Los Angeles, the Riots and the Strange Beauty of Hetero-architecture*. London: Academy Editions. See also: Betsky, A., Chase, J., & Whiteson, L. (1991) *Experimental architecture in Los Angeles*. New York: Rizzoli.

[2] Flyvbjerg, B. (2006) Design by deception: the politics of megaproject approval. In Saunders, W. S. (ed.), *Urban Planning Today: A Harvard Design Magazine Reader*. Minneapolis: University of Minnesota Press.

[3] Cf. Lazzarato, M. (1996) Immaterial Labour. In Virno, P., & Hardt, M. (eds), *Radical Thought in Italy: A Potential Politics*. Minneapolis: University of Minnesota Press. Available online at: http://www.generation-online.org/c/fcimmateriallabour3.htmSee also: Moulier Boutang, Y. (2011) *Cognitive Capitalism*. Cambridge: Polity Press. For various (tentative) applications of the term 'cognitive capitalism' in architectural discourse, see: Hauptmann, D., Neidich, W., & Angelidakis, A. (2010) *Cognitive Architecture: from Bio-politics to Noo-politics ; Architecture & Mind in the Age of Communication and Information*. Rotterdam: 010 Publishers.

[4] Unless otherwise noted, all references to Eric Owen Moss are from a personal interview with him on June 28, 2012.

[5] Dreyfuss, J. (1979, December 12) Gallery Stirs Up Architects. *Los Angeles Times*. Available online at: http://socalarchhistory.blogspot.com.es/2010/04/frederick-fisher-and-venice-rat-pack.html

[6] Cf. Deleuze, G. (1992) Postscript on the Societies of Control. *October*, 59, pp. 3–7.

[7] See for instance *Arts and Architecture* magazine's Case Study House program. Cf. Kaplan, W. (2011) Introduction: 'Living in a Modern Way'. In Kaplan, W., Tigerman, B., & Adamson, G. (eds), *California Design, 1930–1965: Living in a Modern Way*. Los Angeles: Los Angeles County Museum of Art.

[8] One of the most suggestive illustrations of this institutionalized, bureaucratic post-war technocracy can be found in Jacques Tati's allegorical movie, *Play Time* (1967). For

an academic discussion of post-war technocratic American architecture, see Martin, R. (2003) *The Organizational Complex: Architecture, Media, and Corporate Space.* Cambridge: MIT.

[9] As early symptomatic examples, see these items conceived in the 1960s: Johnson, P. (1979) The Seven Shibboleths of Our Profession. In *Philip Johnson: Writings.* Oxford: Oxford University Press. Rudofsky, B. (1964) *Architecture Without Architects: An Introduction to Nonpedigreed Architecture.* New York: Museum of Modern Art.

[10] Cf. Kaplan, Introduction: 'Living in a Modern Way'.

[11] See Scott, D. E. F. (2007) Chapter 4: Designing Environment. In *Architecture or Techno-Utopia: Politics After Modernism.* Cambridge: MIT Press.

[12] In this sense, an interesting comparative analysis is to look at the California Institute of the Arts which was also founded at the same time as SCI-Arc and also had a School of Design imparting architecture. The author has pursued this analysis elsewhere, see: Shvartzberg, M. (2012) *What is Radicality? The Aesthetics and Politics of the 'L.A. School' of Architecture,* Valencia: California Institute of the Arts; and also, Shvartzberg, M. (2012) CalArts 1970: Art, Radicality, and Critique in the 'New Economy'. In De Boever, A., & Kearney, D. (eds), *In/Form: Arche,* Valencia: California Institute of the Arts.

[13] Kappe, R., Coate, R., Zimmerman, B., & Slert, C. (1974, April 22) Conversation on the 'LA 12'. Available online at: http://www.sciarc.edu/sciarc_player.html?vid=http://www.sciarclive.com/Lectures/1974_Kappe.flv&title=Ray%20Kappe

[14] These included Thom Mayne and Michael Rotondi.

[15] Kappe et al. (1974) Conversation on the 'LA 12'.

[16] For more on this tension between political idealism and diverse other (apolitical) architectural approaches in this context, see the epochal series of 1970s interviews, discussions, exhibitions and publications known as the 'Los Angeles 12'. Instigated by Kappe's friend and colleague at Pomona, architect Bernard Zimmerman and his student Charles Slert, these events provided a forum and a cross-section of Los Angeles architectural discourse by bringing together 12 architects (established and emerging) of the 1970s: Roland Coate, Daniel Dworsky, Craig Ellwood, Frank Gehry, John Lautner, Jerrold Lomax, Anthony Lumsden, Leroy Miller, Cesar Pelli, James Pulliam and Bernard Zimmerman. The project began with talks at SCI-Arc in 1974, the exhibition was hosted at the Pacific Design Center in 1976, and the movement's book was published in 1978.

[17] Zimmerman, B., Dillon, M., & Hacker J. (ed.) *The LA 12 Revisited, interview with architect Bernard Zimmerman.* Available online at: http://www.volume5.com/bz/html/architect_bernard_zimmerman_in2.html

[18] Among Schiller's contemporary critics is French philosopher Jacques Ranciere. See for instance, Rancière, J. (2010) The Aesthetic Revolution and its Outcomes. *Dissensus: On Politics and Aesthetics.* London: Continuum. See also: Kester, G. H. (2011) *The One and the Many: Contemporary Collaborative Art in a Global Context.* Durham: Duke University Press.

[19] Iovine, J. V. (2004, May 17) An Iconoclastic Architect Turns Theory Into Practice. *New York Times.* Available online at: http://www.nytimes.com/2004/05/17/arts/an-iconoclastic-architect-turns-theory-into-practice.html?src=pm

[20] Day, M. (2009, Thursday 17) Frank Gehry: 'Don't call me a starchitect'. *Independent*.
      Available online at: http://www.independent.co.uk/arts-entertainment/architecture/frank-
      gehry-dont-call-me-a-starchitect-1842870.html

[21] Cf. Gehry, F. O., Pollack, S., & Guilfoyle, U. (2006) *Sketches of Frank Gehry*. Culver City:
      Sony Pictures Classics.

[22] Martin, R. (2010) Postscript. In Deamer, P., & Bernstein, P. (eds), *Building (in) the Future:
      Recasting Labor in Architecture*. New Haven: Yale School of Architecture, p. 204.

[23] Italian philosopher Giorgio Agamben also explores the issue of political de-
      subjectification in relation to contemporary technology in his short essay, 'What is
      an Apparatus?'. Cf. Agamben, G. (2009) *What Is an Apparatus?: And Other Essays*.
      Stanford, Calif: Stanford University Press.

[24] *Architects Newspaper Blog*. (2011, April 29) Roche Unleashes on SCI-Arc. Available
      online at:
      http://blog.archpaper.com/wordpress/archives/16219

[25] Cook, P. (2011) Peter Cook Recalls a Transatlantic Spat between SCI-Arc and a Highly-
      strung French Guest. *Architectural Review London*.

[26] Ibid.

[27] Cf. Jencks, *Heteropolis: Los Angeles, the Riots and the Strange Beauty of Hetero-
      Architecture*. Jencks explicitly addresses liberalism in the context of the 'L.A. School',
      but his focus is on trying to synthesize the diverse polemics of 1990s multiculturalism
      and ecology with his avowed 'Post-modern Liberalism' rather than decentering the
      legacy of liberal individualism per se.

[28] Cf. Arendt, H. (1998) *The Human Condition*. Chicago: University of Chicago Press. For
      Arendt, the archetypical agent of the political is the citizen of the *polis*, who is equal
      and free at the same time: neither ruling nor ruled. Equality in freedom is the structuring
      principle of political subjectivization for Arendt, the condition of citizenship where
      individuals are liberated from the administrative tasks of the home or of work, to be able
      to publically express their singularity through speech and deed –what she calls a 'space
      of appearance'.

[29] This is precisely one of Frederick Jameson's programmatic conclusions to his famed
      Postmodernism, or, the Cultural Logic of Late Capitalism: 'an aesthetic of cognitive
      mapping – a pedagogical political culture which seeks to endow the individual subject
      with some new heightened sense of its place in the global system.' Cf. Jameson, F.
      (1984) Postmodernism, or, the Cultural Logic of Late Capitalism. *New Left Review*, I/146.
      Available online at: http://newleftreview.org/I/146/fredric-jameson-postmodernism-or-
      the-cultural-logic-of-late-capitalism

[30] As Ranciere explains, 'the process of emancipation is the verification of the equality of
      any speaking being with any other speaking being. It is always enacted in the name of
      a category denied either the principle or the consequences of that equality: workers,
      women, people of color, or others. But the enactment of equality is not, for all that, the
      enactment of the self, of the attributes or properties of the community in question. ...
      Equality exists, and makes universal values exist, to the extent that it is enacted. Equality
      is not a value to which one appeals; it is a universal that must be supposed, verified,
      and demonstrated in each case. ... The logical schema of social protest, generally

speaking, may be summed up as follows: Do we or do we not belong to the category of men or citizens or human beings, and what follows from this? The universality is not enclosed in *citizen* or *human being*; it is involved in the "what follows," in its discursive and practical enactment. ... What is a process of subjectivization? It is the formation of a one that is not a self but is the relation of a self to an other. Let me demonstrate this with respect to an outmoded name, "the proletarian." ... *Proletarians* was the name given to people who are together inasmuch as they are between: between several names, statuses, and identities; between humanity and inhumanity, citizenship and its denial; between the status of a man of tools and the status of a speaking and thinking being. Political subjectivization is the enactment of equality – or the handling of a wrong – by people who are together to the extent that they are between.' Rancière, J. (1992) Politics, Identification, and Subjectivization. *October*, 61, pp. 58–64.

[31] It must be noted that this kind of free-market architectural determinism has been most brashly upheld by the 'postcritical' turn of architectural discourse since the early 2000s. Interestingly, the L.A. School may in fact be considered precursory to this movement (i.e. note Rotondi's 'cleaning' of 'social thinkers' at SCI-Arc in the 1980s, or Gehry's many-times-avowed rejection to reading publications or engaging in critical intellectual dialogue). For a review of the postcritical turn see: Saunders, W. S. (2007) *The New Architectural Pragmatism: A Harvard Design Magazine Reader.* Minneapolis: University of Minnesota Press. For the most virulent attack on critical theory in postcritical architectural discourse, see: Speaks, M. (2005) After Theory – in Architecture Schools, Debate Rages about the Value of Theory. *Architectural Record*, 193, 6, p. 72.

[32] Fisher, M. (2009) *Capitalist Realism: Is there no alternative?* London: Zero Books.

[33] Rancière, J. (1999) *Disagreement.* Minneapolis: University of Minnesota Press, p. 132.

[34] Ibid. p. 102.

[35] Cf. Rancière, J. (2006) Democracy, Republic, Representation. *Constellations Volume 13*, No 3.

[36] Cf. Aureli, P. V. (2011) *The Possibility of an Absolute Architecture.* Cambridge: MIT Press.

[37] Harvey, D. (2008) The Right to the City. *New Left Review 53*, Sept–Oct. See also: Harvey, D. (2012) *Rebel Cities: From the Right to the City to the Urban Revolution.* New York: Verso, p. 32. Interestingly, one of the LA School's most famed early projects, Frank Gehry's Santa Monica residence (1977) 'reflects' a certain paranoid border or territoriality condition. In this, it metaphorically approximates (though not literally) the work of neo-conservative planner Oscar Newman, who in the early '70s developed the doctrine of 'Defensible Space'. Newman, O. (1972) *Defensible Space; Crime Prevention Through Urban Design.* New York: Macmillan. See also: Davis, M. (1990) *City of Quartz: Excavating the Future in Los Angeles.* London: Verso.

[38] This remark is not intended as an attack on a possible 'pornographic architecture' (which would certainly be an interesting proposition). Rather it is meant to illustrate the shift from what Norman M. Klein calls the modernist 'industrialization of desire' to what I call a 'totalization of desire' in the hegemonic architecture of contemporary cognitive capitalism. See: Klein, N. M. (2004) *The Vatican to Vegas: A History of Special Effects.* New York: New Press, p. 325.

[39] Rancière, op. cit. *Disagreement,* p. 29.

[40] However, Moss distances himself from the 1960s counterculture and socio-political movements, insisting on the uniqueness of the individual characters making up the L.A. School, and rejecting any kind of social, political, historical, or theoretical determinations on the group's uprising. As he told me: 'You are not *given permission* to be creative, experimental and free, you have to *take it yourself*.'

[41] Marcuse theorised and advocated 'the Great Refusal', arguing for 'individual rebellion and opposition to the existing system of domination and oppression; avant-garde artistic revolt that creates visions of another world, a better life and alternative cultural forms and style; and oppositional thought that rejects the dominant modes of thinking and behavior.' Marcuse, H., & Kellner, D. (2005) *The New Left and the 1960s*. London: Routledge, p. 10. For this rhetoric's specific traction at CalArts, see the Design School's second Associate Dean's classic book-manifesto on the politics of design: Papanek, V. J. (1972) *Design for the Real World: Human Ecology and Social Change*. New York: Pantheon Books.

[42] CalArts radical founders were: first president Bob Corrigan; first provost Herb Blau; first Dean of the Design School Richard Farson; first Dean of Critical Studies Maurice Stein. For a review of CalArts Design School's institutional politics, see: Hodgetts, C. (2011) Experimental Impulse Interview with Ben Tong, available online at http://www. eastofborneo.org/archives/craig-hodgetts-experimental-impulse-interview-2011. Hodgetts was founding Associate Dean of the CalArts Design School. See also: Farson, R. (2011) Experimental Impulse Interview with Ben Tong, available online at: http://www. eastofborneo.org/archives/experimental-impulse-interview-richard-farson-2011. Farson was founding Dean of the Calarts Design School. See also: Wharton, D. (1990, April 15) A Tradition of Tradition-Be-Damned: CalArts at 20: It sprang from a Disney family gift and has grown from its euphoric beginnings to respectability. *Los Angeles Times*. Available online at: http://articles.latimes.com/1990-04-15/entertainment/ca-1889_1_ waltdisney.

[43] 'Mayne returned to the SCI-Arc fold this month as trustee. Other board members include architects Frank Gehry, Michael Rotondi and William Fain, and real estate developers Kevin Ratner and Tom Gilmore.' Vincent, R. (2011, April 22) L.A. architecture school SCI-Arc buys its unorthodox home. *Los Angeles Times*. Available online at: http://articles. latimes.com/print/2011/apr/22/business/la-fi-downtown-deal-20110422.

[44] Other L.A School figures, such as Thom Mayne, also seem to have significantly shifted emphasis from their early 1970s aesthetic radicalism to include the realm of politics and social context in their rhetoric, as became evident at SCI-Arc's 2012 Raimund Abraham Lecture, where Mayne surprisingly extolled 'the importance of the collective, of the city, of planning, of (gasp) clients and neighbours, and even of pushing Modernism forward by letting go of some of its utopianism and paying attention to reality.' Lubell, S. (2012, March 27) An Evening with the Mayne Man. *Architectural Review London*. Available online at: http://www.architectural-review.com/reviews/an-evening-with-the-mayne-man/8628359.

[45] On political 'disenchantment', see Virno, P. (1996) The Ambivalence of Disenchantment. In op. cit. *Radical Thought in Italy: A Potential Politics*. On 'the Great Refusal' and this discourse's influence on CalArts School of Design, see endnote 41.

[46] Op. cit. Scott, F.D.E. (2007) *Architecture or Techno-Utopia: Politics After Modernism*, p. 253.

[47] For more on this argument, see Shvartzberg, M. (2012) Mythopoetics of the Kunsthalle. *Architecture, Media, Politics, Society*, Vol. 1, No. 2. Available online at: http://architecturemps.com/back-issues/.

[48] As French political thinker Claude Lefort famously put it: 'democracy is instituted and sustained by the *dissolution of the markers of certainty*.' Lefort, C. (1991) The Question of Democracy. *Democracy and Political Theory*. Cambridge: Polity Press, p. 19.

[49] Cook, P. (1983) City of Dreams. In Goldstein, B., & Cook, P. (eds), *Los Angeles Now: an Exhibition*. London: Architectural Association, p. 6.

[50] '12 L.A. Architects', L.A. 12 exhibition poster (1976) Available to view online at: http://socalarchhistory.blogspot.com.es/2010/03/1976-los-angeles-12-exhibition-at_26.html.

[51] See for instance the L.A. 12 interview with Gehry at SCI-Arc, 1976. Available online at: http://www.sciarc.edu/sciarc_player.html?vid=http://www.sciarclive.com/Lectures/1976_Gehry.flv&title=Frank%20Gehry.

[52] A fantastic survey of aesthetic (performance) projects centered squarely on socio-political questions (rather than as ancillary afterthoughts) can be found in Shannon Jackson's *Social Works*. Jackson, S. (2011) *Social works: performing art, supporting publics*. New York: Routledge.

[53] See for instance the L.A. 12 poster cited earlier, and Gehry's introduction, 'Let a thousand flowers bloom' in Betsky, A., Chase, J., & Whiteson, L. (1991) *Experimental Architecture in Los Angeles*. The L.A. School obviously had other non-artistic influences (mainly architectural, such as Venturi's *Complexity and Contradiction*, or Banham's *Four Ecologies*) which *have* been the subject of many critical evaluations and are thus not a central part of my remit here.

[54] As art critic Karen Moss notes regarding these practices emerging in the 1970s in Southern California: 'With their concerted effort to de-institutionalize institutions and/or create work in the public sphere, often in eccentric locations, artists worked "outside the frame." As they eschewed the gallery system and the commodification of their art, many artists took an activist, antimaterialist, politically engaged position vis-à-vis critical cultural, social, and political issues. … It is this goal of educating the public that is shared by all of these artist collectives. In these socially engaged events, audiences are not only active participants but also co-learners in an investigative process that is informed by a sense of critical pedagogy.' Moss, K. (2011) Beyond the White Cell: Experimentation/Education/Intervention in California circa 1970. In Lewallen, C., Moss, K., Bryan-Wilson, J., & Rorimer, A. (eds), *State of Mind: New California Art circa 1970*. Berkeley: University of California Press, pp. 189–190. See also: Donis, A., & Bryan-Wilson, J. (2011) *Collaboration Labs: Southern California Artists and the Artist Space Movement*. Santa Monica: 18th Street Arts Center; Clark, R., & Auping, M. (2011) *Phenomenal: California Light, Space, Surface*. Berkeley: University of California Press; Chavoya, C. O., & Gonzalez, R. (2011) Elite of the Obscure: An Introduction. In Chavoya, C. O., & Gonzalez, R. (eds), *Asco: Elite of the Obscure: a Retrospective, 1972–1987*. Ostfildern: Hatje Cantz.

[55] Lippard, L. R. (1973) *Six Years: the Dematerialization of the Art Object from 1966 to*

1972: A Cross-Reference Book of Information on Some Esthetic Boundaries. New York: Praeger.

[56] Such as the one Walt Disney intended with his funding of CalArts; see, for instance, Shvartzberg, M. (2012) CalArts 1970: Art, Radicality, and Critique in the 'New Economy'.

[57] Note, for instance, that 'performance art' came into its own in California, with the initially Los Angeles-based publications *Artforum* and *High Performance* engaging this 'dematerialized' practice in a critical context, allowing it to reach a wide audience.

[58] Cf. Bourriaud, N. (2008) *Relational Aesthetics.* Dijon: Presses du réel; Bishop, C. (2006) *Participation.* London: Whitechapel; and Kester, G. H. (2004) *Conversation Pieces: Community and Communication in Modern Art.* Berkeley: University of California Press.

[59] See for instance: Rogoff, I. (2010) Turning. *E-flux Journal,* No. 0. Available online at: http://www.e-flux.com/journal/turning/. See also: O'Neill, P., and Wilson, M. (eds) (2010) *Curating and the Educational Turn.* London: Open Editions.

[60] A very partial sample of theorists and practitioners embodying and extending this legacy in Southern California today would include art critic Grant Kester; artists Andrea Fraser, Ashley Hunt, Sam Durant, Michelle Dizon; urban thinkers such as Norman M. Klein, Edward Soja, and Mike Davis; and artist–activist–architects like Teddy Cruz or Fritz Haeg.

[61] Of course, this is a generalisation intended to capture the overall attitude of the original 'L.A. School' approach as the dominant regional force on architectural discourse (with a global influence). There is a minority of L.A. architects who engage in these political issues as an integral part of their practice, for instance, Michael Maltzan Architects. See: Maltzan, M., & Varner, J. (eds) (2011) *No More Play: Conversations on Urban Speculation in Los Angeles and Beyond.* Ostfildern: Hatje Cantz Verlag; Lepik, A. (2010) *Small Scale, Big Change: New Architectures of Social Engagement.* New York: Museum of Modern Art.

[62] Giovannini, J., Martínez, D., & Sewell, T. (eds) (1984) *Real Estate as Art: New Architecture in Venice.* Venice: Sewell Archives.

[63] Cf. Deamer, P., & Bernstein, P. (eds), *Building (in) the Future: Recasting Labor in Architecture.*

[64] Op. cit., Cook, P. (1983) City of Dreams, p. 4.

[65] Op. cit., Lubell, S. (2012, March 27) An Evening with the Mayne Man.

[66] As Foucault put it, 'We are not talking about a gesture of rejection [i.e. Marcuse's "Great Refusal"]. We have to move beyond the outside–inside alternative, we have to be at the frontiers. Criticism indeed consists of *analyzing and reflecting upon limits.* ... to grasp the points where change is possible and desirable, and to determine the precise form this change should take. ... What is at stake, then, is this: How can the growth of capabilities be disconnected from the intensification of power relations?' Foucault, M. (1984) What is Enlightenment? In Rabinow, P. (ed.), *The Foucault Reader.* New York: Pantheon Books.

[67] Lubell, Sam. op. cit.

[68] Lazzarato, M. (1996) Immaterial Labour.

[69] Fisher, M. (2009) *Capitalist Realism: Is There No Alternative?*

[70] Italian philosopher Paolo Virno borrows this notion from Marx's *Grundrisse* to critique

the 'post-Fordist' commodification of common intellectual potential, as in 'formal and informal knowledge, imagination, ethical tendencies, mentalities and "language games". Thoughts and discourses function in themselves as productive 'machines' in contemporary labour and do not need to take on a mechanical body or an electronic soul. ... General intellect needs to be understood literally as intellect in general: the faculty and power to think, rather than the works produced by thought – a book, an algebra formula etc.' Virno, P. (2001) On General Intellect. In Zanini, A., Fadini, U., & Herold, C. (eds), *Lessico postfordista: dizionario di idee della mutazione*. Milano: Feltrinelli. Available in English online at: http://libcom.org/library/on-general-intellect-paulo-virno. See also: Berardi, F., 'Bifo' (2009) *The Soul at Work: From Alienation to Autonomy*. Los Angeles: Semiotext(e).

Bibliography

Agamben, G. (2009) *What Is an Apparatus?: And Other Essays*. Stanford, CA: Stanford University Press.

Architects Newspaper Blog (2011, April 29) Roche Unleashes on SCI-Arc. Available online at: http://blog.archpaper.com/wordpress/archives/16219

Arendt, H. (1998) *The Human Condition*. Chicago: University of Chicago Press.

Aureli, P. V. (2011) *The Possibility of an Absolute Architecture*. Cambridge: MIT Press.

Berardi, F., 'Bifo' (2009) *The Soul at Work: From Alienation to Autonomy*. Los Angeles: Semiotext(e).

Betsky, A., Chase, J., & Whiteson, L. (1991) *Experimental Architecture in Los Angeles*. New York: Rizzoli.

Bishop, C. (2006) *Participation*. London: Whitechapel.

Bourriaud, N. (2008) *Relational Aesthetics*. Dijon: Presses du reel.

Chavoya, C. O., & Gonzalez, R. (2011) Elite of the Obscure: An Introduction. In Chavoya, C. O., & Gonzalez, R. (eds), *Asco: Elite of the Obscure: a Retrospective, 1972–1987*. Ostfildern: Hatje Cantz.

Clark, R., & Auping, M. (2011) *Phenomenal: California Light, Space, Surface*. Berkeley: University of California Press.

Cook, P. (1983) City of Dreams. In Goldstein, B., & Cook, P. (eds), *Los Angeles Now: an Exhibition*. London: Architectural Association.

Cook, P. (2011) Peter Cook Recalls a Transatlantic Spat between SCI-Arc and a Highly-Strung French Guest. *Architectural Review London*.

Davis, M. (1990) *City of Quartz: Excavating the Future in Los Angeles*. London: Verso.

Day, M. (2009, Thursday 17) Frank Gehry: 'Don't call me a starchitect'. *The Independent*. Available online at: http://www.independent.co.uk/arts-entertainment/architecture/frank-gehry-dont-call-me-a-starchitect-1842870.html

Deleuze, G. (1992) Postscript on the Societies of Control. *October*, 59, pp.3–7.

Donis, A., & Bryan-Wilson, J. (2011) *Collaboration Labs: Southern California Artists and the Artist Space Movement*. Santa Monica: 18th Street Arts Center.

Dreyfuss, J. (1979, December 12) Gallery Stirs Up Architects. *Los Angeles Times*. Available online at: http://socalarchhistory.blogspot.com.es/2010/04/frederick-fisher-and-venice-rat-pack.html

Farson, R. (2011) Experimental Impulse Interview with Ben Tong. Available online at: http://www.eastofborneo.org/archives/experimental-impulse-interview-richard-farson-2011

Fisher, M. (2009) *Capitalist Realism: Is there no alternative?* London: Zero Books.

Flyvbjerg, B. (2006) Design by deception: the politics of megaproject approval. In Saunders, W. S. (ed.), *Urban Planning Today: A Harvard Design Magazine Reader.* Minneapolis: University of Minnesota Press.

Foucault, M. (1984) What is Enlightenment? In Rabinow, P. (ed.), *The Foucault Reader.* New York: Pantheon Books.

Gehry, F. O. (1976) L.A. 12 interview with Gehry at SCI-Arc. Available online at: http://www.sciarc.edu/sciarc_player.html?vid=http://www.sciarclive.com/Lectures/1976_Gehry.flv&title=Frank%20Gehry

Gehry, F. O., Pollack, S., & Guilfoyle, U. (2006) *Sketches of Frank Gehry.* Culver City: Sony Pictures Classics.

Giovannini, J., Martínez, D., & Sewell, T. (eds) (1984) *Real Estate As Art: New Architecture in Venice.* Venice: Sewell Archives.

Harvey, D. (2012) *Rebel Cities: From the Right to the City to the Urban Revolution.* New York: Verso.

Harvey, D. (2008) The Right to the City. *New Left Review 53,* Sept–Oct.

Hauptmann, D., Neidich, W., & Angelidakis, A. (2010) *Cognitive architecture: from bio-politics to noo-politics; architecture & mind in the age of communication and information.* Rotterdam: 010 Publishers.

Hodgetts, C. (2011) Experimental Impulse Interview with Ben Tong. Available online at: http://www.eastofborneo.org/archives/craig-hodgetts-experimental-impulse-interview-2011

Iovine, J. V. (2004, May 17) An Iconoclastic Architect Turns Theory Into Practice. *The New York Times.* Available online at: http://www.nytimes.com/2004/05/17/arts/an-iconoclastic-architect-turns-theory-into-practice.html?src=pm

Jackson, S. (2011) *Social Works: Performing Art, Supporting Publics.* New York: Routledge.

Jameson, F. (1984) Postmodernism, or, the Cultural Logic of Late Capitalism. *New Left Review,* I/146. Available online at: http://newleftreview.org/I/146/fredric-jameson-postmodernism-or-the-cultural-logic-of-late-capitalism

Jencks, C. (1993) *Heteropolis: Los Angeles, the Riots and the Strange Beauty of Hetero-architecture.* London: Academy Editions.

Johnson, P. (1979) The Seven Shibboleths of Our Profession. In *Philip Johnson: Writings.* Oxford: Oxford University Press.

Kaplan, W. (2011) Introduction: 'Living in a Modern Way'. In Kaplan, W., Tigerman, B., & Adamson, G. (eds), *California Design, 1930–1965: Living in a Modern Way.* Los Angeles: Los Angeles County Museum of Art.

Kappe, R., Coate, R., Zimmerman, B., & Slert, C. (1974, April 22) Conversation on the 'LA 12'. Available online at: http://www.sciarc.edu/sciarc_player.html?vid=http://www.sciarclive.com/Lectures/1974_Kappe.flv&title=Ray%20Kappe

Kester, G. H. (2004) *Conversation Pieces: Community and Communication in Modern Art.* Berkeley: University of California Press.

Kester, G. H. (2011) *The One and the Many: Contemporary Collaborative Art in a Global Context.* Durham: Duke University Press.

Klein, N. M. (2004) *The Vatican to Vegas: A History of Special Effects*. New York: New Press.

Lazzarato, M. (1996) Immaterial Labour. In Virno, P., & Hardt, M. (eds), *Radical Thought in Italy: A Potential Politics*. Minneapolis: University of Minnesota Press. Available online at: http://www.generation-online.org/c/fcimmateriallabour3.htm

Lefort, C. (1991) The Question of Democracy. *Democracy and Political Theory*. Cambridge: Polity Press.

Lepik, A. (2010) *Small Scale, Big Change: New Architectures of Social Engagement*. New York: Museum of Modern Art.

Lippard, L. R. (1973) *Six Years: the Dematerialization of the Art Object from 1966 to 1972: A Cross-Reference Book of Information on Some Esthetic Boundaries*. New York: Praeger.

Lubell, S. (2012, March 27) An Evening with the Mayne Man. *Architectural Review London*. Available online at: http://www.architectural-review.com/reviews/an-evening-with-the-mayne-man/8628359

Maltzan, M., & Varner, J. (eds) (2011) *No More Play: Conversations on Urban Speculation in Los Angeles and Beyond*. Ostfildern: Hatje Cantz Verlag.

Marcuse, H., & Kellner, D. (2005) *The New Left and the 1960s*. London: Routledge, p. 10.

Martin, R. (2003) *The Organizational Complex: Architecture, Media, and Corporate Space*. Cambridge: MIT.

Martin, R. (2010) Postscript. In Deamer, P., & Bernstein, P. (eds), *Building (in) the Future: Recasting Labor in Architecture*. New Haven: Yale School of Architecture, p. 204.

Moss, K. (2011) Beyond the White Cell: Experimentation/Education/Intervention in California circa 1970. In Lewallen, C., Moss, K., Bryan-Wilson, J., & Rorimer, A. (eds), *State of Mind: New California Art Circa 1970*. Berkeley: University of California Press.

Moulier Boutang, Y. (2011) *Cognitive capitalism*. Cambridge: Polity Press.

Newman, O. (1972) *Defensible Space; Crime Prevention through Urban Design*. New York: Macmillan.

O'Neill, P., and Wilson, M. (eds) (2010) *Curating and the Educational Turn*. London: Open Editions.

Papanek, V. J. (1972) *Design for the Real World: Human Ecology and Social Change*. New York: Pantheon Books.

Rancière, J. (1992) Politics, Identification, and Subjectivization. *October*, 61, pp.58–64.

Rancière, J. (1999) *Disagreement*. Minneapolis: University of Minnesota Press.

Rancière, J. (2006) Democracy, Republic, Representation. *Constellations Volume 13*, No 3.

Rancière, J. (2010) The Aesthetic Revolution and Its Outcomes. *Dissensus: On Politics and Aesthetics*. London: Continuum.

Rogoff, I. (2010) Turning. *E-flux Journal*, No. 0. Available online at: http://www.e-flux.com/journal/turning/

Rudofsky, B. (1964) *Architecture Without Architects: An Introduction to Nonpedigreed Architecture*. New York: Museum of Modern Art.

Saunders, W. S. (2007) *The New Architectural Pragmatism: A Harvard Design Magazine Reader*. Minneapolis: University of Minnesota Press.

Scott, D. E. F. (2007) *Architecture or Techno-Utopia: Politics After Modernism*. Cambridge: MIT Press.

Shvartzberg, M. (2012) *What is Radicality? The Aesthetics and Politics of the 'L.A. School' of Architecture*, Valencia: California Institute of the Arts.

Shvartzberg, M. (2012) CalArts 1970: Art, Radicality, and Critique in the 'New Economy'. In De Boever, A., & Kearney, D. (eds), *In/Form: Arche,* Valencia: California Institute of the Arts.

Shvartzberg, M. (2012) Mythopoetics of the Kunsthalle. *Architecture, Media, Politics, Society*, Vol. 1, No. 2. Available online at: http://architecturemps.com/back-issues/

Speaks, M. (2005) After Theory – in Architecture Schools, Debate Rages About the Value of Theory. *Architectural Record*, 193, 6, p. 72.

Tati, J., et al. (1967) *Playtime*. London: BFI Video Pub.

Vincent, R. (2011, April 22) L.A. architecture school SCI-Arc buys its unorthodox home. *Los Angeles Times*. Available online at: http://articles.latimes.com/print/2011/apr/22/business/la-fi-downtown-deal-20110422

Virno, P. (2001) On General Intellect. In Zanini, A., Fadini, U., & Herold, C. (eds), *Lessico postfordista: dizionario di idee della mutazione*. Milano: Feltrinelli. Available in English online at: http://libcom.org/library/on-general-intellect-paulo-virno

Virno, P. (1996) The Ambivalence of Disenchantment. In op. cit. *Radical Thought in Italy: A Potential Politics*.

Wharton, D. (1990, April 15) A Tradition of Tradition-Be-Damned: CalArts at 20: It sprang from a Disney family gift and has grown from its euphoric beginnings to respectability. *Los Angeles Times*. Available online at: http://articles.latimes.com/1990-04-15/entertainment/ca-1889_1_waltdisney

Zimmerman, B., Dillon, M., & Hacker, J. (ed.) *The LA 12 Revisited, interview with architect Bernard Zimmerman*. Available online at: http://www.volume5.com/bz/html/architect_bernard_zimmerman_in2.html

'12 L.A. Architects', L.A. 12 exhibition poster (1976) Available online at: http://socalarchhistory.blogspot.com.es/2010/03/1976-los-angeles-12-exhibition-at_26.html

Jefa GREENAWAY, Janet McGAW,
Jillian WALLISS

CHAPTER 2
DESIGNING AUSTRALIA – CRITICAL ENGAGEMENT WITH INDIGENOUS PLACE MAKING

The Challenges of Today and Tomorrow in Australia: Framing a Post-colonial Design Response

As the crisis of global environmental change unfolds, we are becoming increasingly aware of the difficult and continuing legacy of Australia's history as a settler society. Australia was colonised by the British just over 200 years ago on the land of the oldest continuing culture in the world. Settlement occurred with minimal understanding of our environmental context and no acknowledgement of a prior occupation. While Australia shares a settler legacy with South Africa, Canada, the United States and New Zealand, it is the only settler society without a treaty with its Indigenous inhabitants.

From their very first encounters in 1788, Europeans have struggled to understand the Australian landscape and its Indigenous owners. Joseph Arnold proclaimed in 1810 that the landscape of NSW 'was as strange to me as if I had become an inhabitant of the moon.'[1] Environmental concerns, combined with the forced migration of convicts between 1788 and 1856, created an image of the Australian colonies as inferior to other European ones. Some scientists considered the landscape and its Indigenous occupants so 'environmentally primitive' that they feared the development of a 'half-caste society'.[2] These attitudes shaped the colonial relationships with Indigenous people, with the Australian Aboriginal relegated to the lowest of the primitive and perceived as an ancient relic. This assessment was influential in the decision not to negotiate a Treaty between the colonisers and Indigenous peoples of Australia; an act that positioned Australia as 'the exception to the British formula of securing consent from Indigenous people by a treaty of cessation.'[3] Instead, the doctrine of *terra nullius* was applied, which denied the land rights of the traditional owners.[4]

Two hundred years on, we still struggle to understand our unique ecology and the complex and diverse culture of Indigenous Australia. In the case of Melbourne, Australia's second-biggest city, a focus on technical and economic issues rather than cultural and ecological understanding of place continues to guide the development of Melbourne's urban, suburban and peri-urban areas. Acknowledgement of a pre-European history and ecology is lacking, despite the fact that European settlers arrived in Melbourne 175 years ago. The ecological and cultural blindness of settler colonists, and what Tony Birch describes as 'an anxious attachment to the land', led to a rapid and new kind of place making in the 1800s: the building of streets, monuments and dwellings that ignored the more subtle characteristics of Melbourne's landscape and ecology.[5]

An aerial image of Melbourne reveals a dense urban fabric and a fixation on an urban grid. These are the dominant patterns and understanding which inform many design decisions, responding to lines of occupation and development. Yet in the case of Melbourne this dominant representation is only 175 years old. We are puzzled when, after extensive periods of rain, certain streets in Melbourne flood. Unaware of the extensive disruption and filling-in of wetland systems that occurred during that period, we fail to understand the complex ecological systems that are now subsumed under the ground as well as other much older stories and narratives of occupying place. These attitudes continue to shape urban development and are indeed heightened by a global design practice where, increasingly, design is produced within the culturally and ecologically abstract space of the digital.

Universities offer important avenues for exploring new models of urbanism and place making which encompass Indigenous perspectives and knowledge. While tertiary institutions around the country have had faculties of Australian Indigenous Studies for a number of decades, it is only recently that Indigenous discourses have been embedded in other faculties. In architecture however, it has not taken hold. Architectural anthropologist, Paul Memmot, heads an Aboriginal Environments Research Centre at the University of Queensland, which has led the archaeological and anthropological research into pre-colonial Indigenous architecture in the country. It is the only one of its kind.

In 1995 the State Public Works department in New South Wales formed an Aboriginal design unit led by Dillon Kombumerri and Kevin O'Brien, the first Indigenous-run architecture practice in Australia. Greenaway is one of only nine Indigenous architects in Australia and the only registered architect in Victoria. Given the rich craft traditions and lauded contemporary visual and performing arts practitioners in Australia, this lack of representation amongst designers of the built environment is perplexing. It demonstrates the importance of institutions working more actively to make space for Indigenous knowledge systems so that architecture might be perceived as a desirable professional pathway for Indigenous Australians. In the meantime, it also highlights the need for non-Indigenous architects to develop modes of practice and representation that are both respectful of, and meaningful to, Aboriginal people.

In 2009, the University of Melbourne established an Institute for Indigenous Development, Murrup Barak, which has a mandate to increase the University's engagement with Indigenous culture, support active recruitment of Indigenous staff, enhance Indigenous content in academic programs across all faculties and support partnerships with external Indigenous communities. In the past two years, both the Australian Institute of Architects and the University of Melbourne, in close consultation with Indigenous stakeholders, have developed Reconciliation Action Plans that include key performance indicators for implementing changes that will facilitate reconciliation with Indigenous Australians. Since its inception, the Melbourne School of Design (MSD), a multi-disciplinary graduate school encompassing architecture, landscape architecture, urban design and planning, has sought to engage with research and design studios that address the mandate of Murrup Barak, including David O'Brien's award-winning Bower Studios and their on-site design and build projects with Indigenous communities in remote Western Australia and the Northern Territory.

In line with the principles underlying these studios, many other related projects and design studios have emerged. These include 'Indigenous Placemaking in Melbourne', run by Janet McGaw, the architectural historian Anoma Pieris and the cultural theorist Emily Potter. Its aim is the establishment of a cultural knowledge and education centre in Melbourne. Design studios that share the same ethos include those discussed here: 'Re-making Place in the Sites of Flow and Passage', 'Re-making Place in the Academe' and 'Re-making Place in the City'. Central to these studios were two questions. Firstly, what new strategies might emerge for architecture and landscape architecture in Melbourne if time and place were conceptualised through an Indigenous lens? Secondly, how do we as designers, in the absence of many Indigenous architects to guide our way, engage with other ways of knowing place?

Intrinsic to the question of re-making place is a critique of Western conceptions, of time and the 'passivity' of the site, that underpin architectural design. Creative research offered an important means for investigating these very particular issues for which Western design precedents offer minimal guidance. Unlike other forms of research, which use linear argument and repeatable, generalisable experiments, creative research of the type discussed here is usually local, specific, unrepeatable and poetic. Paul Carter and others have argued that when creative methods are used to enable the lateral leaps required to see our designed environments in new ways, they become a form of research in and of themselves.[6]

Three creative research methods informed the studio framing in this regard: deep listening, mapping and critical spatial practices. These methods offered the means for engaging with Indigenous perspectives, demystifying Aboriginality and broadening the frame of reference of what it means to represent Aboriginal culture. At every turn, they challenged Western conceptualisations of space, history and time.

Creative Research Method 1: Deep Listening

Indigenous artist Treanha Hamm and non-Indigenous scholar Laura Brearley have developed a mode of research that sits between Indigenous and non-Indigenous knowledge systems that they call 'deep listening'. It refers to both an intuitive listening to the land and a respectful listening to one another based on a concept that appears in a number of Aboriginal languages. In the Ngungikurungkurr language of the Daly River it is referred to as *Dadirri*, and in the Yorta Yorta language of the Murray River it is *Gulpa Ngawal*.[7] Through their use of deep listening, Hamm and Brearley ask: 'What would it look like to create spaces in the academe for research incorporating Indigenous ways of knowing – without appropriating or colonising? How might we engage in different ways of seeing and listening to each other?'[8] 'Deep listening', then, challenges traditional research approaches in academic institutions which privilege Western textual scholarly conventions. In 'deep listening', the interpersonal space of storytelling is centralised and listeners are encouraged to recognise their own participatory connectedness to the narrative.

The medium in which we work is not linguistic, but formal, spatial and material. As a result, part of this process has involved considering how stories might materialise in built form. Traditional Aboriginal culture is generally regarded as an oral one; a culture in which stories were handed down through speech and song. However, material practices of storytelling proliferated as well – markings with ochre, lime and charcoal on rocks and bark, carvings into wood and inscriptions onto animal hide all functioning as a kind of 'writing'.

This is important because, in recent decades, specific critique of 'essentialising practices' in linguistics have prioritised 'writing' over 'non-writing' cultures.[9] Rousseau's categorisation of languages into three stages of increasing sophistication, from pictographic to ideographic to phonographic, has been widely challenged for its Eurocentrism.[10] In culturally stable settings, with tight contextual controls, it is likely that pictographic and ideographic symbols carried a less ambiguous meaning than has been presumed by Western scholars and, as such, Indigenous material practices of painting, drawing and inscribing can be considered a kind of writing that communicates a rich and complex culture. Penny Van Toorn argues that all writing systems are mixtures of phonetics, image and idea.[11] The reader/listener is now understood to have a pivotal role in attributing meaning to any form of 'writing', be it alphabetic or symbolic.

In light of this, the design projects discussed in detail later begin with multiple opportunities for students to 'listen' through a range of media. They were encouraged to find their own points of connection with the stories they heard. In parallel with the design studios, we offered a seminar series where Indigenous partners, stakeholders, artists and architects spoke about their culture, aspirations, place-making traditions and what they thought were appropriate and inappropriate architectural responses. Speakers told 'Dreaming' stories, stories of post-colonial dispossession, referenced scholarship into Aboriginal place-making practices, brought along examples of Aboriginal craft work and inscriptions, showed contemporary art from Victoria and gave students consent to use these stories as springboards for their design work. [12] Students were also encouraged to access the Koorie Heritage trust library which includes oral histories, and the 'Koorie Voices' collection at the Melbourne Museum as well as online collections of recordings and transcripts.

Through exploring Indigenous narratives, students discovered that place is linked to pathways of movement that connect sites of significance, rather than discrete and bounded territories marked with built structures. In traditional Aboriginal culture, movement between places was a ritual marking of the relationship between land and the Ancestral spirits, who are enduringly present. That is, Ancient dreaming time, generational cycles, seasonal and ecological cycles play out simultaneously in the rituals of movement and song that mark the connections between places and that together make up one's 'country'.[13] An important task was therefore to locate these sites of Indigenous significance in the urban landscape of Melbourne where the traces of pre-colonial culture are now barely visible.

Creative Research Method 2: Mapping Place and Time

Creative mapping techniques operate across multiple scales of space and histories, grounding design issues within an ecological and cultural context that is often absent in architectural explorations. They also provide a valuable means for recasting the way history is understood within Western architecture – a tradition that privileges evidence of built fabric. This is a particularly problematic bias within Australia given that it is shaped by a combination of the oldest continuing living culture on the most ancient continent, and has a recent colonial history. With Indigenous Australia operating with a light, ephemeral footprint, it is very easy for history to be conceptualised from the foundational colonial moment.[14] Creative mapping techniques allow students to disrupt the orthodox national histories premised on progress and enable them to recast their reading of a site within a much longer temporal continuum.

Creative mapping exercises have had a significant impact within landscape architecture where, since the 1990s, landscape architects have adopted more exploratory approaches to mapping that recognise their generative capabilities. As theorist James Corner states, 'new and speculative techniques of mapping may generate new practices of creativity, practices that are expressed not in the invention of novel form, but also in the productive reformulation of what is already given.'[15] Corner encourages designers to explore the map, firstly as a means of 'finding', then as a means of 'founding', new projects which effectively rework what already exists. He argues that processes of mapping should be valued for both their revelatory and productive potential. In the case of Aboriginal Australia, it is often what has not been mapped and what is left unsaid that are most revealing.

'The thoroughfares of Melbourne, dignified
by the names of streets, are worse than
ever; they form one mass of liquid mud, varying
from 3 inches to 3 feet deep'.

The Herald 1843 in Robyn Annear (2005)
Bearbrass: Imagining Early Melbourne
(Melbourne: Black Inc.) p40

A shower of rain caused a little rivulet to run
along the centre of Elizabeth St; after a day's,
rain, the rivulet turned into a 'brawling torrent'.

Annear, *Bearbrass* p42.

Red indicates site of Indigenous significance
Yellow indicates site of Colonial significance

Taking these practices into the architecture studio was especially productive. Architecture students, more familiar with diagramming or the reductive figure ground image, initially struggled to be open to exploring site for potential in these ways. These explorations, however, not only fundamentally challenge how site is perceived, they also unsettle perceptions of Australian history and culture and a composite mapping technique is thus critical in re-establishing these relationships. Rather than mapping information within different layers, composite maps require different information to be brought into a singular representation. The designer must actively curate and manipulate narratives to produce a new map which is premised on relationships and co-existence. Creating maps from text, image, photographs, places of known Aboriginal occupation and ecological systems, as well as traditional cartography, allowed for voices and ecologies to emerge that are normally excluded from geographic representations of Melbourne.

Addressing the erasure of the Wurrundjeri people and culture from the city, for example, began with developing a composite map focusing on central Melbourne. Denis Byrne argues that the 'invisibility' of Aboriginal people has been affected in two ways: through physical marginalisation and through discursive erasure.[16] He maintains that heritage professionals in general have not 'deployed their skills and knowledge in the interests of revealing the historical coexistence and entanglement of settler and Aboriginal cultures.'[17] The dominant narrative within architectural and urban history positions the pre-colonial conditions of the site and its Indigenous presence at the beginning of the narrative and quickly subsumes it by the heralding of subsequently influential people, designers and builders.[18]

The maps produced in this studio revealed new sites of significance invisible to the eye. For example, the map series of Melbourne's inner city (Figure 1) reveals the disconnect between the early colonial grid of streets and the natural seasonal waterways – particularly along Elizabeth street, which was originally a creek line. Further research into the point where this creek discharges into the Yarra River revealed a site of sacred significance for the Wurundjeri; a place of fertility and 'women's business'. It also heightened the significance of a former one-metre-high waterfall that divided the freshwater upper reaches of the Yarra from the salty estuarine mouth.

The explorations of the sea and monsoon in Mumbai by Anuradha Mathur and Dilip da Cunha gave us insights into how Melbourne's hidden waterways might be mapped. Mathur and da Cunha comment on the difficulty of the British administrators in conceiving Mumbai during the south-west monsoon period, which they considered the 'foul-weather season'.[19] For over two hundred years, planning, administrative decisions and surveying occurred during the 'fair weather', with the monsoon, despite occurring annually, being considered an 'externality'. It was this inability to conceive of this natural process that contributed to the massive flood of July 2005 'when the monsoon and sea refused to follow the lines of maps.'[20] This conceptualisation of the monsoon as external to the fabric and terrain of the city mirrors the externalisation of the water systems of pre-colonial Melbourne, also a city conceived in isolation from the peculiarities of its uncomfortable reality.

Creative Research Method 3: Critical Spatial Practices

Traditional cartography has been systematically critiqued since the 1960s and it is out of this critique that the innovations in creative mapping by Corner and others have developed.[21] However, Michel de Certeau points out that the aerial view that is fundamental to the map is a device that keeps the designer aloof from a site and which misses the way ordinary people often make use of spaces in ways that cannot be seen from above. He describes the 'migrational city' as one that is discovered through the spatial practice of walking.[22] His writings – and those of others such as Guy Debord, Francesco Careri and Bernard Tschumi – have invited design practitioners to embrace performative practices with a view to understanding site differently.

Methods for recording an experiential knowledge of a site have been developed by a range of artists, architects and landscape architects. These include intuitive wandering, making informal notes, site sketching and photographing the unexpected and also include increasingly disciplined approaches that connect map and experience. The Situationists' practice of *derive*, for example, tended toward the informal and intuitive, while Italian architecture group, Stalker, and artist Laura Ruggeri in Berlin disciplined their wandering to follow a specific line drawn on a map. Architect Mie Miyamoto's 17.6 km passage through *London: Section* is similar, though she introduces a representational technique that connects a scaled plan of her walk with an informal photomontage of sketches.

While these techniques vary in the extent to which a Cartesian order organises the process of encountering the eye-level view, they all remain contained to some extent by a post-industrial Western paradigm of logic. South Australian Indigenous scholar Irene Watson argues that the Western understanding of place, and its emphasis on boundaries and land ownership, runs counter to the relational understanding of the land that is central to Indigenous culture. The performative practice of walking 'songlines' and re-telling creation stories is an enactment of respect to the enduring creator spirits who reside within the land.[23]

Michel de Certeau describes the practice of marking a boundary of ownership around a place as a 'strategy' and the use of movement and timing to appropriate place 'owned' by someone else, even for a moment, as a 'tactic'.[24] While these terms denote a particular type of power relation that is arguably not a feature of traditional Indigenous place-making practices, it is a characteristic of post-colonial Indigenous place making. Tactics of temporary re-appropriation of territory have been used by Aboriginal activists over the past 40 years, most notably in the Aboriginal Tent Embassy, first erected in 1972 on the lawns of Parliament House in the nation's capital. As with Deep Listening and the Mapping of Space and Time, these critical spatial practices were used by students to explore their understanding of the site more deeply and to disengage themselves from the Western and modern architectural prejudices regarding their reading of place.

Studio 1: Re-making Place in the Sites of Flow and Passage

Jane Rendell articulates a mode of practice between architecture and public art that allows architectural academics and practitioners to engage with social critique outside the usual programmatic constraints of practice and the isolation of the academe. She coins the term 'critical spatial practices' to describe such works that include temporary material installations and immaterial performances with a deliberately spatial quality. [25] Throughout the post-colonial period, Aboriginal activists in Australia have adopted this mode of practice to make visible their protest against the legal and economic constraints placed on them by government legislation. Examples include the Freedom Rides of 1965, Fiona Foley's *Lie of the Land* (an installation outside the Town Hall in 1997 that has since become a permanent piece at the Museum of Melbourne), *Camp Sovereignty* (a 60-day occupation of the Kings Domain Melbourne in 2006 supported by Breakdown Press's *Stolenwealth* posters) and Ilbijerri Theatre's *Dirty Mile* (a walking tour of Aboriginal Fitzroy in 2008).

In each of these events and installations, artists and activists have used movement and timing to claim place in Australia's urban realm. Using these as precedents, the students of these design studios were challenged to create a temporary 'place' in Melbourne that challenged non-Indigenous assumptions about the land and the colonising practices of European settlers, and helped create spatial opportunities in which important Indigenous stories might re-emerge. There were two criteria: firstly, that the site for the installations be appropriated (consent from landowners or council would need to be sought, but no exchange of money could take place); and secondly, that the material value of the 'tactic' had to be less than $100. Reflecting on stories that the students had heard, they identified sites of Indigenous significance using critical mapping and then engaged with them experientially at different times of the day and week before developing a transformational response. Rather than a heroic architectural gesture, the production of such small-scale ephemeral installations within Melbourne's urban context challenged students to reconsider the scope and agency of architecture. In so doing, the focus of the student shifts from 'architecture as object' to 'architecture as experiential and performative'. Consequently, they are confronted immediately with the reaction of the wider community, enabling them to learn from the experience and hone their approach.

The waterfall mentioned earlier became a focus for many students who, through further mapping investigations, uncovered a correlation between the waterfall and the site of the Turning Basin used to by settlers to turn their tall ships after disembarking goods and passengers to the Customs House in the new colony. The falls were the only natural crossing point for several kilometres and were used by the Wurrundjeri for hunting on the southern marshy riverbanks at dusk. Within 30 years of settlement, the falls were destroyed with dynamite to mitigate against seasonal flooding upstream and the ecological consequences of mixing salt and freshwater went largely unnoticed by colonial settlers for many decades.

This site is now occupied by Flinders Street Station, Melbourne's central railway hub. An underpass beneath the rail lines leads from Elizabeth Street, down steps to an underground access passage and out to a podium above the river's edge. The original creek that ran along this street now flows out of a drain beneath. Research revealed that it was not only a site of 'women's business' for the Wurrundjeri but also a space

Figure 2: The Passing. Nadia Combe

Figure 3: The Falls. Evan Dimitropoulous

of spiritual transition where the spirits of the unborn young wait to be brought into the living world. The confluence of this place of importance for Indigenous peoples and a place of passage in the post-colonial metropolis is one that occurs uncannily in a number of places across the city.[26]

The project developed for this site was a performance entitled *The Passing* (Figure 2). It was inspired by a story about a wrapped Dja Dja Wurrung child's remains left in a spiritual burial spot and later removed to a museum by colonialists.[27] The story was told by Gary Murray from the Victorian Traditional Owners Land Justice Group who had encouraged the students to let it inspire their creative work. Although the final 'design proposal' here was a performance, the process of developing the design response worked within the disciplinary traditions of landscape architecture augmented by the new methods taught in the studio. Narratives were uncovered through listening, reading, visiting collections held at the Koorie Heritage Trust, and studying photographic evidence of tradition Indigenous ceremonies. Creative mapping revealed the site as one of Indigenous significance and studies of the site in plan and section identified the confluence of flows: a river, a creek hidden within a drain, a pedestrian underpass and a train line overhead.

Studies of the site at different times of the day revealed the daily ebbs and flows of pedestrian movement and the passage of the sun. Positioned through a reading of Jan Gehl's *Life Between Buildings*, the specific site made use of a wall, which, given its scale, position and orientation, almost invited appropriation as a stage set. Extensive material studies were made: white clay was traditionally collected upstream, by the Wurrundjeri and used for ceremony and ritual. Casaurina She-Oak branches, traditionally burnt in smoking ceremonies, were used to sweep the site. A range of prototypes of bundles were produced, reflecting on Indigenous weaving traditions. In addition, scene-by-scene choreographic plans were produced to instruct the 'tactics' of appropriation. Stories erased by the 'strategies' of urbanisation were usurped for a moment in time.

Another critical spatial practice, *The Falls* (Figure 3), drew connections between the changes to the natural waterways since colonisation and the commercialisation of water more generally. Prior to the establishment of the colony, the falls were the only crossing point on the Yarra for many kilometres. They enabled hunting and gathering on the southern marshy banks in the early evening while affording an opportunity to retreat to higher dry ground to the north when needed. Commercial trade emerged around water in Melbourne as far back as 1839, just five years after settlement. A group of entrepreneurs installed pumps along the Yarra and hired water carriers to distribute fresh water to the colony at a price of around 1s 6d per 100 gallons.[28] Attempts at damming the Yarra above the falls failed after flood damage; and schemes to pipe water were abandoned. High tides would often rise above the fall line making the water at this point brackish. Outbreaks of water-borne diseases, including cholera, typhoid and dysentery, occurred throughout the 1840s from the discharge of raw sewerage into the Yarra but a sewerage system was not installed for another 50 years. As a result of commercial colonial intervention, the water became undrinkable.[29] This century, commercial trade in water has re-emerged as an escalating phenomenon and, despite Melbourne now having one of the least contaminated and chlorinated water supplies in the world, bottled-water consumption has risen dramatically in recent years. By 2005, Australians drank 550 million litres of bottled water, almost 30 litres per capita, with only a small fraction of the plastic containers being recycled.[30]

The Falls was a spatial performance that recreated the lost waterfall and highlighted environmentally destructive settler–coloniser practices around waterways; its highlight involved participants pouring bottled water from Queensbridge to create a modern version of the waterfall.[31] The Koorie Heritage Trust have requested a copy of the work in which participants, following detailed instructions, collected their water bottles on the deck above the Tuning Basin and walked single file onto the bridge. At a signal, they opened their bottles and poured their water into the river, recreating for a moment the lost waterfall. Again, like *The Passing*, this performance was a carefully choreographed tactic, timed precisely and performed by the crowd that had gathered in perfect unison.

Studio 2: Re-making Place in the Academe

A review of the discursive history of the University of Melbourne reveals the narrow focus of academics and heritage professionals in conceiving urban and spatial history. Accounts of the campus heritage, produced during a period where issues of native title and reconciliation have been at the forefront of public and academic discourses, offer minimal acknowledgement of the site's history or physicality prior to the University's foundation. History begins in 1853, conceived as a celebration of key developmental moments such as the laying of the foundation stone, the many shifts in education that have followed and the construction of major buildings. This narrative mode aligns the construction of the University of Melbourne with the development of Australia as a modern space. While common in Australia's historical discourse, this framing is highly problematic for incorporating Indigenous people within nation and history. It is a position that, as Chris Healy argues, 'ignores the simple fact that being fully in the time and space of Australia could only be conceived in relation to the place and time of Indigenous people in Australia.'[32]

In these studios, students were asked to insert an Indigenous space into the physical fabric of the University campus. Creative mapping techniques formed a valuable starting point for extending the campus's history into a longer temporal and spatial continuum. These mappings revealed the campus as part of a former grassy woodland plain positioned on a high point located between three water bodies. The inclusion of contour lines over the early campus plan reveals that the University's first building, the Gothic-inspired Quadrangle, was constructed on a prominent ridgeline. This ran adjacent to a major creek line which was, in turn, linked into a swampy area. Further archival research into this swampy area revealed an extraordinary history, some of which is highlighted in the map, *Patchy Past* (Figure 4). Events included the Crown Surveyor Hodgkinson extending the boundary of the University to encompass two good trees and swamp (1854); the transformation of the swamp into a lake (1861); Socialist student Guido Baracchi being reprimanded for criticising Australia's involvement in WWI (1917); students re-enacting first contact on the lake, with Captain Cook, King Billy and a treaty (1938); and the final erasure of the lake (1939).

While some historians might argue that these new maps lack the accuracy and rigour of textual histories, their strength is both in their ability to engage simultaneously with

Figure 4: Patchy Past. Fiona Johnson

multiple sources of history, and to uncover new stories, narratives and relationships. The spatialisation of history immediately creates a space of co-existence that addresses Byrne's concern that historians traditionally compose 'a version of the Australian historical landscape which is a fictional space in which races do not interrelate; a space where Aborigines do not even exist.'[33] However, the rich narratives of the site revealed in this way contrast with the limited account offered by the official campus history which frames the swamp as 'an open site, a swampy part of which had probably been a food-gathering area for the local Wurundjeri people' and an 'inhibitor to development.'[34] Today the swamp site forms part of the Union Court known as 'the concrete lawn', erased by post-May '68 design strategies that aimed to riot proof the University campus. Yet our maps revealed a site of significance for both the Indigenous and non-Indigenous, hidden beneath the concrete. Consequently many students chose this area as the site for their proposed intervention.

One scheme, for example, proposed a new flow of paths and surfaces through the built fabric which invited 'an evolving Aboriginal authorship of space through habitation, use and expression.' Ramps carved into the ground plan lead to a new subterranean space and outdoor courtyard that offer multiple canvasses for interactive art, adaptable architecture, new technologies and media (Figure 5). A focus on

Figure 5: An undulating ramp leads into subterranean spaces and a new courtyard. Jacqui Monie

new technologies challenges old notions of primitivism and instead emphasises a continually evolving and highly urbanised Aboriginal culture. The use of technology also facilitates connections beyond the site and provides for the writing of new futures and stories with a strengthened collective voice; it also offers a broader audience.

The ambition to connect the diverse and multiple layers of Indigenous culture also informed an intervention for the student union building, located adjacent to the concrete lawn. This proposal was premised on connecting the isolated pockets of Indigenous presence found within and outside the University. It included the Melbourne Museum, visiting Indigenous academics and the Koori community of Carlton and Murrup Barrack, within the major hub of campus activity in the union building.

This design strategy was informed by the research of Australian architect Shaneen Fantin who advocates for a focus on social practices, rather than the abstraction of Aboriginal semiotic devices into design.[35] It is a response that shifts from presenting Aboriginal culture as an object, to the creation of an architecture based on daily events, activities, use and occupation. Accordingly, the proposal (Figure 6) realigned the existing architectural fabric of the union building to the true cardinal points of east and west which was a reference to the tracking of the sun. It provided opportunities for opening up the internal structure to surrounding spaces and light and allowed for the interweaving of new programs that incorporated Indigenous culture into the structure through the use of natural materials, transitional spaces and external programs. While these spatial and programmatic interventions remain within the realm of speculation, the new mappings and histories uncovered as part of the studio have now been incorporated in a new walking tour of the campus. The 'Billibellary Walk' offers an understanding of how the Wurundjeri people continue to understand the land on which the University was constructed. The extraordinary history of the swamp uncovered as part of the studio will feature as one of the eleven points of interest.

Figure 6:
Interweaving new programs and a new orientation into the existing student union building.
Sarah Delamore

Re-making Place in the City

In 2008, representatives from the Victorian Traditional Owners Land Justice Group (VTOLJG), Reconciliation Victoria (RecVic) and the Melbourne City Council (MCC) Arts and Culture branch joined forces to form a working group to promote a proposal for an Aboriginal cultural precinct in the heart of Melbourne. The proposal has received support in principle from key agencies in the Aboriginal community and local government, and is currently gathering broader support. Such a precinct would be a profoundly significant step in Melbourne, marking a new recognition of the centrality of Aboriginal culture to the national identity. Until now, Aboriginal Cultural Centres have been dispersed, small and, on the whole, located in regional Australia. Although the City of Melbourne has boasted a 'China Town' and a 'Greek Precinct' for decades, Aboriginal culture has been confined to specific facilities, such as Bunjilaka in the Melbourne Museum and the Koorie Heritage Trust, located in a converted office building in the north-west corner of the Central Activities District (CAD). This is the first proposal for a major civic precinct owned and managed by – and for – all Victorian traditional owners.

The students of the third studio worked on a design for a Victorian Cultural Education and Knowledge Centre that would showcase a variety of traditional cultures, both in their traditional and contemporary expressions. It was intended to help boost tourism in south-east Australia and house spaces for education, entertainment, exhibitions, performances, conferences and public events. Students were asked to include office space for Aboriginal organisations and a central commercial precinct for Aboriginal business initiatives. Most significantly, however, they were asked to dedicate space for the cultural expression of each of the almost forty traditional-owner language groups in south-east Australia. It was to be designed as a place that all Victorian Aboriginals could call 'home'.

Defining Aboriginal architecture, which is both rooted in history and reflective of an ever-evolving identity, is extremely challenging. The lack of an identified architectural tradition responding to the majority of urbanised Aboriginals is manifest. Given the dispersal of Aboriginal connectedness, the notion of an Aboriginal gathering place is gaining great currency. However, it is also fraught: what exactly constitutes the notion of 'Aboriginality' and how is it best represented through built form? This studio engaged with these issues and examined the use of appropriate signifiers and representations of different cultural groups.

Relying on or adapting to another's architecture eliminates a culture's ability to define its own voice. Indeed, for Indigenous Australians, the dominant experience has been the need to rely on another's built form, resulting in the need to adapt, renovate or be dominated by culturally inappropriate forms of space making. It was discovered throughout the studio that the current generation of Aboriginals assert themselves in reviving tradition in new ways and, as a result, architecture becomes symbolically powerful. But the key question is how to determine a semiotics of authenticity. It was posited that Indigenous buildings nearly always deal with the interrelated

Figure 7: Proposal for an Indigenous Cultural Knowledge and Education Centre for Melbourne.
Eleanor Fenton

Figure 8: The Yarra River, re-aligned to follow its old course, flows into the ground floor plan of a
proposed Indigenous Cultural Knowledge and Education Centre for Melbourne. Katelin Butler

**+ RE-MAPPING THE
SALTWATER BASIN**

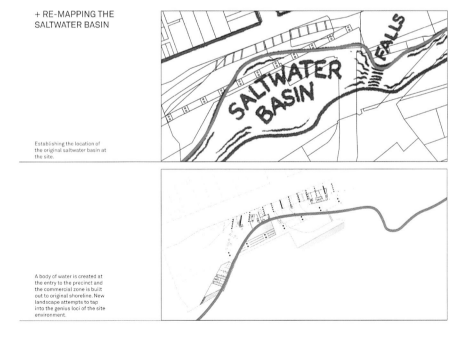

Establishing the location of
the original saltwater basin at
the site.

A body of water is created at
the entry to the precinct and
the commercial zone is built
out to original shoreline. New
landscape attempts to tap
into the genius loci of the site
environment.

issues of sovereignty, economic self-sufficiency and cultural self-determination. We envisaged the potential that a certain distinctiveness borne out of a desire to avoid the universality of global and international forces, which often take away the uniqueness of place and culture, could evolve from this. We dared to think that future Aboriginal architects and their non-Aboriginal collaborators could cherry pick those elements of existing architectural traditions which truly reflected the way in which they wish to be represented, while potentially enabling new and unique hybrids to emerge.

One design was proposed for what is now known as Enterprise Park, originally the site of the first landing by settlers, next to the Turning Basin and opposite the original Customs House, now a museum for Immigration (Figure 7). The design referred to the pre-colonial material practice of making cloaks out of possum skin as inspiration; a practice barred later by colonial authorities and which is only now tentatively re-emerging.[36] The design responded, both symbolically and pragmatically, to the brief and re-imagines Aboriginal place in the heart of urban Melbourne without resorting to the organic forms and rustic materials that are typically associated with Aboriginal Cultural Centres. Conceived as an embassy of sorts, the design embraces the complexity of creating a centre that reflects the variety of language groups, each with different cultural traditions, on the country of the Wurundjeri. Each language group was to be offered one fragment of the façade, like the skin of a possum, that a representative artist would design to represent their group. The assemblage would form a complex whole that represented a craft practice common to all language groups in the south-west of Australia.

While this example emphasises an approach to form-making and visual representation of Indigenous culture, another design explored the relationship of an Indigenous cultural centre to its site, the Yarra River (Figure 8). The Yarra River has been re-aligned a number of times since colonisation, initially to enable ships to travel deeper up the river, but also to manage seasonal silting and to eliminate marshlands which were believed to be associated with disease and ill health.[37] However, it also has a deep indigenous history and, in 2001, Indigenous artist Kimba Thompson, of Sista Girl Productions, developed an installation called *Scar Tree* on the site. Using poles reclaimed from the Queensbridge that were carved by a different Aboriginal artist, the installation pays homage to the breadth of Aboriginal language groups in Victoria prior to colonisation. [38] A second Cultural Centre also responded to the site by re-instating the pre-colonial alignment of the river so that the river penetrates the ground floor of the proposed building. The undulating bank of the river is also re-created, *Scar Tree* is re-positioned along its edge, thus heralding the entry to the new building. Old landscapes merge with new architecture to challenge binaries of architecture–landscape and highlight the cultural significance of living ecologies in Indigenous culture.

These and other projects sought to embrace the complexity of positioning Indigenous culture in the heart of the city, finding contemporary representations of Indigeneity that were neither fixed in a pre-colonial past nor entirely represented through Western practices. As Mathilde Lochert writes, 'complex representations tend to be undermined by stereotypes, i.e. the "traditional", the "real", the "authentic" Aborigine' but, in reality, can never be 'fixed'.[39] Contemporary Aboriginality is indeed complex and diverse and any single expression of culture that purports to unite will not go uncontested; particularly one that is designed by a non-Indigenous designer. As Jenny Williams puts it, the majority of creative industries are invariably 'owned, defined and represented through the lens of the white gaze'. In other words, it is owned by a singular white world view which subsumes the 'authentic' non-white voice.[40] Testing methods such as deep listening, creative mapping and critical spatial practices are a start to changing this but involving Indigenous Australians in teaching is also critical. However, it is not until we have significant participation in the architectural profession by Indigenous designers that we will see new and authentic expressions of contemporary Aboriginality through architecture and landscape architecture emerge.

Conclusion

Although representation by Indigenous Australians in the academe is small, and within the architectural profession is barely existent, Australia has been moving towards reconciliation between settler society and Aboriginal and Torres Strait Islanders since the late 1960s. However, progress has been slow. An Apology to Australia's Indigenous peoples was given by Prime Minister Rudd in 2008 and universities and the Institute of Architects only began developing Reconciliation Action Plans as recently as 2010. It is within this context that new design educational curricula for students of architecture and landscape architecture at the University of Melbourne are being framed. While there are always limitations with student design work, universities are a formative environment wherein the concerns of the next generation of designers are shaped. This is the generation of graduates who will be designing the future and, as we conclude this chapter, we can legitimately ask, what will be the implications of this education for Australia's built environment in decades to come?

We suggest that there are two broad issues at stake, the second contingent on the first. The first is epistemological: to what extent can and should a non-Indigenous 'outside' engage critically with Indigenous knowledge? The second issue is material and spatial: what do we learn about the limitations of settler coloniser practices from our encounter with Indigenous cultural ecologies? There is a third, more specific issue that has also been tested in these studios: how might Indigenous culture claim space within the settler city? Where should it be sited, what form might it take and what new architectural typologies emerge? Non-Indigenous architects have a well-founded anxiety about engaging with Indigenous culture. There is a long history of dispossession and paternalism in Australia and a well-articulated affirmation of Aboriginal people's right to speak for themselves. At times architects have engaged in robust discourse around the successes and failures of architecture for Indigenous culture – particularly in housing and cultural centre design.

The outcomes of these debates have highlighted the difficulties of the binary constructions of Indigenous/non-Indigenous inherent in our professions. One question we must ask then, is whether this kind of design studio is another form of colonisation?

Do we look to Aboriginal culture to enact a new form of capture only when we see the failures of our own? At times, perhaps it is. However, following Lochert, we suggest that non-Indigenous culture is not static either. Australian architectural and landscape architectural practices have changed significantly over two hundred years through an evolving understanding of our environmental conditions, critical encounters with the diaspora of many settler societies, and a growing awareness of the limitations of post-industrial lifestyles. Yet critical engagement with our host culture is only in its infancy. We anticipate that Australian design in the future will continue to change as we develop this process of de-colonisation.

'Listening' to Indigenous narratives of place can occur through many media. We argue that stories are not only read or heard, but take material form in practices of inscription previously regarded as 'non-writing'. By mapping place through layers of time we see a new landscape emerge below the settler city; one in which watery channels and marshlands have been buried beneath bitumen to make more predictable surfaces for building. We begin to understand why, as climate change progresses, these waterways surface with flooding rains and buildings crack in times of drought. However, we also begin to see sacred places disrupted by our practices.

The effects of these studios have rippled out beyond the walls of the faculty, and indeed University of Melbourne at large. The University is now implementing campus tours that are informed by the students' work and which acknowledge the University's Indigenous history. The research project, *Indigenous Placemaking in Melbourne*, continues and outcomes will include a precedent study of Indigenous Cultural centres in Australia and a state-wide 'creative consultation' project that is experimenting with new ways of 'listening'. Greenaway Architects, based in Melbourne, now employs an Indigenous graduate in architecture and they have also launched a consultancy to provide support and advice to architects about Indigenous issues: Indigenous Architecture Victoria. This Consultancy is hosting a Summer School at the Koorie Heritage Trust in 2013 to entice Indigenous youth to consider architecture as a viable career option. They have also been engaged by the Barenji Gadgin Land Council to design a Knowledge and Education Centre in the Wimmera to consider the site selection based on the importance of 'place'. As the twenty-first century unfolds, new opportunities are emerging in Australia for reconciliation between the first peoples of this land and settler society that raise questions about design for a post-colonial city. How to eschew the Western concepts of time and place that appear to be failing us and look to Indigenous knowledge for alternatives is one of its key challenges. This is a challenge that may well be repeated across the world in places dealing with similar issues.

Acknowledgements

We would like to acknowledge the following people and organisations: Emeritus Professor Graham Brawn, Gary Murray from the Victorian Traditional Owners Land Justice Group, Janina Harding and Shona Johnson from The Melbourne City Council Indigenous Arts Program, the Australian Research Council, Reconciliation Victoria and the Melbourne School of Design.

In addition we would like to thank all the students who participated in the design studios, with special thanks to John Mounsey, Nadia Combe, Evan Dimitriopoulous, Jacqui Monie, Fiona Johnson, Sarah Delamore, Eleanor Fenton and Katelin Butler, whose work illustrates this paper.

Notes

[1]   Neville, R. (1997) *A Rage for Curiosity: Visualising Australia 1788–1830*. Sydney: State Library of New South Wales Press, p. 17.

[2]   Griffiths, T. (1996) *Hunters and Collectors: The Antiquarian Imagination in Australia*. Melbourne: Cambridge University Press, p. 151.

[3]   Denoon, D., Mein-Smith, P., and Wyndham, M. (2000) *A History of Australia, New Zealand and the Pacific*. Malden, Mass: Blackwell Publishers, p. 123.

[4]   At no time did any Indigenous group in Australia cede their sovereignty to foreign or Australian governments. Indigenous Australians were considered to have no rights under native title until the 1992 Supreme Court ruling on the Mabo case.

[5]   Birch, A., in conversation, 5 August 2010.

[6]   Carter, P. (2004) *Material Thinking*. Melbourne: Melbourne University Publishing, 2004.

[7]   Brearley, L., & Hamm, T. (2009) Ways of Looking and Listening. In Grierson, E., & Brearley, L., (eds) *Creative Arts Research: Narratives of Methodologies and Practices*. Rotterdam: Sense Publishers, p. 37.

[8]   Brearley & Hamm, 2009, p. 33.

[9]   Van Toorn, P. (2006) *Writing Never Arrives Naked: Early Aboriginal cultures of writing in Australia*. Canberra: AIATSIS, p. 71.

[10] Van Toorn, 2006, p. 72.

[11] Van Toorn, 2006, pp. 72–92.

[12] Indigenous Placemaking in Melbourne: Representations, Practices and Creative Research, is an Australia Research Council funded Linkage project. Melbourne City Council Indigenous Arts Program, Victorian Traditional Owners Land Justice Group and Reconciliation Victoria. Chief investigators include Janet McGaw, one of the authors of this paper, Dr Emily Potter from the School of Communication and Creative Arts at Deakin University, and Dr Anoma Pieris from the Faculty of Architecture Building and Planning at University of Melbourne. It is also supported by Emeritus Professor Graham Brawn, who is a mentor for the project and research assistants Naomi Tootell, Carolynne Baker and Fiona Johnson.

[13] Meucke, S. (2004) *Ancient and Modern: Time, culture and indigenous philosophy*. Sydney: UNSW Press, p. 17.

[14] Recent critical histories by historians such as Boucher and Russell, Edmonds and architectural anthropologist Greenop are emerging that argue an Aboriginal presence continues throughout the process of urbanisation. Physical traces in the built fabric of the urban centres are largely invisible, however. The usual explanation for this is that they built temporary dwellings from sticks and bark; however, the stone architectural remains in south-west Victoria challenge this. Referring to Bulith's archaeological work in this area, Memmot suggests that these may have been far more extensive, and the stones pilfered by settlers to construct paddock fences. Memmott, P. (2007) *Gunya Goondie + Wurley: The Aboriginal Architecture of Australia.* St Lucia: University of Queensland Press, pp. 189–193.

[15] Corner, J. (1999) The Agency of Mapping: Speculation, Critique and Invention. In Cosgrove, D. (ed.) *Mappings.* London: Reaktion Books, p. 17.

[16] Byrne, D. (2003) The Ethos of Return: Erasure and Reinstatement of Aboriginal Visibility in the Australian Historical Landscape. *Historical Archaeology, 37*(1), p. 74.

[17] Byrne, 2003, p. 73.

[18] Goad and Willis have made a case for the writing of a new history of Australian architecture on the grounds that the only comprehensive history of architecture in Australia, J.M. Freeland's *Architecture in Australia* (Melbourne: Penguin Books, 1968), is outdated and excludes a range of national conditions, the foremost being Indigenous architecture. Goad, P., & Willis, J., A Bigger Picture: Reframing Australian Architectural History, *Fabrications: The Journal of the Society of Architectural Historians Ausralia and New* Zealand. St Lucia: The University of Queensland Press, pp. 7–10.

[19] Mathur, A., & da Cunha, D. (2010) The Sea and Monsoon Within: A Mumbai Manifesto. In Mostafavi, M., with Doherty, G. (eds) *Ecological Urbanism.* Switzerland: Lars Muller Publisher, p. 196.

[20] Mathur & da Cunha, 2010, p. 196.

[21] Harmon, K. (2009) *The Map as Art: Contemporary Artists Explore Cartography.* New York: Princeton Architectural Press. This is an extensive survey of a range of critical maps that disrupt dominant geographies.

[22] De Certeau, M. (1984) trans Rendall, S. *The Practice of Everyday Life.* Berkley: University of California Press, p. 93.

[23] Watson, I. (2009) Sovereign Spaces, Caring for Country, and the Homeless Position of Aboriginal Peoples, *South Atlantic Quarterly* 108(1), Durham, NC: Duke University Press, pp. 37–38.

[24] De Certeau (1984) p. xix.

[25] Rendell, J. (2006) *Art and Architecture: A Place Between.* London: IB Taurus, p. 9.

[26] Melbourne Cricket Ground, Melbourne's largest and most iconic stadium was a corroboree site for the 'wurrung' language groups prior to displacement by colonists.

[27] In 1904, a woodcutter discovered the remains of a child wrapped in a possum skin in the fork of a tree. The skin also contained 130 artefacts, both Aboriginal (apron, tool belt and possum skin pegs) and European (button, axe head and bootie), and was determined by the coroner to have died between 1840 and 1860. The remains were kept in storage in the Melbourne Museum until 2003, when after years of campaigning, they were returned to the Dja Dja Wurrung community, which placed them back in the fork of a tree

on the child's 'country', a return to place for remains and spirit. This was a significant step of recognition by a settler institution in recognising its complicity in dispossession and marked a new era of respect of different cultural traditions. The Passing was a performance that transformed the underpass to Flinders St Station one evening during peak hour by recalling these hidden stories. Four characters, a grieving woman, a cleaning woman, an oblivious woman and a hurried woman, participate. A pram is wheeled in, carrying not a child but a box full of ash. The grieving woman opens it and rhythmically sprinkles the ash over the site. A cleaner appears, erecting signs warning passers-by that 'cleaning is in progress' and proceeds to draw buckets of water from the Yarra River below. She begins to mop the platform, the ash and water mixing to turn the bluestone pavement milky white, evoking the materials used in some Indigenous burial ceremonies. A seemingly oblivious woman on her mobile phone on the fringe slowly becomes aware and begins to help. A woman carrying bags and books rushes through, apparently on her way to the station. Dropping her things as she walks through the milky site, she bends to collect them, and a bundle that had been earlier suspended above the scene slowly and magically lowers next to her. The women converge, unwrap the bundle and discover it contains a rabbit skin pelt, beads and trinkets. They join together and silently and reverently re-wrap the bundle, carry it tenderly to the river's edge and lower it into the Yarra River where it is taken by the current. The critical spatial practice celebrates this place once again as a site of womens' business and transition from the living to the spirit world. It challenges the hurried passer-by to consider the numinous in spite of the busyness of their everyday pressures and remembers a different material presence in the ordered surfaces of the contemporary city.

[28] Lewis, M. (1995) *Melbourne: The City's History and Development*. Melbourne: The City of Melbourne, pp. 31–32.

[29] Together with filth, the destruction of the falls that allowed salt water to travel further upstream led Melbournians to look elsewhere for their fresh-water supply. The Yarra River and its fresh-water supply had been one of the key reasons Fawkner and Lancey had selected this site for a new settlement and it is ironic that it took only a decade for settlers to foul the water to the point that it became undrinkable. By 1857, a reticulated water supply fed by a dam in the hills on the outskirts of the city was turned on and, by 1862, all Melbourne's suburbs were connected to free water (Lewis, 1995, pp. 31–49).

[30] Potter, E., Mackinnon, A., McKenzie, S., & McKay, J. (eds) (2007) *Fresh Water: New Perspectives on Water in Australia*. Carlton: Melbourne University Press.

[31] Social media was used to invite people to Queensbridge, the site where the falls once stood, on Saturday 23 October 2010 at 3pm. Each participant received a bottle of water that had been carefully re-labelled. The new labels were a collage of archival ethnographic photographs of Aboriginals with excerpts from letters between Melbourne's surveyor Robert Hoddle and colonial secretary and police magistrate, William Lonsdale, in 1838–39 regarding an attempt to dam the river at the point where the falls once stood. It references the work of Aboriginal artist, Leah King-Smith, Patterns of Connection, that re-contextualised similar portraits with her own paintings and photographs of Australia's bush. One of the guest speakers, Indigenous academic Tony Birch, had shown similar images in the seminar series.

[32]   Healy, C. (2008) *Forgetting Aborigines*. Sydney: UNSW Press, p. 49.

[33]   Byrne, 2003, p. 81.

[34]   Goad, P., & Tibbits, G. (2003) *Architecture on Campus: A Guide to the University of Melbourne and Its Colleges*. Carlton: Melbourne University Press, p. 97.

[35]   Fantin, S. (2003) Aboriginal Identities in Architecture, *Architecture Australia* 92(5), p. 86.

[36]   Details of the historical practice are scarce and can only be gleaned from settlers' diaries and some oral histories; however, many early photographs show Victoria's first inhabitants wearing these cloaks. See Haw, P., & Munro, M. (2011) *Footsteps over the Loddon Plains: A Shared History*. Boort: Boort Development Incorporated. Accounts describe them as garments to keep warm in the chilly winters and as bedding for sleeping on. But they could also be described as a mapping of 'country'. On the back of the skins, using mussel shells heated in fire, Aboriginal people inscribed the place stories of their country using image and symbol and, in so doing, identified their personal connection to clan and tribe. Each person's cloak was different, depending on the knowledges they were responsible for. Skins were added to cloaks over time as children grew to become adults and, when they died, they were buried in them. In the early colonial period, possum-skin cloaks were outlawed and Aboriginals were instead issued with European clothes and woollen blankets. By the late twentieth century, only eight possum-skin cloaks remained, two of which were held in the Melbourne Museum. Over the past decade there has been a resurgence in the practice, led by artists Couzens, Daroch and Hamm, and a number of contemporary cloaks have been made. Gary Murray brought along one that his daughter Ngarra Murray had produced for the Dhudhuroa language group to show the students.

[37]   The Saltwater basin, at what was the foot of the falls, is now covered over with a timber deck and the edge of the river is defined by a bluestone wall and footpath. There are other significant challenges on the Enterprize Park site: two elevated rail bridges hover above, one a Victorian brick overpass, the other a late-twentieth-century concrete addition along the river's edge. The park is cut off from pedestrian access by heavy traffic to the north and east and the Melbourne aquarium is to the west. Although called a park and named after the ship that brought the first wave of colonising settlers to the banks of the Birrarung in 1834, it now functions as an interstitial space.

[38]   There is also a small copse of eucalypts on the site, a reminder of the vegetation of Melbourne before Elm trees were planted along the colonial city's boulevards and streets. These are significant moments of recognition in Melbourne's fabric that are remarkably inaccessible to pedestrians.

[39]   Lochert, M. (1997) Mediating Aboriginal Architecture, *Transition*, 54–55, pp. 8–19.

[40]   Williams, J. (2010) Black Leadership and the white gaze. In Kay, S., & Veneer, K., with Burns, S., & Schwarz, M. (eds) *A cultural leadership reader*. London: Arts Council England, p. 40.

Bibliography

Birch, A., in conversation, 5 August 2010.

Brearley, L., & Hamm, T. (2009) Ways of Looking and Listening. In Grierson, E., & Brearley, L., (eds) *Creative Arts Research: Narratives of Methodologies and Practices* Rotterdam: Sense Publishers.

Byrne, D. (2003) The Ethos of Return: Erasure and Reinstatement of Aboriginal Visibility in the Australian Historical Landscape. *Historical Archaeology, 37*(1).

Carter, P. (2004) *Material Thinking*. Melbourne: Melbourne University Publishing, 2004.

Corner, J (1999) The Agency of Mapping: Speculation, Critique and Invention. In Cosgrove, D. (ed) *Mappings*. London: Reaktion Books.

De Certeau, M. (1984) trans Rendall, S., *The Practice of Everyday Life*. Berkley: University of California Press.

Denoon, D., Mein-Smith, P. and Wyndham. M. (2000) *A History of Australia, New Zealand and the Pacific*. Malden, Mass: Blackwell Publishers.

Fantin, S. (2003) Aboriginal Identities in Architecture, *Architecture Australia* 92(5).

Lochert, M. (1997) Mediating Aboriginal Architecture *Transition,* 54-55.

Griffiths, T. (1996) *Hunters and Collectors: The Antiquarian Imagination in Australia*. Melbourne: Cambridge University Press.

Goad, P., & Tibbits, G. (2003) *Architecture on Campus : A Guide to the University of Melbourne and Its Colleges*. Carlton: Melbourne University Press.

Goad, P., & Willis, J. A Bigger Picture: Reframing Australian Architectural History, *Fabrications: The Journal of the Society of Architectural Historians Ausralia and New Zealand*. St Lucia: The University of Queensland Press.

Harmon, K. (2009) *The Map as Art: Contemporary Artists Explore Cartography*. New York: Princeton Architectural Press.

Healy, C. (2008) *Forgetting Aborigines*. Sydney: UNSW Press.

Lewis, M. (1995) *Melbourne: The City's History and Development*. Melbourne: The City of Melbourne.

Mathur A & da Cunha, D (2010) The Sea and Monsoon Within: A Mumbai Manifesto. In Mostafavi, M with Doherty, G (Eds) *Ecological Urbanism*. Switzerland: Lars Muller Publisher.

Memmott, P. (2007) *Gunya Goondie + Wurley: The Aboriginal Architecture of Australia*. St Lucia: University of Queensland Press.

Meucke, S. (2004) *Ancient and Modern: Time, culture and indigenous philosophy*. Sydney: UNSW Press.

Neville, R. (1997) *A Rage for Curiosity: Visualising Australia 1788-1830*. Sydney: State Library of New South Wales Press.

Potter, E., Mackinnon, A., McKenzie, S., & McKay, J. (Eds) (2007) *Fresh Water: New Perspectives on Water in Australia*. Carlton: Melbourne University Press.

Rendell, J. (2006) *Art and Architecture: A Place Between*. London: IB Taurus.

Van Toorn, P. (2006) *Writing Never Arrives Naked: Early Aboriginal cultures of writing in Australia*. Canberra: AIATSIS.

Watson, I. (2009) Sovereign Spaces, Caring for Country, and the Homeless Position of Aboriginal Peoples, *South Atlantic Quarterly* 108(1). Durham, NC: Duke University Press.

Williams, J. (2010) Black Leadership and the white gaze. In Kay, S., & Veneer, K., with Burns, S., & Schwarz, M. (Eds) *A cultural leadership reader*. London: Arts Council England.

Mary DELLENBAUGH,
Prof Dr Andrea HAASE

CHAPTER 3

DESIGNING IN SHRINKING CITIES – THE CASE OF EASTERN GERMANY

The Shrinking City

According to Karina Pallagst, a leading expert on shrinking cities, every sixth city in the world is shrinking.[1] However, not all shrinking is equal. Reasons, degrees, rates and types of shrinkage vary from place to place and between eras. The primary reasons behind shrinkage in the 1950s in the US, for example, 'white flight' and post-war suburbanisation, were not the reasons for shrinkage in the 1970s: the collapse of heavy industry in many areas.[2] Shrinkage and growth, concentration and distribution, have to do with migration, and the reasons for migration vary based on social, political and economic contexts. In addition, trigger events such as the opening of borders, the changing of laws or economic fluctuations can change the attractiveness of various areas for different groups, thus unleashing the selective migration seen in the 'white flight' studies.

Twenty-three years after Germany's reunification, East German cities present unique opportunities to develop innovative approaches to the conditions presented by shrinking cities. The legacy of forty years of socialist influences on urban development plus the ensuing dramatic demographic changes in the years after the fall of the Berlin Wall have created an individual set of challenges for professionals in the fields of urban design, architecture and urban planning. The changes in Germany were not only sudden but also drastic, with Karina Pallagst speaking of a net migration of over one million East German residents to West Germany between 1991 and 2004.[3]

Figure 1: Vacant Plot in Magdeburg, Saxony-Anhalt

Some studies describe a net loss of 1.6 million people between 1989 and 2009 – 12 per cent of the total population[4] – while others quote figures of up to 2 million between 1989 and 2011.[5] In the cities of East Germany an average of 12 per cent of the population emigrated in the years after the fall of the Wall but, for the three case study cities in Saxony-Anhalt that will be discussed in this paper, the proportions were much higher, averaging 20 per cent.[6,7] In addition, a disproportionately high number of the émigrés in the East German case are women under thirty-five – a particularly significant figure given that this demographic grouping is key to natural population growth and its absence is one of the more specific characteristics of German population decline.

In Germany, the interest in addressing the shrinking phenomenon from the perspective of urban redevelopment (*Stadtumbau*) began in February 2000 when a special commission was formed by the government. It was set up by the Federal Minister for Traffic, Building and Housing, the State Minister of the Chancellery, and the Federal Commissary for Affairs of the New German States.[8] The commission, formed to assess the problem of vacant apartments in the new German states, declared in their report in November 2000 that, 'ten years after reunification, approximately one million apartments, or around 13 per cent of the housing stock in East Germany, stood empty', and suggested a 300,000 to 400,000 unit reduction in housing stock over the course of 10 years in order to stabilise the housing market.[9]

The removal of housing units concentrated, above all, on the newest housing stock: the socialist post-war housing estates on the outskirts of the cities. In 2002, the joint federal–state program *Stadtumbau Ost* (Urban Redevelopment East) was officially begun. It hosted competitions and provided funding for urban regeneration projects and programmes. In order to be able to take part in the program, towns had to have developed an integrated urban planning concept (*Integrierten Stadtentwicklungskonzept – ISEK*). Thus the program, which ran from 2002 to 2009, did not just intend to remove housing stock, it aimed at ensuring this occurred as part of an integrated plan for the long-term betterment and stabilisation of the East through holistic planning measures. [10]

German academic research about shrinking cities and *Stadtumbau Ost* has run parallel to this program, and the growing demands on planners and urban designers have been increasingly discussed in academic circles in the last few years.[11] Furthermore, there has been increased interest in landscape ecology studies that deal with both the ecological goods and services of abandoned land[12] and the possibilities around urban forestry.[13] Indeed, an interest in these issues has come together to form a rich vein of research in the context of the former East Germany.

German Reunification and the East German Shrinking City

The fall of the Berlin Wall was the beginning of a great many changes in Eastern Europe. In Germany, forty years of separate development had created a critical economic difference between the states of the Federal Republic of Germany (FRG – West Germany) and the former German Democratic Republic (GDR – East Germany). In fact, the construction of the Berlin Wall, which began in August 1961, was in part a reaction to the differential development of the two Germanys and the political side effects created by it. According to official numbers, between 1949 and 1961, the population of the GDR fell from 18.3 million to 17 million: a loss of 7 per cent of the population in just 12 years.[14] Other sources indicate that this number may be too low, suggesting that up to one quarter of the population emigrated before the Berlin Wall was finished in 1961.[15] The emigration was not equal across all professional and age groups, however, but was primarily composed of young, highly skilled and highly educated citizens; a phenomenon aptly termed 'brain drain'.[16]

The solidification of the border through the construction of the Berlin Wall and the inner-German border stopped the initial loss of skilled workers and young families, although birth rates remained very low. In the West, the post-war economic boom continued well into the 1970s and involved the establishment of industrial centres throughout West Germany. Good examples of this are the banking headquarters in Frankfurt am Main, the concentration of television and radio studios in Cologne, and the grouping of publishing houses in Bavaria.

German reunification doomed the inefficient and superfluous socialist industrial complex to closure and, at the same time, crippled the job market in the East.[17] This meant that the 'new German states', as the former East is called in German, were disadvantaged in two regards in 1990: they had fewer skilled workers and no established industrial centres. The collapse of the socialist industrial complex in the first few years after the fall of the Wall meant unemployment rates were as high as 40 per cent in some areas[18] and, as a result, emigrating job seekers were one of the main sources of shrinkage in these areas in the early 1990s.

These structural conditions, and their resulting developments, also had significant effects on the landscape. The socialist industrial building complexes had consisted not only of factories and warehouses, but also of corollary structures for workers such as vacation settlements, kindergartens, worker housing and administrative buildings, all of which were state owned.[19] These facilities were all abandoned with the collapse of East German industry, leaving a proportionally high number of vacant and abandoned buildings blotting the landscape of the East almost overnight. In light of population decline, lack of demand, lack of industry and a lack of funding, these buildings could only be repurposed to a very limited extent, if at all.[20]

Another issue affecting the renovation of buildings at the time was the restitution clause in the reunification contract. This stated that properties seized or abandoned during the regimes of either the Nazis or the socialists must be returned to their original owners. [21] The main problem with this was the fact that the restitution clause covered a time span of over sixty years, during which several legitimate owners may have owned the buildings in question. Disputes over restitution rights dominated the early '90s and deeply complicated the renovation or adaptation of these properties, since no steps could be taken until the legitimate owners were found or determined.[22] In the case of Jewish properties seized by the Nazis, the original owners were often no longer alive and in these cases, the property was generally returned to their heirs; a fact that complicated matters even further.[23]

The fundamental economic changes that went along with reunification were also catastrophic for Eastern Germany. The economic logic of socialism did not favour the accumulation of capital in the form of savings, for example, as it did and still does (in general) under capitalism. Hence, East German citizens were wholly at a disadvantage in comparison to their West German counterparts, who had not only benefited from the post-war economic boom, but also from being part of the fundamentally different, and ultimately victorious, economic system. All of this saw the value of earnings in the East halved with the adoption of the new currency.[24] To this day, wages, but also living costs, are much lower in the new German States.[25] In this economic and labour context, emigration to West Germany (or elsewhere) became increasingly common and is a phenomenon which has left consequences that are still being dealt with today.

East German cities have become trapped in a downward spiral in which those who could both revive the inner cities and bring tax revenue to state coffers, the skilled workers and educated young people with families, are the ones who continue to move away. The remaining population is ageing and a larger proportion of them is retiring than entering the workforce – yet one more factor increasing the economic burden that the new states seem to pose.[26]

While discussions of shrinking cities in countries such as the United States centre around privatisation and revitalisation – such as the transforming of old warehouses into loft apartments, the replacement of high-density housing with low-density housing, and the incorporation of empty lots into large city parks, for example[27] – East German cities are confronted with a very different set of issues. As described above, such redevelopments cannot be realised in East Germany for the simple reasons of extremely low demand and a dearth of investors. All of this constitutes a constellation of negatively developing characteristics: the lack of tax revenue means that the abandoned lots remain abandoned; the lack of young women means that the birth rate drops further; the average age of the population continues to rise meaning that more people retire rather than join the workforce; and the unattractiveness of areas of derelict landscape compound the problems by doing little to stem the tide of emigration.

A Framework for Solutions – Stadtumbau Ost and 'Less is Future'

Several top-down planning instruments have been used in the last two decades to attempt to combat these problems, the first and probably most important of which was *Stadtumbau Ost*, (Urban Regeneration East). This federal program was intended to speed up the development of integrated urban development plans in the new German states. Several projects and laws were nested under the larger *Stadtumbau Ost*, among them the 'International Building Exhibition Urban Redevelopment Saxony-Anhalt 2010' (*International Bauausstellung Stadtumbau Sachsen-Anhalt 2010*), an international design competition aimed at fomenting urban planning ideas, whose name was later shortened to 'Less is Future' (*Weniger ist Zukunft*).[28] This programme, intended to provide the towns with planning instruments for the period up to 2010, not only informed practice but also forms the backdrop of many educational projects such as the case studies and student projects discussed here.

In the summer of 2001, the Bauhaus foundation in Dessau, which is housed in the same campus as the *Hochschule Anhalt* (The Applied University [Hochschule] Saxony-Anhalt), presented a concept for an international building exhibition to the federal minister of building.[29] The programme proposed a design competition for sites in nineteen cities and towns in the state of Saxony-Anhalt between 2003 and 2010.[30] The proposal was approved in November 2002 and the resultant projects subsequently formed the backbone of architecture, urban-design and landscape-design teaching in the area in the following years[31] – an example of which was the international masters programs in architecture and landscape architecture at *Hochschule Anhalt*.

In discussing education and its response to the phenomenon of the shrinking city, it is important to note that not only the political, economic and industrial infrastructure of the GDR, but also its educational and research infrastructure was fundamentally affected by the political changes of the early 1990s. The education programs were reorganised throughout the East because, amongst other things, the East German higher education and research system was regarded as too influenced by the socialist state.[32]

In this context, four new applied universities, including the *Hochschule Anhalt*, were set up during this period, all focussing on subject-specific, practical and applied skills. These 'applied universities' are state run and financed, and typically divide programs among themselves. As a result, there is only one design program in the state. In addition to the four technical universities, however, two historic universities (*Universitäten*) that primarily focus on the theoretical and 'high-science' aspects of education and knowledge production are also located in the state. Thus, what we have in Saxony-Anhalt is a clear division of the practical and theoretical aspects that is typical of the German academic system.

Setting it apart from the strict traditional German disciplinary approach, the international masters program in architecture at *Hochschule Anhalt* integrates various departments at *Hochschule Anhalt* to provide a framework for interdisciplinary learning. Other characteristics that broaden the learning experience at the school are the mix of students from around the world and its learning-by-doing ethos.[33] In this regard, the teaching methods employed are premised on presenting students with the harsh realities of local site conditions and encouraging them to develop innovative and creative solutions appropriate to the spatial and location-specific conditions of sites in the area.

The subject matter and scope of the lectures and studios offered at *Hochschule Anhalt* are intended to be appropriate for dealing with the very specific and demanding design challenges found in the region and include, amongst other things, the study and response to 'spatial breaks' – the fragmentation of cities resulting from processes of de-industrialisation and de-population which are the result of globalisation, international emigration and local and regional factors such as those discussed earlier.

Numerous studios and courses at *Hochschule Anhalt* deal with, and have dealt with, these and other related issues relevant to German states affected by shrinkage and it is in this context that we see the importance and influence of programs such as *Stadtumbau Ost* in the educational sector and the way in which education is responding to the specific issues affecting the former East Germany. The architecture program alone, for example, conducts four studio projects per year, at least half of which concern the immediate region. They are intended to involve real research and to come up with real proposals, three examples of which are discussed here.

Three Case Studies and Projects

Magdeburg, Dessau and Halle are all cities located in the southern and central parts of Saxony-Anhalt that border the state of Lower Saxony (*Niedersachsen*) to the west, and thus formed the inner-German border between 1949 and 1990[34] (Figure 2). Overall, the population of Saxony-Anhalt has dropped by over half a million since 1990, a sum that represents nearly 20 per cent of the state's population at the time of reunification. [35] All its towns share similar characteristics in terms of their structural conditions and all show evidence of having fallen derelict as a consequence of widespread emigration. That said, as we shall discuss below, although all three towns have been through the

Figure 2. Map of Saxony-Anhalt.

same political changes since 1989, these changes have had different consequences for their local urban character, and their material and immaterial urban conditions and characteristics.

All three towns successfully competed in the *Stadtumbau Ost* design competition in 2001, one of the goals of which was to come up with ideas to help the cities establish an 'urban brand' and new identity. Magdeburg won with the theme *Leben an und mit der Elbe* (Life on and with the Elbe). Halle successfully competed with the theme *Waldstadt Silberhöhe* (Forest city Silberhöhe – a socialist post-war housing estate in Halle) and Dessau won funding with their innovative concept *Stadtinseln* (Urban islands). All three integrated the demands of the design competition and worked towards the reduction of housing stock in different ways.[36]

One of the main foci of the design projects carried out at *Hochschule Anhalt* was the goal set as part of *Stadtumbau Ost*: to increase the significance of the service and knowledge-based economy in the area. All three of the case-study areas contain a higher-education facility, a university or technical university, which has contributed to the current situation of the town and, as we shall argue in detail later, can play a significant role in the redevelopment of this kind of city. The expansion of the university in Magdeburg has gentrified a formerly industrial riverside district near the river Elbe and, as a result, one of the formerly industrial sites near the river has been restructured and integrated into inner urban areas for the first time. Similarly, the development of the university district in Halle has revitalised this part of the city and strengthened the role of the already well-integrated inner-city university as part of the medieval core of the town. The building of the campus in Dessau, and its renewal of public spaces during the last two years, has beautified the portion of Dessau around the Bauhaus and *Hochschule Anhalt* on the western side of the railway track, albeit in a way that visually and spatially underlines the separation of the town into two parts; the industrially influenced east and the arts and science influenced west.

These new developments around the universities have taken place alongside the cities' medieval cores which, in each case, have the potential to facilitate a rich and diverse array of service industries including, but not limited to, knowledge production. In order to broaden local opportunities in accordance with the locally existing structural conditions, the projects dealt with below suggest options for connecting currently derelict and recently regenerated parts of the urban fabric so as to enrich the uses, the image and the concept of urban space in these 'shrinking cities'.

Post-reunification housing development in these cities has concentrated on the redevelopment, redesign or partial demolition of mono-functional socialist large-scale housing estates and the promotion of its opposite: single-family houses. In practice, this means the case-study areas are witnessing a post-reunification emergence of suburban neighbourhoods that continues unabated today. Within this range of general characteristics, the case studies and projects carried out at *Hochschule Anhalt* worked with a framework of five specific design criteria seen as being of key importance for successful redevelopment.[37]

The first of these criteria can be defined as the distribution of large urban open spaces and their interconnection with the surrounding region. The cities in question are perforated by large ecologically significant urban spaces whose integration with the surrounding countryside is critical for wildlife migration, air circulation and the alleviation of the heat-island effect. The second important design criteria identified was the proximity of, and the relationship between, urban areas and river banks. Each of the case study areas is located on a river whose banks provided the backdrop for industrial expansion. Discontinuation of industrial uses has meant that the large quantities of industrial buildings located here are derelict and, in some cases, that the associated sites are contaminated. These waterways and their respective wetlands are ecologically, historically, culturally and socially significant and must form a major area of interest in any future development.

Thirdly, the readability of history and different periods of urban development in the urban profile is considered an important design criterion. The case studies, which were all significant industrial centres in the first half of the twentieth century, have been periodically destroyed and rebuilt over the years; both the First and Second World Wars in particular left significant 'scars' on the landscape. In addition, the substantial visual and structural differences between pre- and post-WWII architecture and urban planning means that the landscape feels very fragmented, and that the sense of place or *genius loci* is diffuse and impalpable. Finding ways to remedy this is fundamental.

The fourth point to be considered is the distribution and character of central and de-central public spaces in the case study areas. Open spaces play an important ecological role in the urban environment, as mentioned above, but are also important for recreation and thus a sense of general well-being for inhabitants. It is important to ensure that any new developments offer a just distribution of open space for recreation to all inhabitants and not just those in more well-to-do neighbourhoods.

The fifth and final point to bear in mind is the usability, legibility and changeability of urban conditions in settled areas. The fact that the case-study towns have been partially destroyed and rebuilt in several waves means that it has been difficult to ensure the integration of buildings and areas into an overall coherent plan; a fact that impedes orientation, the integration of services and movement, amongst other things. In addition, this lack of integration has hindered future-oriented changes and the urban responsiveness which are needed to adapt these towns to the changing demands for living and working in today's economic and social climate.[38]

Case Study 1: Magdeburg

Magdeburg is located on the River Elbe. It is the state capital and, spatially, the densest of the case-study cities. The River Elbe cuts deeply into the lowlands of the *Magdeburger Börde* region and, whereas the riverside to the east merges with woodlands and wetlands, to the west it forms a clear edge which was an important urban and industrial core in the past. The river valley connects the large-scale greenways in the area and separates the wilderness in the east from the controlled agricultural lands to the west.

The research carried out as part of this project identified that the former fishing villages that form the core of the pre-industrial city on the western bank of the Elbe have clearly defined access to the river. It showed that the former industrial sites are frequently located on polluted and derelict ground and are separated by transport routes from the river and that 'readability' in the major urban core is primarily based on medieval landmarks such as churches and marketplaces (Figure 3). It also identified that the edges of the former villages were transformed by ribbon development in the GDR period that has fragmented the main core of the city, and that the cores of these former villages have been strongly influenced by single-family house development since reunification; a fact that has further exacerbated their already existent mono-functional spatial arrangement.

The research conducted here also revealed that the central public spaces are fragmented and dominated by commercial activities, and that decentralised public spaces like paths along the river and village cores derive their meaning from frequent use by residents. Mixed in with all this are suburban areas that have direct access to open spaces, and thus allow for a small-grained spatial integration of new uses and activities.

Figure 3: Magdeburg. Housing and the Towers of Magdeburg Cathedral in the historic centre.

Figure 4: Water Tower and proposed decentralised development.

In response to these conditions, the projects develop by the university students involved the redesign of a former industrial site between a major traffic route and river. The core of the project was a broad strategy that would allow for the preservation, maintenance and renewal of the city's historic water tower; this would intensify the land use on and around the site so as to make it a viable location for investment and redevelopment. The historical water tower is a site with various inherent advantages such as the beauty of the adjacent riverside landscape. The importance of the landmark is highlighted by its nickname: 'The Cathedral of the South of Magdeburg' (Figure 4).

The projects put forward by the architectural students for this site involved, firstly, arguing architecturally, technically and economically for the maintenance of the tower itself; and then for developing the surrounding site for decentralised residential housing. In this way, the site was to be developed with a differentiated hierarchy of public spaces that would combine and integrate the water tower as the main public space, the residential area as a semi-public space, and pathways to river Elbe as the main public network of connections to the waterside. The combination of these ideas not only met the design criteria identified in the early stages of the project, but their perspective was widened even more through the proposal to establish a 'business improvement district' (BID) which would gain funding from the state.

Case Study 2: Halle

Halle is built around the River Saale. Its main medieval centre is located to the south of the river and the main post-war housing settlement, *Halle-Neustadt*, forms a satellite to the west of the main agglomeration. The historic city and *Halle-Neustadt* are separated by the north–south path of the river which meanders within the inner urban area and provides an extension of the riversides there. Our students suggested that, in addition, it connects 'two different worlds': the multifunctional pre-industrial core with its extensions in the east and the large mono-functional ribbon of post-war housing complexes in the west.

They identified that the potential to connect the inner-city areas and the riversides exists and, indeed, that many such attempts had been made in the past. Research indicated that the 'readability' of the urban fabric attains its highest levels in the central core of the city and that the central public spaces are clearly defined in the central core, but not yet in the areas around the watersides. Decentralised public spaces, in both urban and suburban settings, suffer from the effects of industrialisation and, since reunification, have also suffered from complete spatial fragmentation. These features are most obviously seen on the edges of the medieval villages that form the core of the city (Figure 5).

South of the medieval core, the outskirts of the medieval fortification have been rebuilt several times, most recently during the 1960s, when the elevated highway that turned *Halle-Neustadt* into an area for the extension of industrial housing in the GDR period was also built. West of the River Saale, there are several high-rise towers that have fallen derelict due to shrinking-related demographic changes and changing demands

LIVERPOOL JOHN MOORES UNIVERSITY
LEARNING SERVICES

Figure 5: Halle. View towards the inner city.

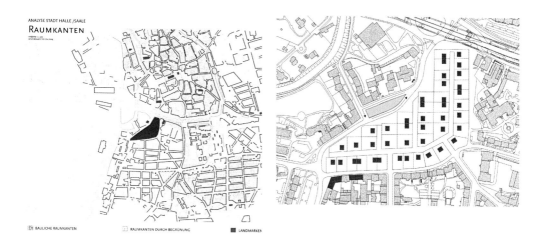

Figure 6: Position of proposed 'human-scale' housing (left); and the same shown in close up (right).

for housing. The projects developed in response to these developments attempted to restructure this housing and create a more 'human-scale' environment that connected the medieval core with the southern suburban areas of *Halle-Neustadt* through landscaping schemes and the creation of public spaces. Consequently, the projects concentrated on an arrangement of open 'interim' spaces that could become a new core-cell for urban life between the medieval core and the south-western outskirts (Figure 6).

Case Study 3: Dessau

Dessau is located at the juncture of the Elbe and Mulde rivers. The River Elbe flows from east to west and has a distinct oxbow bend between the satellite centre Roßlau to the north and Dessau's urban core to the south. In the 1950s, a highway was built that cut through the riverside and through the former castle garden, disturbing the flow of the river in the urban core. In the north and east, areas dominated by green spaces that integrate well with the surrounding landscape (Figure 7), the Mulde and the Elbe frame the city.

The research conducted in this project identified that fragments of the city's pre-industrial history remain, although the landscape is mostly dominated by industrial relics and buildings with mono-functional uses. The most obvious central public space is the city park (*Stadtpark*) in the middle of the town which, however, needs to be better integrated into the surrounding built space in order to work well at an urban scale (Figure 7). Most public spaces are decentralised and are more or less invisible to visitors not familiar with the area. They are, however, well known and well used by inhabitants. The architectural students' projects here focused on the interconnection of the park and the surrounding urban areas and identified three levels of intervention defined as slight support, modest renewal and strong intervention.

Slight support referred to opportunities to identify, localise and strengthen existing spatial characteristics; *modest renewal* referred to enriching these conditions by adding new components; while *strong intervention* involved replacing areas with new designs that would facilitate new connections between built forms and open spaces. Different

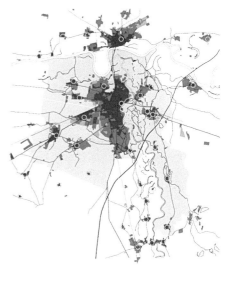

Figure 7: Dessau. The poorly integrated city park.

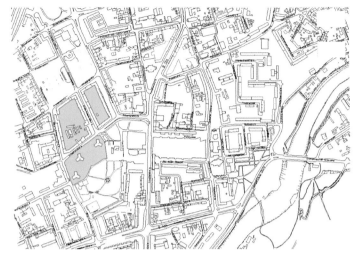

Figure 8:
Proposed plan of
Dessau – 'strong
intervention' to
create a new
block and better
integration of the
city park.

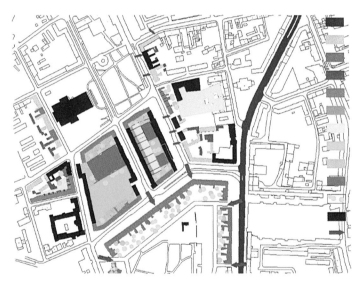

urban forms were proposed relative to the intensity of intervention proposed in different areas. In one case, for example, the *Stadtpark* was 'framed' by built forms arranged around open spaces. In another, major mono-functional buildings, such as the local shopping mall were removed and replaced by smaller structures that offered a mixture of uses and opened up movement around them (Figure 8).

Each of these specific proposals and the broader studio projects from which they emerged were intended to address three aspects of development in post-socialist Germany: derelict historic buildings, disruptive post-war development, and the integration of urban planning from different eras. In Magdeburg, the students' projects involved the preservation of a historic landmark through the extension of contemporary mixed-used development. In Halle, they saw the creation of 'interim' settlements that soften the edges between pre-war and post-war urban planning; and lastly, in Dessau, the case study most significantly affected by fragmentation through loss of population, the projects focused on strengthening the city core and the creation of a central meeting and gathering place.

These are all projects that reflect the need to transform large-scale, mono-functional housing zones in the area, whether they be urban post-war housing estates or suburban, post-reunification, single-family dwelling areas. They reflect the need to find new uses for abandoned industrial sites and seek to enrich existing urban spaces by redeveloping the 'spaces' or 'gaps' between existing centres of activity. They also seek to restructure and integrate the existing well-frequented urban and suburban public spaces, semi-natural landscapes and greenways into their new proposals; all through small-scale spatial interventions that instigate and guide processes of self-organisation and support the functional characteristics of the landscapes.

They are projects that support the postulation that holistic and socially sustainable interventions by urban planners, architects and landscape architects in this type of city suffering from shrinkage need to break up, enrich and combine areas of mono-functional use by integrating new activities and structures that make places meaningful, recognisable and create a unique sense of place, or *genius loci*. As a result, a move from large blocks of mono-functional buildings to diverse small-scale patterns is proposed to allow dynamic shrinkage and growth to take place as necessary. This is important because diverse, small-scale urban development and design allow for the restructuring of buildings and their uses in new ways as changing conditions dictate in the future.

Summary: The Double Role of Education

Although the opportunities for implementing these plans in the current climate are very limited due to a complete lack of funding and a general lack of capital flow in the region, each of these projects was seen as a genuine investigation and a realistic proposal capable of either being implemented or forming the basis of more developed proposals at a later date. As a result, they are important in that they provide a deeper understanding of the problems and possibilities offered by the region and thus represent the foundation of future possible developments. They are also important in that they encourage students, and universities as institutions, to engage in the 'realities' of their region which, in these cases, means more than just setting projects there.

The move from mono-functional to more adaptive spatial arrangements in such contexts represents the spatial expression of a fundamental social and cultural turn in Europe – from an industrial, product-based economy to a post-industrial, service- and knowledge-based economy. Solutions in shrinking cities like those of the former East

Germany must continue to be future-oriented and focus on structural organisations that bring the development of knowledge-based infrastructures to the fore. Typical in this regard are creative individuals such as artists and designers, but also institutions such as universities, research complexes and facilities.

This involves seeing the creative industries and education as active economic factors as well as the sites of theoretical and practical research investigations.[39] In contexts such as those described here, the university itself is an active economic driver in regeneration and, as a result, it is important to respond appropriately to make sure it remains so. On one level, this involves ensuring that infrastructure such as housing, public transportation and open spaces are appropriate and contemporary in order to attract students and keep young skilled workers in the area upon the completion of their degree. On another level, however, it involves a reconsideration of the curriculum and approaches to teaching.

In today's complex economies, in which the factors that affect the success, or otherwise, of any initiative or region are multiple, diverse and interrelated, we would argue that it is important that professionals be trained in systems thinking – so as to better understand a range of different disciplines and ideas.[40] The educational programs at Dessau and *Hochschule Anhalt* seek to break out of the traditional, hierarchical and disciplinary approach in Germany to rise to the challenges presented by shrinking cities. The success of *Stadtumbau Ost* further highlights the fact that an integrated and interdisciplinary approach is appropriate for dealing with the complex and multiple structural specifics in Eastern Germany.

The architecture and landscape architecture programs at *Hochschule Anhalt* have made the first step in this direction and continue to strive for locally specific integration of this approach. This should, however, be done with an eye on international lessons through both international and regional projects that help understand and dynamically define the innate qualities of urban life and character in shrinking cities.

The educational program must also be revised and extended to accommodate these requirements. Concrete steps to improve teaching so as to contribute to the tackling of the challenges presented by shrinking cities in our context include; a yearly symposium to refine the existing approaches to teaching and design; extending the existing program to PhD level; employing PhD students for teaching; and introducing a new practical office on site in Dessau.[41]

This type of development will be the next step of an on-going engagement of education in the challenges of the future in Germany that will add to the potential of universities to work with local and regional areas and the issues and problems they face. They will add value to the type of project described here in which education has already been involved in the 'production' of new ideas and initiatives and the 'reproduction' or reworking of existing projects, initiatives and infrastructures inherent to the economy of the country and its regions. These must be the goals followed in any design or planning program, particularly one dealing with the phenomenon of shrinking cities.

Notes

[1]   El Nasser, H. (2006, December 27) As older cities shrink, some reinvent themselves. *USA TODAY*. Retrieved from: http://www.usatoday.com/news/nation/2006-12-26-shrinking-cities-cover_x.htm

[2]   Ibid.

[3]   Ibid.

[4]   Kulish, N. (2009, June 19) In East Germany, a Decline as Stark as a Wall. *The New York Times*. Retrieved from: http://www.nytimes.com/2009/06/19/world/europe/19germany.html

[5]   Bauer, 2011.

[6]   Statistisches Landesamt Sachsen-Anhalt (2012, August 6) Entwicklung der Deutschen und Ausländer in Sachsen-Anhalt seit 1990. Retrieved from: http://www.stala.sachsen-anhalt.de/Internet/Home/Daten_und_Fakten/1/12/124/12411/Entwicklung_der_Deutschen_und_Auslaender.html

[7]   These shrinking tendencies had different sources in the three case-study areas examined and were linked back to three causes that were present in different proportions in the three cities: natural population decline (death rate > birth rate), emigration and suburbanisation (Haase, 2011).

[8]   Pfeiffer, U., Simons, H., & Porsch, L. (2012, August 29) Wohnungswirtschaftlicher Strukturwandel in den neuen Bundesländern – Bericht der Kommission. Retrieved from: http://www.schader-stiftung.de/docs/kommission_strukturwandel_kurzfass.pdf

[9]   Pfeiffer, U., Simons, H., & Porsch, L. (2012, August 29) Wohnungswirtschaftlicher Strukturwandel in den neuen Bundesländern – Bericht der Kommission. Retrieved from: http://www.schader-stiftung.de/docs/kommission_strukturwandel_kurzfass.pdf

[10]   Institut für Regionalentwicklung und Strukturplanung. (2012, August 6) Bund-Länder-Programm Stadtumbau Ost. Retrieved from: http://www.stadtumbau-ost.info/

[11]   Bontje, M. (2004) Facing the challenge of shrinking cities in East Germany: The case of Leipzig. *GeoJournal*, 61(1) pp. 13–21; Hollander, J. B., Pallagst, K., Schwarz, T., & Popper, F. J. (2009) Planning shrinking cities. *Progress in Planning*, 72(4), pp. 223–232; Kühn, M., & Liebmann, H. (eds) (2009) *Regenerierung der Städte: Strategien der Politik und Planung im Schrumpfungskontext*. Wiesbaden: VS Verlag für Sozialwissenschaften; Müller, B., & Siedentop, S. (2012, August 29) Growth and Shrinkage in Germany – Trends, Perspectives and Challenges for Spatial Planning and Development, Berlin. Retrieved from: http://www.difu.de/publikationen/growth-and-shrinkage-in-germany-trends-perspectives-and.html; Pallagst, K. (2010) Viewpoint: The planning research agenda: shrinking cities – a challenge for planning cultures. *Town Planning Review*, 81(5), pp. i–vi; Rieniets, T. (2012, August 27) Shrinking cities – growing domain for urban planning? Retrieved from: http://aarch.dk/fileadmin/grupper/institut_ii/PDF/paper_presentation_EURA2005.pdf

[12]   Langer, M., & Endlicher, W. (eds) (2007) *Shrinking cities: Effects on urban ecology and challenges for urban development*. Frankfurt am Main: Peter Lang.; Müller, N., Werner, P., Mathey, J., & Rink, D. (2010) Urban Wastelands – A Chance for Biodiversity in Cities? Ecological Aspects, Social Perceptions and Acceptance of Wilderness by Residents.

In N. Müller, P. Werner & J. G. Kelcey (eds), *Urban Biodiversity and Design*. Oxford: Wiley-Blackwell; Rink, D. (2009) Wilderness: the nature of urban shrinkage? The debate on urban restructuring and restoration in eastern Germany. *Nature and Culture*, 4(3), pp. 275–292.

[13] Dettmar, J. (2005) Forests for Shrinking Cities? The Project 'Industrial Forests of the Ruhr'. In I. Kowarik & S. Körner (eds), *Wild Urban Woodlands: New Perspectives for Urban Forestry*, Berlin/Heidelberg: Springer, pp. 263–276; Kowarik, Ingo (2005) Wild urban woodlands: Towards a conceptual framework. In I. Kowarik & S. Körner (eds), *Wild Urban Woodlands: New Perspectives for Urban Forestry*, Berlin/Heidelberg: Springer, pp. 1–32.

[14] –. (1989) *Statistisches Jahrbuch der DDR. 1. Auflage*. Berlin (Ost): Staatsverlag der DDR.

[15] Laar, M. (2010) *The Power of Freedom, Central and Eastern Europe after 1945*. Tallinn: Unitas Foundation.

[16] Haase, A. (2011, May 30) Magdeburg, Halle, Dessau – Gegenwart und Zukunft der Stadtentwicklung in Sachsen-Anhalt. Retrieved from: http://www.stadtentwicklung-sachsen-anhalt.de/

[17] Bahrmann, H., & Links, C. (2005) *Am Ziel vorbei*. Berlin: Ch. Links Verlag.

[18] Kern, S. (2006) Auswirkungen der Wiedervereinigung. GRIN Verlag. Retrieved from: http://www.grin.com/de/e-book/51246/auswirkungen-der-wiedervereinigung

[19] Bahrmann, H., & Links, C. (2005) *Am Ziel vorbei*. Berlin: Ch. Links Verlag.

[20] Dissmann, C. (2010) *Die Gestaltung der Leere: Zum Umgang mit einer neuen städtischen Wirklichkeit*. Bielefeld: transcript Verlag.

[21] Goschler, C., & Lillteicher, J. (2002) *'Arisierung' und Restitution – Die Rückerstattung jüdischen Eigentums in Deutschland und Österreich nach 1945 und 1989*. Göttingen: Wallstein Verlag; Hockerts, H. G., & Kuller, C. (2003) *Nach der Verfolgung*. Göttingen: Wallstein Verlag; Leupolt, S. (2003) *Die rechtliche Aufarbeitung des DDR-Unrechts*. Münster: LIT Verlag.; Reimann, B. (1997) The transition from people's property to private property: Consequences of the restitution principle for urban development and urban renewal in East Berlin's inner-city residential areas. *Applied Geography*, 17(4), pp. 301–313.

[22] Häußermann, H., Glock, B., & Keller, C. (2000) *Eigentumsstrukturen zwischen Persistenz und Wandel : zu den Folgen der Restitution in suburbanen und innerstädtischen Gebieten*. Plymouth: University of Plymouth; Reimann, B. (1997) The transition from people's property to private property: Consequences of the restitution principle for urban development and urban renewal in East Berlin's inner-city residential areas. *Applied Geography*, 17(4), pp. 301–313.

[23] Goschler, C., & Lillteicher, J. (2002) *'Arisierung' und Restitution – Die Rückerstattung jüdischen Eigentums in Deutschland und Österreich nach 1945 und 1989*. Göttingen: Wallstein Verlag.

[24] Bahrmann, H., & Links, C. (2005) *Am Ziel vorbei*. Berlin: Ch. Links Verlag.

[25] Abraham, K. G., & Houseman, S. (1995) Earnings inequality in Germany. In R. B. Freeman & L. F. Katz (eds), *Differences and Changes in Wage Structures*, Chicago: University of Chicago Press, pp. 371–404; –. (2009, August 28) Despite Progress, Former East Germany Still Lags Behind. Spiegel Online. Retrieved from: http://www.

spiegel.de/international/germany/20-years-of-investment-despite-progress-former-east-germany-still-lags-behind-a-645596.html

[26] Bos, D., & Von Weizsacker, R. K. (1989) Economic consequences of an aging population. *European Economic Review*, 33(2–3), pp. 345–354.

[27] El Nasser, H. (2006, December 27) As older cities shrink, some reinvent themselves. *USA TODAY*. Retrieved from: http://www.usatoday.com/news/nation/2006-12-26-shrinking-cities-cover_x.htm

[28] Bauer, U. C. (2011) Weniger ist Zukunft. *STANDORT – Zeitschrift für Angewandte Geographie*, 35(1), pp. 2–5.

[29] Bauer, U. C. (2011) Weniger ist Zukunft. *STANDORT – Zeitschrift für Angewandte Geographie*, 35(1), pp. 2–5.

[30] The federal program worked through a system in which a state or agency 'pitched' a concept for an IBA to the federal ministry of building, who then granted funding or initiated a joint-funding programme.

[31] Bauer, U. C. (2011) Weniger ist Zukunft. *STANDORT – Zeitschrift für Angewandte Geographie*, 35(1), pp. 2–5.

[32] Fuchs, H.-W. (1997) *Bildung und Wissenschaft seit der Wende: zur Transformation des ostdeutschen Bildungssystems*. Opladen: Leske + Budrich.

[33] The teaching methods are mostly indirect and project-oriented, allowing the students to develop their own solutions and interventions based on the knowledge gained in their Bachelor Degree and the local conditions of the site. The principle of learning-by-doing is given specific emphasis, above all because of the varying experience levels and educational background of the students. Working in mixed groups on studio projects allows for the exchange of experience between various cultures of learning. Architecture students who have completed their Bachelors in Dessau, for example, with its combination of courses, projects and practical experience (internship), come into contact with students who have been taught on courses with different formats. This usually forms a mutually beneficial and synergistic condition.

[34] Saxony-Anhalt comprises the western-central portion of former East Germany and shares a border to the south with Thuringia (*Thüringen*), to the east with Saxony (*Sachsen*) and to the east and north with Brandenburg. Magdeburg, the largest of the three cities and the capital of the state, lies approximately 130 kilometres west-southwest of Berlin.

[35] The two largest drops in population occurred between 1990 and 1995 (135,029 residents or 4.7%) and 1995 and 2000 (123,553 residents or 4.5%). Since 2001, the population has dropped steadily – by approximately 1% per year (Statistisches Landesamt Sachsen-Anhalt, 2012). The state statistical office predicts a continuation of this trend.

[36] Sonnabend, R., & Stein, R. (2006) *Die anderen Städte: Profilierung von Städten/The other cities: Urban distinctiveness*. Berlin: Jovis.

[37] The analysis discussed in the following section stem from the German-language study *Magdeburg, Halle, Dessau – Gegenwart und Zukunft der Stadtentwicklung in Sachsen-Anhalt* (Magdeburg, Halle, Dessau – Present and Future of Urban Development in Saxony-Anhalt), which ran from 2000 to 2003 and was funded by the *Bundesministerium*

für Bildung und Forschung (German Ministry for Education and Research). Further information (in German) is available here: http://www.stadtentwicklung-sachsen-anhalt. de.

[38] Bentley, I., Alcock, A., Murrain, P., McGlynn, S., & Smith, G. (1985) *Responsive environments: A manual for designers.* Oxford: Architectural Press.

[39] Florida, R. (2002) *The rise of the creative class and how it's transforming work, leisure, community and everyday life.* New York: Basic Books.

[40] In this regard we suggest that ideas related to Henri Lefebvre's arguments on the production of space, as both a physical and metaphysical (symbolic, conceptual or ideological) good are important. These processes of learning, and above all 'discovery', need to be guided by the design program in order to promote the concept put forward by the Dessau-born Jewish philosopher Moses Mendelssohn: *enlightenment through education.*

[41] This, we suggest, should be in close and officially acknowledged cooperation with the Bauhaus Foundation in order to harness the design potential present at the university.

Bibliography

–. (1989) Statistisches Jahrbuch der DDR. 1. Auflage. Berlin (Ost): Staatsverlag der DDR.

–. (2009, August 28) Despite Progress, Former East Germany Still Lags Behind. *Spiegel Online.* Retrieved from: http://www.spiegel.de/international/germany/20-years-of-investment-despite-progress-former-east-germany-still-lags-behind-a-645596.html

Abraham, K. G., & Houseman, S. (1995) Earnings inequality in Germany. In R. B. Freeman & L. F. Katz (eds), *Differences and Changes in Wage Structures,* Chicago: University of Chicago Press, pp. 371–404.

Bahrmann, H., & Links, C. (2005) *Am Ziel vorbei.* Berlin: Ch. Links Verlag.

Bauer, U. C. (2011) Weniger ist Zukunft. *STANDORT – Zeitschrift für Angewandte Geographie,* 35(1), pp. 2–5.

Bentley, I., Alcock, A., Murrain, P., McGlynn, S., & Smith, G. (1985) *Responsive Environments: A Manual for Designers.* Oxford: Architectural Press.

Bontje, M. (2004) Facing the challenge of shrinking cities in East Germany: The case of Leipzig. *GeoJournal.* 61(1), pp. 13–21.

Bos, D., & Von Weizsacker, R. K. (1989) Economic consequences of an aging population. *European Economic Review,* 33(2–3), p. 345–354.

Dettmar, J. (2005) Forests for Shrinking Cities? The Project "Industrial Forests of the Ruhr". In I. Kowarik & S. Körner (eds), *Wild Urban Woodlands: New Perspectives for Urban Forestry,* Berlin/Heidelberg: Springer, pp. 263–276.

Dissmann, C. (2010) *Die Gestaltung der Leere: Zum Umgang mit einer neuen städtischen Wirklichkeit.* Bielefeld: transcript Verlag.

El Nasser, H. (2006, December 27) As older cities shrink, some reinvent themselves. *USA TODAY.* Retrieved from: http://www.usatoday.com/news/nation/2006-12-26-shrinking-cities-cover_x.htm

Florida, R. (2002) *The rise of the creative class and how it's transforming work, leisure, community and everyday life.* New York: Basic Books.

Fuchs, H.-W. (1997) *Bildung und Wissenschaft seit der Wende: zur Transformation des ostdeutschen Bildungssystems*. Opladen: Leske + Budrich.

Goschler, C., & Lillteicher, J. (2002) *"Arisierung" und Restitution – Die Rückerstattung jüdischen Eigentums in Deutschland und Österreich nach 1945 und 1989*. Göttingen: Wallstein Verlag.

Haase, A. (2011, May 30) *Magdeburg, Halle, Dessau – Gegenwart und Zukunft der Stadtentwicklung in Sachsen-Anhalt*. Retrieved from: http://www.stadtentwicklung-sachsen-anhalt.de/

Häußermann, H., Glock, B., & Keller, C. (2000) *Eigentumsstrukturen zwischen Persistenz und Wandel : zu den Folgen der Restitution in suburbanen und innerstädtischen Gebieten*. Plymouth: University of Plymouth.

Hockerts, H. G., & Kuller, C. (2003) *Nach der Verfolgung*. Göttingen: Wallstein Verlag.

Hollander, J. B., Pallagst, K., Schwarz, T., & Popper, F. J. (2009) Planning shrinking cities. *Progress in Planning*, 72(4), p. 223–232.

Institut für Regionalentwicklung und Strukturplanung. (2012, August 6) Bund-Länder-Programm Stadtumbau Ost. Retrieved from: http://www.stadtumbau-ost.info/

Kern, S. (2006) *Auswirkungen der Wiedervereinigung*. GRIN Verlag. Retrieved from: http://www.grin.com/de/e-book/51246/auswirkungen-der-wiedervereinigung

Kowarik, Ingo (2005) Wild urban woodlands: Towards a conceptual framework. In I. Kowarik & S. Körner (eds), *Wild Urban Woodlands: New Perspectives for Urban Forestry*, Berlin/Heidelberg: Springer, pp. 1–32.

Kulish, N. (2009, June 19) In East Germany, a Decline as Stark as a Wall. *The New York Times*. Retrieved from: http://www.nytimes.com/2009/06/19/world/europe/19germany.html

Kühn, M., & Liebmann, H. (eds) (2009) *Regenerierung der Städte: Strategien der Politik und Planung im Schrumpfungskontext*. Wiesbaden: VS Verlag für Sozialwissenschaften.

Laar, M. (2010) *The Power of Freedom, Central and Eastern Europe after 1945*. Tallinn: Unitas Foundation.

Langer, M., & Endlicher, W. (eds) (2007) *Shrinking cities: Effects on urban ecology and challenges for urban development*. Frankfurt am Main: Peter Lang.

Leupolt, S. (2003) *Die rechtliche Aufarbeitung des DDR-Unrechts*. Münster: LIT Verlag.

Müller, B., & Siedentop, S. (2012, August 29) *Growth and Shrinkage in Germany – Trends, Perspectives and Challenges for Spatial Planning and Development*. Berlin. Retrieved from: http://www.difu.de/publikationen/growth-and-shrinkage-in-germany-trends-perspectives-and.html

Müller, N., Werner, P., Mathey, J., & Rink, D. (2010) Urban Wastelands – A Chance for Biodiversity in Cities? Ecological Aspects, Social Perceptions and Acceptance of Wilderness by Residents. In N. Müller, P. Werner & J. G. Kelcey (eds), *Urban Biodiversity and Design*. Oxford: Wiley-Blackwell.

Pallagst, K. (2010) Viewpoint: The planning research agenda: shrinking cities–a challenge for planning cultures. *Town Planning Review*, 81(5), pp. i–vi.

Pfeiffer, U., Simons, H., & Porsch, L. (2012, August 29) Wohnungswirtschaftlicher Strukturwandel in den neuen Bundesländern – Bericht der Kommission. Retrieved from: http://www.schader-stiftung.de/docs/kommission_strukturwandel_kurzfass.pdf

Reimann, B. (1997) The transition from people's property to private property: Consequences of the restitution principle for urban development and urban renewal in East Berlin's inner-city residential areas. *Applied Geography, 17*(4), p. 301–313.

Rieniets, T. (2012, August 27) Shrinking cities – growing domain for urban planning? Retrieved from: http://aarch.dk/fileadmin/grupper/institut_ii/PDF/paper_presentation_EURA2005.pdf

Rink, D. (2009) Wilderness: the nature of urban shrinkage? The debate on urban restructuring and restoration in eastern Germany. *Nature and Culture*, 4(3), p. 275–292.

Sonnabend, R., & Stein, R. (2006) *Die anderen Städte: Profilierung von Städten/The other cities: Urban distinctiveness.* Berlin: Jovis.

Statistisches Landesamt Sachsen-Anhalt (2012, August 6) Entwicklung der Deutschen und Ausländer in Sachsen-Anhalt seit 1990. Retrieved from: http://www.stala.sachsen-anhalt.de/Internet/Home/Daten_und_Fakten/1/12/124/12411/Entwicklung_der_Deutschen_und_Auslaender.html

Yelena McLANE,
Lisa WAXMAN

CHAPTER 4
DESIGNING FOR GOOD

Context

In the United States, the interior-design profession is relatively young; yet it has evolved to encompass a broad range of skills and applications, and its practitioners ply their trades in diverse fields – health care, education, residential, hospitality, retail, exhibit and museum design – the goals and objectives of which may differ significantly. The interior-design profession has matured, at least in part, due to profound and ongoing changes in educational methods that emphasise the acquisition of technical skills, health and safety concerns, and empirical knowledge of users' needs alongside the cultivation of individual aesthetic sensibilities and connoisseurship vis-à-vis historical styles, the fine arts and crafts, and furniture and finishes. Today's interior-design educators are charged with propagating in their students an expansive range of aptitudes that will enable them to solve complex design problems utilising research, creativity, technical skills, and sustainable business and construction practices, with an understanding that the function of *good design* is to foster human welfare.

For too long, interior-design professionals (and associated educational curricula) disproportionately favoured designing spaces used primarily by people with higher socio-economic status: specialty shops, restaurants and lounges, salons, luxury residences, museums and galleries.[1] Yet even as interior-design education has moved away from these high-end studio projects in favour of more socially relevant design, most non-designers still assume that interior designers work pretty much exclusively in contexts of granite-topped counters, crystal chandeliers and velvet curtains.[2] Admittedly, these projects are fun, with their unrestrained budgets and opportunities to showcase artsy flourishes, but are they really *good* projects? For some time now, the consensus among educators is that interior-design practice and education is not well served by promulgating the idea that good and worthwhile design is always opulent design.[3] Survey a typical cohort of interior-design students today, however, and the number of respondents whose career goals trend towards high-end residential and hospitality design remains far in excess of the number of jobs for which these students could reasonably hope to compete.[4] The current generation of educators is striving to impart to the next generation of design professionals a desire to apply their skills and training to jobs worth doing in a more global and meaningful sense,[5] centring on issues of social justice – like low-income housing, urban schools and medical clinics. Despite their undying love of boutique-hotel studio assignments, students are showing an inspiring readiness to reach out through practicums and work-study programs to deliver good design to historically underserved communities.

Today's leading design educators are focused on enhancing both students' and the public's understanding of the meaning of good design. At the risk of sounding tautological, the consensus appears to be that good design is *designing for good*. In the context of interior design, this first means designing work spaces, study spaces, living spaces, play spaces and liminal spaces that nurture good work, good studying, good living, good playing and, to every practical extent, good in-betweening. In other words, this means designing spaces that work well for their intended uses – spaces that are good at facilitating what they are designed to facilitate. A second meaning is that the designer of good spaces should aim for users of the spaces to have their needs met while using the spaces (i.e. work spaces that enhance productivity while encouraging worker collegiality; preschool classrooms that offer flexibility to teachers and are durably constructed and safe without stifling young learners' explorations; kitchens that are energy efficient and allow for people to gather comfortably and spend time cooking, eating and washing up together). A third meaning is designing for good, as in designing for a long period of productive use – not ephemeral design, not faddish design, not conspicuous consumption of the latest design doohickeys, but design that is efficient and lasting, and which must incorporate applications that can be changed out or adapted to unanticipated uses while maintaining a core of reusable construction. In short, good design is not wasteful design, it is design that is considerate of the environment in which it is located, that uses only as much energy and material as is needed to achieve its purpose and, in the event that the design must be dismantled, is poised to return to the building stream where it can be recycled or reapplied to new construction.

Given the built-out status of so many urban areas and commercial districts, the issues of space and energy conservation and efficient functioning of buildings are acute and will very likely play a much larger part in interior designers' practices in years to come. [6] As population trends in the United States suggest a reversal of the historic migration away from large cities, and more young people and families desire to live and work closer to the heart of the city, the need for well-designed homes, offices, stores, clinics and educational facilities will only increase. Although projects mandating green design certification from the U.S. Green Building Council[7] and sustainability in materials and energy use are not yet the norm in the larger world of commercial and residential construction, they are no longer the whims of a few eccentric clients. In major urban centres, green projects have entered the mainstream of architectural and interior-design practices, particularly in the context of federal-,[8] state- and local-government commissions.[9] A rapid and irreversible integration of sustainable design methods, including remodelling and retrofitting, into both practice and educational curricula is fully underway, with the U.S. Green Building Council leading the promotion and support of these efforts. Much has been written in both academic literature and the mainstream media on green design, sustainability and related practices.[10] Here, the focus is on the less-prominent issues of public interest and welfare that, although often considered in design efforts, are often couched in bland terms of user health and safety or welfare[11] instead of heralded as the raison d'être of design as a service.

To these ends, designing for good *may* be green and sustainable design in a technical sense of the term, but it *must* be affordable, dependable and respectful of its users. As such, the first goal of interior-design education should be to train thinkers and problem solvers to be ready to design sturdy spaces that people can afford to inhabit (with regard both to financial and environmental impacts) and will gladly inhabit. Good designers realise that people will live, work and play, as well as give birth, receive an education, meet new friends, build careers, recover from illness, grow old and eventually die in the spaces that they have designed. Good designers are cognisant of the economic forces that increasingly necessitate reuse, retrofitting, adaptation and the lowering of energy profiles. Although, interior-design educators are working towards achieving these goals, there is much work to be done if the profession is to make itself sustainable.

Exploring the current state of design practice and education around the globe will allow for a better understanding not only of design, but of the broader range of issues facing us all in what should be a collective effort to yield 'good' through design. Gathering the thoughts of diverse designers and design educators will undoubtedly result in the discovery of many common, as well as contrasting, issues that warrant lengthier discussions. With increasing globalism, intellectual and even cultural barriers between nations are less clear, and issues facing one group are often issues facing everyone working in design professions, including architecture, interior design, product and industrial design, and environmental graphic design.[12] Just as advances in material, construction and design technologies inspire practitioners to innovate, downtrending economic forces retard designers' ability to realise capital intensive design goals and force them to be more creative with their resources. As such, as a profession, we must periodically assess whether the trends in design education are squaring up with market trends, meeting the public's needs and responsive to students' career interests and likeliest employment scenarios.

In this text, this is considered in the context of the United States – with a focus on major factors influencing practice and education including: the influence of trade organisations and initiatives; the impact of the economy; changes in client expectations and perceptions; considerations for human welfare and well-being; the value of multidisciplinary collaboration; changes in the student population; and the need to balance design theory and research with hands-on technical skills training. All of this is done with an eye to advancing the goal of *designing for good*.

Factors and Forces Impacting Interior-design Education and Practice in the United States

Organisations and Initiatives

If designers and design educators are to succeed in increasing the emphasis on designing for good (i.e. designing with public interest and social welfare objectives in mind), there must be partnerships between practitioners and trade groups and the public, whose money and consent are needed in equal measure to realise any project. Public perception of the profession of interior design in the United States has improved significantly over the last fifty years, before which time interior designers were caricatured as pillow-and-picture consultants. Despite this, there is still much work to be done to make clearer in the public's imagination the services that interior designers actually provide. To that end, a number of organisations and initiatives are helping to define the profession and establish a strong foundation for high-quality interior-design education.

The major organisations serving practitioners, educators and the interior-design community in the United States and Canada are all members of a group called the Issues Forum. Although the Issues Forum is an informal group, the leaders of seven major interior-design organisations meet twice each year to discuss issues of importance to the profession. These organisations include:

- The practitioner organisations: the American Society of Interior Designers (ASID), the Interior Designers of Canada (IDC) and the International Interior Design Association (IIDA)

- The Council for Interior Design Accreditation (CIDA), the accrediting body for interior-design education

- The Interior Design Continuing Education Council (IDCEC), which coordinates the continuing education for interior designers

- The Interior Design Educators Council (IDEC), the foremost organisation for interior-design educators in North America, and

- The National Council for Interior Design Qualification (NCIDQ), which manages the examination process used to identify qualified interior designers.

The Issues Forum partners have worked hard to raise the level of professionalism and to better inform the public regarding the role that interior designers play in the design of the built environment. One joint project is the Careers in Interior Design website, which offers resources relating to careers, and preparation for careers, in interior design.[13] The Issues Forum has also funded the latest version of *The Interior Design Profession's Body of Knowledge*, written by Caren Martin and Denise Guerin, professors at the University of Minnesota.[14] There have been three editions of the *Body of Knowledge* (2000, 2005 and 2010). One of the goals of the 2010 *Body of Knowledge* was more clearly to define the scope of work that interior designers perform, the responsibilities of interior designers to clients and to the wider public community, and to identify health, safety and welfare issues involved in interior-design practice. *Body of Knowledge* also serves as a guide to state and provincial lawmakers in helping them better to understand the profession as they draft interior-design-related legislation.[15]

Another important initiative that has advanced the interior-design profession is the creation of the website InformeDesign, which has been instrumental in linking practice and education by taking research articles and summarising them for easy use by interior-design practitioners.[16] Its founders, again Martin and Guerin, were concerned that so much research conducted in academia never finds its way to practitioners and the site is intended to respond to this, although it is also widely used by students for their pre-design research and programming of projects, and for graduate-student research.

The driving force behind quality interior-design education in the United States is the Council for Interior Design Accreditation (CIDA) (originally named the Foundation for Interior Design Education Research [FIDER]), which was formed in the 1970s as the accrediting body for interior-design education in colleges and universities. CIDA standards are generally accepted as the most significant measure of the quality of an interior-design education, and these standards have shown to be reliable markers of successful programs.[17] CIDA currently has sixteen standards that serve as the measure that most programs use to frame their curricula. The most recent CIDA standards[18] include categories that define the minimum competencies required for an interior-design program to be accredited. These standards address the mission and goals of the program as well as ensure that curricula include global perspectives on design, an understanding of human behaviour, an emphasis on design process and critical thinking, opportunities for collaboration and the development of good communication skills. In addition, in their course offerings, there is also an emphasis on professionalism; business practices; history; space and form; colour; furniture, fixtures and equipment; finish materials; environmental systems and controls; building systems; regulations; and assessment and accountability. At the time of this writing, more than 170 interior-design programs in the United States are accredited.[19]

The Economy

Conversations between interior-design practitioners and educators in the United States over the last four years have often centred upon the sluggish economy and its dour financial implications for design firms and students' ability to find jobs. Design firms report that the old ways of doing business are not working.[20] Many interior designers described their business in terms of 'before and after' 2008 and presented two very different practice and financial scenarios. A common refrain is the extent to which practices have coped by eliminating costs that were not immediately necessary, including personnel. In interviews, interior designers have identified that they have furloughed staff one day a week and adjusted salaries accordingly as one response. Others have reduced their staff pool directly. One possible positive thing to emerge in the mist of such cuts has been identified, however: extra time to 'focus on design details and seek more creative solutions – to play with design more.'[21]

In a session at NeoCON in Chicago in 2011, titled *Navigating the New Normal*,[22] sponsored by the International Interior Design Association (IIDA), design leaders explained how they are managing in the down economy. Speakers stressed the importance of leveraging partnerships and utilising technology to help partnering occur. They also said they expect designers have an 'all hands on deck' attitude, meaning everyone needs to be ready to step up and get the work done. Many firms have laid off administrators, human resources staff and marketing specialists, with those roles filled by designers or architects. If a firm needs specialised expertise in a particular area, they are more likely to hire consultants rather than full-time employees. Designers also stressed the need to be nimble and to hire designers who are crossed-trained with diverse managerial and technical aptitudes. They want designers who can do pre-planning, construction documents, space planning, sketching, many types of computer-aided design, as well as possess strong speaking, writing and listening skills.

The American Society of Interior Designers (ASID), in its 2010 *Interior Design in the New Economy: Lessons Learned from the Great Recession*, reported that members were altering their work habits to become 'leaner, meaner, and greener.'[23] The report indicated that, by becoming leaner and reducing the overheads associated with office space, equipment and perquisites that had become commonplace, firms were saving money. Firms are also becoming more strategic when deciding which jobs to accept by weighing the cost and time involved and accepting those that will be most profitable. Some practices also started seeking out complimentary professional expertise from outside consultants who could collaborate on projects. Designers are becoming credentialed as LEED-APs (Leadership in Energy and Environmental Design Accredited Professional) or opting to take the National Council for Interior Design Qualification Exam; and some are going back to school for MBAs and other specialised business training.

The global economy continues to be a change agent for North American design culture and practice. Several designers have opined that the United States is perceived internationally as a 'throw-away culture',[24] while clients from many other nations are interested in building for the long term. Building and construction codes in the United States support the disposable, quick turnover approach[25] and must change to support long-term occupancy and maximise beneficial use of material and energy resources. The rising interest in sustainable design focuses more on long-lasting sustainable

Figure 1: After School Arts Centre – student project designed to function as a refuge and a place of self-exploration. It provides a positive environment for behaviour modification. Student designer, Tracie Kelly, FSU

building practices and, as more designers and builders embrace this, more buildings will be built to last. This change is 'good design' in that it requires fewer resources in long run and puts less stress on the environment.

All of these issues have come to the fore in practice due to the economy. However, the poor economy of the United States has also affected students. At present, there is a severe shortage of paid employment opportunities available to new graduates. Students must have extensive internship experience to have any chance at getting a job. Many offer to work as non-paid interns or as research assistants on projects. These interns and research assistants report that, their unpaid status notwithstanding, they are expected to bring knowledge and 'hands-on' technical skills to their work for the firm.[26] Firms are looking for students who possess a strong work ethic, who are open to criticism and who display emotional maturity. They must also be able to speak well, write well and know how to find information. Although hand sketching is still valued, technological skills, including building information modelling (BIM) computer skills, must be current. Practitioners and design teams need deep, subject-specific knowledge and good critical thinkers now more than ever, as designers are no longer tasked only with completing projects under commission, but with devising new and creative approaches to enhancing revenue.[27]

Given these changes in the economy, students and practitioners would be well advised to follow the lead of designers who have realised that fewer commissions enhances opportunities 'to play more with design'.[28] If the profession transitions – both mentally and in its business models – away from pursuing only conventional fee-for-service projects towards more entrepreneurial modes in which the designer reads the markets and anticipates design needs,[29] it will be better able to weather what may well be a permanent shift in the economics of the provision of architectural and interior-design services away from blocks and buildings and towards renovations and retrofits. ASID reported that 'the growing popularity of "green lifestyles" made it socially acceptable to turn the necessities of lowering expectations and making do with less into chic virtues',[30] and added that clients in nearly all sectors of the economy are 'holding back'.[31] In these circumstances, designers are encouraged to reach out to clients and expand the conversation beyond simply the aesthetics of design to topics such as sustainability, health, safety, privacy, security, productivity, profitability, employee and customer satisfaction, and finally welfare, which are all part of good design.

Collaboration, Multidisciplinary Approaches and Interdisciplinary Thinking

As design projects, products and services become increasingly complex and the management of each requires a wide range of professional expertise, design solutions as the creations of the 'lone creative genius'[32] are slipping into myth. As Steve Badanes identifies, 'in the real world, little happens without collaboration'.[33] Increasingly, multidisciplinary design teams are the norm when addressing complex design problems. Finding people who have the skills, knowledge and temperament to work as a team allows a design firm to bid on a greater variety of projects.[34] Looking outside interior design to related design fields can help enrich a project with new thinking and approaches to design solutions, thus fostering a professional culture of collaboration. Such practice models could serve as a constant reminder to designers that there are numerous others, including the end users, whose different thoughts, feelings, intuitions and subjective preferences must be factored into viable design solutions. Ultimately this leads to a professional culture of 'designing for good'.

We have moved away from the manual drafting board. The design process is no longer linear. It can jump back and forth between design phases, skip steps, look back to reassess, add new components and result in better design outcomes.[35] Depending on the project goals, size and contractual arrangements, a diverse and multidisciplinary collaborative team approach allows for a greater flexibility in developing design objectives, selecting methodologies and solving problems.[36] In many ways, the multidisciplinary team is like an orchestra conducted by a leader who understands the big picture while guiding what the other team members are doing. The ability to collaborate and work as a team member is a skill, the development of which requires training and practice. Successful collaboration is always a challenge, and people (and creative people in particular) can find it hard to listen to and hear their partners, to negotiate, compromise and, ultimately, take ownership of a design solution arrived at collaboratively.

Although it may appear that the profession is dominated by large architecture and design firms, the majority of American interior-design program graduates work as solo practitioners.[37] Even the best soloists, however, must know how to be part of an orchestra. As such, the well-trained designer should emerge from his or her degree program accustomed to collaboration, familiar with the practices common to a range of design disciplines (architecture, interior design, graphic design, furniture design and building construction, among others) and open and flexible to the tenets of group thinking as opposed to conceiving the design process as an individual pursuit. Members of a multidisciplinary team must, of course, possess specialised professional expertise in their area, but they should also have a broad understanding of related issues, as well as being open-minded and able to think critically. Having more voices in the process increases the chances that both the client's and end-users' needs will be heard and examined fully by the team members. It also ensures that the team will be able to speak the appropriate professional language and offer problem-solving approaches that yield effective solutions.[38] Among other influential thinkers, Ken Friedman has emphasised that design education needs to move from a craft-oriented approach toward critical inquiry and interdisciplinary studies, and his remarks are an excellent summation of the direction in which program curricula should aim:

> [Every] intelligent design professional in the knowledge era – graphic designer, information designer, design manager, industrial designer – must increasingly be a hybrid professional trained with a broad view. These professionals must draw on a number of disciplines to understand the nature of their task in solving specific problems: design leadership, philosophy, psychology, physiology, sociology of knowledge, research methodology, information, strategic design, combining these with an integrate perspective of critical studies and history of ideas. Is this too broad a range of studies for a single profession? Not in terms of education. It is a matter of practical simplicity in curriculum development.[39]

Friedman's remarks dovetail neatly with the goal of *designing for good* in practice. Truly considerate design draws from the designer's awareness of a broad range of inputs, factors and stimuli. In the current economic climate, although it may seem impractical to incorporate sociological data, strategies of use, reuse and freestyle repurposing into practice, it would deliver new practicalities and efficiencies. Concurrently, students' familiarity with social media, theory, funds of information, historical objects and practices are also highly relevant to *designing for good*; albeit indirectly. In a sense, the modern student's self-education as Internet sage, combined with their eagerness to engage in active dialogues and collaboration[40] reflects the suite of skills upon which future designers will depend in developing good responses to design problems.

Client Perceptions and Expectations

Clients often perceive interior-design services or components of larger architectural projects as those that add cost and time, but no value.[41] Many have only a vague understanding of what interior designers do, or, perhaps worse, misconceive that their scope of services is limited to selecting colours, finishes and furniture. Popular design shows on television reinforce these misconceptions,[42] and create an illusion in the minds of audiences (and eventual clients) that they too are interior-design experts. Who, after all, is not capable of selecting wallpaper and upholstery? The proliferation of design-based entertainment programming centres almost exclusively on high-end residential and hospitality projects. Although this may be an accurate reflection of the direction in which some members of the interior-design industry would like for their own careers to go, it is problematic. The marketing of design through television represents a metastasisation of much of what is wrong about the state of the market for design services today. Its emphasis on wealth, conspicuous consumption and the display of precious materials and building contexts puts it generally far out of reach for the average resident in the economies that support the rich patrons of penthouse and mansion designers featured on TV. There is an on-going battle to show clients that interior design is not, at its core, about luxury, but requires extensive professional training and expertise in a whole range of issues: addressing users' health and safety; adhering to regulatory standards and code requirements in space planning; specifying functional interior components and finishes; and understanding how to enhance the users' welfare by optimising spaces for living and working.

Client expectations and perceptions are also influenced by new economic realities in terms of practicality, sustainability and energy efficiency, in both the commercial and residential sectors. Many interior designers have observed that departing from the relatively affluent decades of the 1990s and early 2000s, clients are stepping back and reassessing what they need, not simply ordering what they want. Clients increasingly expect high-performance interiors that are less costly to operate and maintain, and that are easier to manage than traditionally designed spaces. For instance, they want to integrate surfaces that are easier to clean and lighting that does not need frequent replacement. They also want larger, multi-purpose spaces instead of separate offices and meeting rooms and furniture with modular characteristics that enable adaptation to unanticipated user needs. Many of these changes reflect the stressed economy, as well as the shift in client perceptions of what they need and want. These shifts are also forcing interior designers to provide for enhanced energy efficiency and sustainability among the 'menu items' for design project options. Furthermore, it requires that they integrate holistic efficiency and sustainability goals as baseline standards of their practices. Although many of these design options are good for the environment, as well

Figure 2: Day care centre – student project – designed to nurture and support the activities, learning and comfort of both young children and their carers. Student designer, Tanya West, FSU

as the financial bottom line for clients, they require the designer to be skilled technically and to have expertise in aspects of design and construction.

Human Welfare and Well Being

In recent years another important shift in client expectations has arisen: attention toward the ways in which design affects the welfare and well-being of building users and occupants. Welfare is often listed as part of the total health, safety and welfare package that interior designers must attend to. However, public-interest and welfare issues in interior design have received considerably less attention than health and safety issues. This may be due, in part, to a sense that welfare is intangible and in many ways a personal and cultural construct. Welfare is often subjective in interpretation. However, when welfare-related considerations are integrated into design, the results can contribute greatly to the human experience.[43] The term itself, *welfare*, remains under-defined, even by design professionals, and is poorly understood by the general public. This makes implementing programmatic changes aimed at enhancing designers' sensitivity to welfare issues all the more difficult. We must not, however, be inhibited from centring the idea of 'good design' upon those welfare attributes that are easy to recognise.

The measure of a society's success is often reflected in economic numbers: gross domestic product (GDP), per capita income, and life expectancy.[44] These numbers seldom, if ever, reflect less-evident qualities of people's daily lives, their happiness, or a holistic sense of well-being. Fortunately, attitudes towards these abstract metrics of 'success', devoid of any real human presence, are changing. Changes in thinking that measure *advancement* and *progress* of community and society in terms of people's 'quality of life' are percolating into broader public discourse and government policies. [45] As the U.S. Department of Health and Human Services (2010) has articulated, quality of life and welfare encompass a variety of conditions, including physical, mental, emotional and social functions. Under the national *Healthy People 2020* program, the Department has advocated for the enhancement of quality in people's daily lives as measured by new criteria: the frequency with which individuals feel 'very healthy and satisfied or content with life; the quality of their relationships; their positive emotions; resilience; and the realisation of their potential.'[46] Great Britain, Canada and New Zealand have adopted policies that assess the happiness and well-being of their citizens.[47]

This is a request that human welfare be more than a measure of accrued economic wealth, gross domestic product or protection from criminal harm.[48] As Amartya Kumar Sen, an Indian economist and Nobel Prize winner, has noted, 'a person's well-being is not really a matter of how rich he or she is… [for] commodity command is a means to the end of well-being.'[49] A truly meaningful measure of human welfare must encompass advancements in social, psychological and physical well-being, and be aimed at the realisation of progress in life and the prosperity of individuals and communities. In many ways, welfare is about respecting and maintaining human dignity, as well as bringing joy, identity and meaning into people's lives.[50] Welfare has been an integral part of interior-design practices for a long while,[51] and the term is found in the National Council for Interior Design Qualification (NCIDQ) definition of interior design:

> Interior design includes a scope of services performed by a professional design practitioner, qualified by means of education, experience and examination, to protect and enhance the health, life safety and welfare of the public.[52]

In today's economic climate, however, funds are less available for interior projects while many social and demographic problems are worsening. This should bring a new immediacy and renewed attention to the goal of achieving meaningful gains in human welfare with fewer resources.[53] Increasingly, design practitioners will be tasked with delivering professional services on smaller budgets, or even accept *pro bono* payments. This would cause a shift in the business model of many interior-design practices that would be major. This generation of designers, entering into a marketplace saturated with under-utilised talent, would be well advised to stake claims in the potentially limitless frontier of designing for good.

As many practising designers have noted, today the design of our architectural spaces still revolves around building systems and appearances, but not the welfare of the occupant.[54] The design community must lead the way in educating private- and government-sector clients to invest in such projects, the intangible benefits of which would stimulate the economy in new and exciting ways. Private- and government-sector clients ought to demand not only economically feasible and environmentally sustainable designs, but designs that help to resolve social problems and improve the *quality* of users' lives.[55] It is not sufficient just to update the styles and colour schemes that form the backdrop for users' old lives. Design solutions must go beyond the architecture of a building, the functioning of its physical and mechanical systems, appearances and aesthetics. It must pay equal or greater attention to individual experiences and holistic senses of well-being.

Following on from this, two other critically important and related issues for designers today are the inaccessibility and unaffordability of professional design services to the broader public. As Thomas Fisher has observed, there is a large and growing gap between what people, communities and public institutions need, and what these constituencies can afford to spend to improve living conditions and general welfare. [56] For the most part, professional interior-design practices target and provide services primarily to wealthy clients – individuals, corporations, governmental and private organisations – who can afford customised design services directed to their specific needs. This business model 'greatly limits the number and types of people served by the profession.'[57] As a result, professional interior designers directly affect only a very small percentage of all construction and renovation projects, and thus interior designers' contributions to projects that address the larger public's health, safety and welfare are comparatively insignificant.[58] Economic and social hardships are, however, opening new practice areas for design professionals: community-focused public-interest design. If such a calling does not emerge in force, 'we may soon find that we have too many [designers] skilled at designing museums and mansions and too few able to work with indigent people and communities.'[59] In projects for these clients, the cost-effective provision of life and work spaces, and users' physical and material security and health, eclipse the vapid exercises in style that prevail in the popular imagination as exempla of good design.

A commitment to these positive aims is already found in the NCIDQ definition of interior design that acknowledges the service component of interior design as a multi-faceted profession that 'includes a scope of services performed by a professional design practitioner. It acknowledges that an important aim is to protect and enhance the health, life safety and welfare of the public.'[60] A recommitment to this definition may help to reinterpret the meaning of 'the public' away from moneyed homebuilders or corporate and institutional clients, towards communities or society as a whole. It may help us focus on including health, safety, and welfare of all people, wherever they live and whatever their ability to pay.[61] To that end, interior designers must set out, in a deliberate and constructive fashion, to explain the value and importance of good design in the creation of safer and more enriching environments for children, the elderly

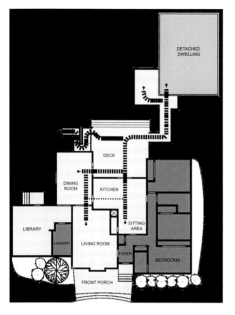
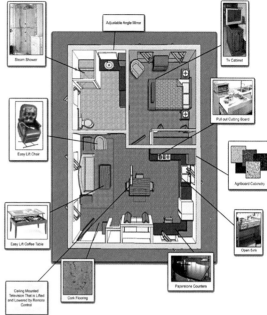

Figure 3: Universal Design Project – student project intended to provide a universal trans-generational dwelling to be attached to existing homes so as to allow for aging-in-place near family members. Student designer, Tessa Menotte, FSU.

and people with chronic health issues, as well as other special-needs groups. It must also explain how good design addresses the issues of psychological comfort, creating positive environments for living, working and recreating.

Designers might begin, for instance, by addressing the three most pressing health problems in the United States and North America – diabetes, heart diseases and obesity – each of which is brought on, in significant part, by sedentary lifestyles. Interior designers, perhaps in collaboration with architects, landscape architects, city planners, public health organisations, government and nonprofit institutions, should seize the opportunity to set the terms of the discussion. They could freely offer prototypes of designed spaces, targeting both the individual user and communities. The aim would be to demonstrate the extent to which design tools may be employed to realise constructive, economically feasible ends that ameliorate the extent to which poorly designed spaces contribute to the proliferation of chronic diseases. As architect John Cary has recently observed:

> We've seen the rise of game-changing non-profit design organizations... both employing human-centered design to improve public services, environments, and lives. Meanwhile, we have mainstream firms... who are strategically integrating pro bono design at unprecedented levels. This collective work, and the field of public

interest design in general, are premised on a conviction that everyone deserves good design and that every human being needs good design in order to live their lives as best as they can.[62]

Preparing Students to Design for Good in a Changing World

All the issues discussed with regard to practice have to find their way into the education system. The new expectations of clients and demands to designers to address public well-being should also be reflected in design education curricula, which should strengthen their advocacy for universal welfare and address issues related to new greater public needs.[63] Design programs should continue to expand course offerings that focus on public-interest design. Design studios should introduce real-life problems for students to think about and find new ways to solve, as well as direct them to other courses related to issues of environmental safety, health, community planning and social organisation. Programs should also focus on providing students with practicums and internship opportunities that promote these kinds of public-interest projects. These would help students learn how these kinds of projects work and understand the challenges of delivering good design to under-served users.

Many students currently enrolled in interior-design programs in the United States fall into the category of millennials: those children born between 1982 and 2002.[64] These students have characteristics unique from those who have come before them. Howe and Strauss have described this generation using descriptors such as 'special', 'sheltered', 'team-oriented', 'confident', 'pressured', 'achieving' and 'conventional'.[65] Diverse as these descriptors may appear, with these character traits come learning traits that researchers suggest should match this generation's unprecedented technical and social aptitudes.[66] These include engagement with interactive technology, a need for immediate instructor feedback, preference for group and team activities, preference for hands-on learning, and opportunities for peer evaluation. The preference for group and team activities will serve this generation well as they will be better prepared to collaborate with others in the profession and in allied areas. In addition to adjusting to new modes of learning, educators are also trying to help students navigate the new culture of multidisciplinary and collaborative practice.

All these issues were raised at Collaborative Think Tank, an event hosted in 2011 by the Council for Interior Design Accreditation (CIDA) which gathered many different types of designers to discuss the importance of collaboration. Educators present at the forum asked what designers are looking for when they hire young designers in today's climate. They reported they want critical thinkers who can problem-solve, frame a topic and facilitate a direction, as well as negotiate, analyse and 'make a case'. They should have had some exposure to other professions while in school and should have knowledge of the many different parties involved in a construction project. Collaboration means thinking of the good of the project as a whole, rather than just a firm's own part of the project. When the project succeeds, the designer succeeds. As such, interior-design educators are continuing to develop group and multidisciplinary studio projects, together with robust instruction on business- and practice-management skills, all of which will help prepare students for effective professional partnerships.

As young interior designers, graduate students will need to follow in the footsteps of design leaders who have gone before them and who continue to elevate the profession. Students should be encouraged to get involved in student design organisations while in university and instructed in the myriad ways that these groups help to lay the foundation for strong, active professional lives and a commitment to service. Students in the United States must know where their state stands in terms of the legal recognition of the interior-design profession and related licensing, certification and registration requirements. They will need to be prepared to become active politically, as needed, so as to protect the interests of the populations that they serve through design. Joining professional design organisations, taking the NCIDQ examination and giving back to the colleges and universities tasked with educating the next wave of students will all pay dividends and will make the profession stronger.

We have noted that many design students expect to graduate into a field replete with high-end hospitality and retail design projects. Students recruited into design programs are best served if they work through curricula that emphasise welfare and the public good over the whims of imaginary affluent clients. There is certainly room for studio projects that allow for students to explore the world of high-end residential, hotel and restaurant design. However, educators will do their students great service if they edify them with an understanding that design work is more fulfilling when it focuses on meeting the needs of individuals whose lives will be 'meaningfully' improved through the design effort. The well-prepared student will embrace the philosophy that everyone deserves good design, that well-designed spaces need not be cost prohibitive, and that many social problems may be ameliorated through the application of smart, informed and no less beautiful articulations of design. Ultimately, among the many jobs of this generation of interior designers will be the conveying to wider audiences that good design is not a luxury, but a necessity.

If interior design is to survive and thrive as a profession, educators and practitioners must hasten to develop in themselves and in their students the suite of skills and knowledge needed to provide diverse and historically underserved publics with more user-friendly, functional, economically feasible, environmentally responsible, sustainable and socially responsible design. As Bryan Bell echoes, 'though it may seem critical of the profession, I am actually extremely optimistic about the future of design. As society evolves, let us strive for the improvement of the lives for all, not just the privileged few. Designers can play key roles as we give new forms to the diverse needs of this future.'[67] Today's consumers do not simply need 'new-fashioned' design reflecting trends in materials, colours and styles; they need 'designs for good'.

Notes

[1] Pable, J. (2010) Socially beneficial design: What can interior designers do? In C. S. Martin & D. A. Guerin (eds), *The state of interior design profession*. New York, NY: Fairchild Books, pp. 8–16; Fisher, T. (2008) Public-interest architecture: A needed and inevitable change. In B. Bell & K. Wakeford (eds), *Expanding architecture: Design as activism*. New York, NY: Metropolis Books, pp. 8–13; Wilson, B. (2008) The architectural Bat-signal: Exploring the relationship between justice and design. In B. Bell & K. Wakeford (eds), op. cit., pp. 28–33.

[2] Waxman, L. & Clemons, S. (2007) Student perceptions: Debunking television's portrayal of interior design. *Journal of Interior Design*, 32(2), pp. v–xi.

[3] See, for example, Pable, J. (2010) op. cit.

[4] Although this claim is not substantiated by hard numbers of a formal study of interior-design job openings and number of interior-design graduates finding jobs, the authors make this argument based on their personal experiences, knowledge and involvement in the industry and from conversations with industry practitioners and interior-design graduates.

[5] Ankerson, K. & Gabb, B. (2010) Benefits of interior design for all. In C. S. Martin & D. A. Guerin (eds), *The state of interior design profession*. New York, NY: Fairchild Books, pp. 30–38; Guerin, D. & Kwon, J. (2010) Welfare: Can you talk about your specialized knowledge? In C. S. Martin & D. A. Guerin (eds), op. cit., pp. 110–118; Pable, J. (2010) op. cit.

[6] McCoy, J. (2012) Sustainability: Environmentally responsible interior design. *Journal of Interior Design*, 37(1), pp.5–6; Sorrento, L. (2012) A natural balance: Interior design, humans, and sustainability. *Journal of Interior Design*, 37(2), pp. ix–xxiv; Lynn, R. & Loehr, D. (2010) Our design responsibility for people and planet. In C. S. Martin & D. A. Guerin (eds), op. cit., pp. 48–58. See also Thorpe, A. (2012) *Architecture & design versus consumerism: How design activism confronts growth*. New York, NY: Earthscan/Routledge.

[7] USGBC (n.d.) Retrieved from: http://www.usgbc.org

[8] US Environmental Protection Agency Green Building Requirements and Policies (n.d.). Retrieved from: http://www.epa.gov/oaintrnt/projects/requirements.htm

[9] Florida Green Building Coalition, nonprofit Florida corporation dedicated to improving the built environment with a mission 'to lead and promote sustainability with environmental, economic, and social benefits through regional education and certification programs.' Retrieved from: http://www.floridagreenbuilding.org/home; Tallahassee Green Building Council (n.d.). Retrieved from: http://tallahasseegreenbuilding.com/

[10] Winchip, S. M. (2011) *Sustainable design for interior environments* (2nd ed.). New York, NY: Fairchild Books; Dennis, L. (2010) *Green interior design*. New York, NY: Allworth Press; Jones, L. (ed.) (2008) *Environmentally responsible design: Green and sustainable design for interior designers*. Hoboken, NJ: Wiley; *Journal of Interior Design* (2012) 37(2), pp. v–xxiv, 1–36.

[11] Pable, J. (2010) op. cit.; Guerin, D. & Kwon, J. (2010) op. cit.

[12] See, for example, Farson, R. (2008) *The power of design: A force for transforming everything.* Ostberg: Greenway Communications LLC.

[13] http://www.careersininteriordesign.com/

[14] Guerin, D.A., & Martin, C.S. (2010) *The Interior Design Profession's Body of Knowledge and its Relationship to People's Health, Safety, and Welfare.* Retrieved from: http://www.idbok.org/PDFs/IDBOK_2010.pdf

[15] Ibid.

[16] InformeDesign (n.d.). Retrieved from: http://www.informedesign.org/

[17] Busch, J.T. (2008, August) Closing the gap. *Contract*, p. 158.

[18] Council for Interior Design Accreditation (CIDA) (2011) Professional Standards 2011. Retrieved from: http://accredit-id.org/wp-content/uploads/Policy/Professional%20Standards%202011.pdf

[19] CIDA (2012) Accredited Programs. Retrieved from: http://accredit-id.org/accredited-programs/

[20] American Society of Interior Designers (ASID) (2010) Interior design in the new economy: Lessons learned from the great recession. Retrieved from: http://www.asid.org/NR/rdonlyres/E24FD5C1-27B6-4077-A1B5-0E9F39483A4B/0/DesigningInTheNewEconomy_FINAL.pdf

[21] Notes from an interview with practitioners conducted by the authors: Y. McLane and L. Waxman in May 2012 for this publication.

[22] International Interior Design Association (IIDA) (2011). Retrieved from: http://knowledgecenter.iida.org/AssetDetails.aspx?assetGuid=04ded3b2-46eb-4fbf-9537-86cf2994b27a

[23] ASID (2010) op. cit., p. 7.

[24] CIDA (2010) *Collaborative strategies report.* Obtained from CIDA by request, p. 5.

[25] Ibid.

[26] Notes from an interview with practitioners conducted by the authors: Y. McLane and L. Waxman in May 2012 for this publication. See also Barnett, A. L. (2010) Advice to gen Y: Become a generation of excellence. In C. S. Martin & D. A. Guerin (eds), *The state of interior design profession.* New York, NY: Fairchild Books, pp. 165–168; Guest, R. C. (2010) Expectations of new graduates: A view from practice. In C. S. Martin & D. A. Guerin (eds), op. cit., pp. 169–173.

[27] Notes from an interview with practitioners conducted by the authors: Y. McLane and L. Waxman in May 2012 for this publication. See also Barnett, A. L. (2010) Advice to gen Y: Become a generation of excellence. In C. S. Martin & D. A. Guerin (eds), *The state of interior design profession.* New York, NY: Fairchild Books, pp. 165–168; Guest, R. C. (2010) Expectations of new graduates: A view from practice. In C. S. Martin & D. A. Guerin (eds), op. cit., pp. 169–173.

[28] Notes from an interview with practitioners conducted by the authors: Y. McLane and L. Waxman in May 2012 for this publication.

[29] Design needs here refers to selling services to publics that do need smart and cost-effective design solutions to everyday problems but who may not need the sorts of vanity projects that used to constitute the bread and butter of many interior-design firms.

[30] ASID (2010) op. cit., p. 4.

[31] Ibid.

[32] Brown, T. (2008, June) Design thinking. *Harvard Business Review*, p. 87.

[33] Badanes, S. (2008) Building consensus in design/build studios. In B. Bell & K. Wakeford (eds), *Expanding architecture: Design as activism*. New York, NY: Metropolis Books.

[34] ASID (2010) op. cit.

[35] Jones, E. E. (2010) A case for interdisciplinary design. In C. S. Martin & D. A. Guerin (eds), *The state of interior design profession*. New York, NY: Fairchild Books, pp. 159–164.

[36] Ibid.

[37] CIDA (2010) op. cit.

[38] Jones, E. E. (2010) op. cit.

[39] Friedman, K. (1997) Design science and design education. In P. McGrory (ed.), *The challenge of complexity*. Helsinki, Finland: University of Art and Design Helsinki UIAH.

[40] This truism is reflected in the popularity of a range of social and professional networking applications.

[41] Connell, J. T. (2010) What is design thinking? In C. S. Martin & D. A. Guerin (eds), *The state of interior design profession*. New York, NY: Fairchild Books, pp. 66–71.

[42] Waxman, L. & Clemons, S. (2007) op. cit.

[43] Pable, J., Waxman, L., & McBain, M. (2011) *Recommendations for design and construction standards for transitional and permanent supportive housing*. Report to the Florida Housing Finance Corporation. Retrieved from: http://lowincomehousingdesign.weebly.com/

[44] Caan, S. (2010, 1 December) International Association of Interior Architects/Designers: President's update. Retrieved from: http://ifiworld.org/presidents_update/?p=97#Homepage

[45] Ibid.

[46] U.S. Department of Health and Human Services (HHS) (2010) *Health-related quality of life and well being. Healthy People 2020*, Washington, DC: U.S. Department of Health and Human Services. Retrieved from: http://www.healthypeople.gov/2020/about/QoLWBabout.aspx

[47] Caan, S. (2010, 1 December) op. cit.

[48] Caan, S. (2010, 1 December) op. cit.

[49] Sen, Amartya (1985) *Commodities and capabilities*. Amsterdam: North-Holland; New York: Elsevier Science Pub. Co., p. 28.

[50] Pable, J., Waxman, L., & McBain, M. (2011) op. cit.

[51] Ibid.; see also Guerin, D., & Kwon, J. (2010) op. cit.

[52] National Council for Interior Design Qualification (NCIDQ) (2004) *Definition of Interior Design*. Washington DC: NCIDQ. Retrieved from: http://www.ncidq.org/AboutUs/AboutInteriorDesign/DefinitionofInteriorDesign.aspx

[53] CIDA (2010) op. cit.

[54] Ibid.

[55] Ibid.

[56] Fisher, T. (2008) op. cit.

[57] Ibid., p. 9.

[58] Ibid.

[59] Ibid., p. 10.

[60] NCIDQ (2004) op. cit.

[61] Fisher, T. (2008) op. cit., p. 10.

[62] Cary, J. (2012, August) From spontaneous to strategic: The rise of public interest design. *Architect*. Retrieved from: http://www.architectmagazine.com/design/from-spontaneous-to-strategic-the-rise-of-public.aspx

[63] Fisher, T. (2008) op. cit.

[64] Howe, N., & Strauss, B. (2000) *Millennials rising: The next great generation*. New York: Vintage Books.

[65] Ibid.

[66] Oblinger, D. (2003) Boomers, gen-xers and millennials: Understanding the 'new students'. *EDUCAUSE Review*, 4, pp. 38–45; Howe, N. (2005, September) Harnessing the power of millennials: New educational strategies for a confident, achieving youth generation. *School Administrator*, 62(8), pp. 18–22; Strauss, W. (2005, September) Talking about their generations: Making sense of a school environment made up of gen-xers and millennials. *School Administrator*, 62(8), pp. 10–14.

[67] Bell, B. (2008) Expanding design towards greater relevance. In B. Bell & K. Wakeford (eds), op. cit., p. 16.

Bibliography

American Society of Interior Designers (ASID) (2010) Interior design in the new economy: Lessons learned from the great recession. Retrieved from: http://www.asid.org/NR/rdonlyres/E24FD5C1-27B6-4077-A1B5-0E9F39483A4B/0/DesigningInTheNewEconomy_FINAL.pdf

Ankerson, K., & Gabb, B. (2010) Benefits of interior design for all. In C. S. Martin & D. A. Guerin (eds), *The state of interior design profession*. New York, NY: Fairchild Books, pp. 30–38.

Badanes, S. (2008) Building consensus in design/build studios. In B. Bell & K. Wakeford (eds), *Expanding architecture: Design as activism*. New York, NY: Metropolis Books.

Barnett, A. L. (2010) Advice to gen Y: Become a generation of excellence. In C. S. Martin & D. A. Guerin (eds), *The state of interior design profession*. New York, NY: Fairchild Books, pp. 165–168.

Bell, B. (2008) Expanding design towards greater relevance. In B. Bell & K. Wakeford (eds), *Expanding architecture: Design as activism*. New York, NY: Metropolis Books, p. 16.

Brown, T. (2008, June) Design thinking. *Harvard Business Review*, p. 87.

Busch, J.T. (2008, August) Closing the gap. *Contract*, p. 158.

Caan, S. (2010, 1 December) International Association of Interior Architects/Designers: President's update. Retrieved from: http://ifiworld.org/presidents_update/?p=97#Homepage

Cary, J. (2012, August) From spontaneous to strategic: The rise of public interest design. *Architect*. Retrieved from: http://www.architectmagazine.com/design/from-spontaneous-to-strategic-the-rise-of-public.aspx

Connell, J. T. (2010) What is design thinking? In C. S. Martin & D. A. Guerin (eds), *The state of interior design profession*. New York, NY: Fairchild Books, pp. 66–71.

Council for Interior Design Accreditation (CIDA) (2010) *Collaborative strategies report*. Obtained from CIDA by request, p. 5.

Council for Interior Design Accreditation (CIDA) (2011) Professional Standards 2011. Retrieved from: http://accredit-id.org/wp-content/uploads/Policy/Professional%20 Standards%202011.pdf

Council for Interior Design Accreditation (CIDA) (2012) Accredited Programs. Retrieved from: http://accredit-id.org/accredited-programs/

Dennis, L. (2010) *Green interior design*. New York, NY: Allworth Press.

Farson, R. (2008) *The power of design: A force for transforming everything*. Ostberg: Greenway Communications LLC.

Fisher, T. (2008) Public-interest architecture: A needed and inevitable change. In B. Bell & K. Wakeford (eds), *Expanding architecture: Design as activism*. New York, NY: Metropolis Books, pp. 8–13.

Florida Green Building Coalition (n.d.) Retrieved from: http://www.floridagreenbuilding.org/ home

Friedman, K. (1997) Design science and design education. In P. McGrory (ed.), *The challenge of complexity*. Helsinki, Finland: University of Art and Design Helsinki UIAH.

Guerin, D. & Kwon, J. (2010) Welfare: Can you talk about your specialized knowledge? In C. S. Martin & D. A. Guerin (eds), *The state of interior design profession*. New York, NY: Fairchild Books, pp. 110–118.

Guerin, D.A., & Martin, C.S. (2010) *The Interior Design Profession's Body of Knowledge and its Relationship to People's Health, Safety, and Welfare*. Retrieved from: http://www.idbok. org/PDFs/IDBOK_2010.pdf

Guest, R. C. (2010) Expectations of new graduates: A view from practice. In C. S. Martin & D. A. Guerin (eds), *The state of interior design profession*. New York, NY: Fairchild Books, pp. 169–173.

Howe, N. (2005, September) Harnessing the power of millennials: New educational strategies for a confident, achieving youth generation. *School Administrator*, 62(8), pp. 18–22.

Howe, N. & Strauss, B. (2000) *Millennials Rising: The Next Great Generation*. New York: Vintage Books.

InformeDesign (n.d.) Retrieved from: http://www.informedesign.org/

International Interior Design Association (IIDA) (2011) Retrieved from: http://knowledgecenter. iida.org/AssetDetails.aspx?assetGuid=04ded3b2-46eb-4fbf-9537-86cf2994b27a

Jones, E. E. (2010) A case for interdisciplinary design. In C. S. Martin & D. A. Guerin (eds), *The state of interior design profession*. New York, NY: Fairchild Books, pp. 159–164.

Jones, L. (ed.) (2008) *Environmentally responsible design: Green and sustainable design for interior designers*. Hoboken, NJ: Wiley.

Journal of Interior Design (2012) 37(2), pp. v–xxiv, 1–36.

Lynn, R., & Loehr, D. (2010) Our design responsibility for people and planet. In C. S. Martin & D. A. Guerin (eds), *The state of interior design profession*. New York, NY: Fairchild Books, pp. 48–58.

McCoy, J. (2012) Sustainability: Environmentally responsible interior design. *Journal of Interior Design*, 37(1), pp. 5–6.

National Council for Interior Design Qualification (NCIDQ) (2004) *Definition of Interior Design*. Washington DC: NCIDQ. Retrieved from: http://www.ncidq.org/AboutUs/AboutInteriorDesign/DefinitionofInteriorDesign.aspx

Oblinger, D. (2003) Boomers, gen-xers and millennials: Understanding the 'new students'. *EDUCAUSE Review*, 4, pp.38–45.

Pable, J. (2010) Socially beneficial design: What can interior designers do? In C. S. Martin & D. A. Guerin (eds), *The state of interior design profession*. New York, NY: Fairchild Books, pp. 8–16.

Pable, J., Waxman, L., & McBain, M. (2011) *Recommendations for design and construction standards for transitional and permanent supportive housing*. Report to the Florida Housing Finance Corporation. Retrieved from: http://lowincomehousingdesign.weebly.com/

Sen, A. (1985) *Commodities and capabilities*. Amsterdam: North-Holland; New York: Elsevier Science Pub. Co., p. 28.

Sorrento, L. (2012) A natural balance: Interior design, humans, and sustainability. *Journal of Interior Design*, 37(2), pp. ix–xxiv.

Strauss, W. (2005, September) Talking about their generations: Making sense of a school environment made up of gen-xers and millennials. *School Administrator*, 62(8), pp. 10–14.

Tallahassee Green Building Council (n.d.) Retrieved from: http://tallahasseegreenbuilding.com/

Thorpe, A. (2012) *Architecture & design versus consumerism: How design activism confronts growth*. New York, NY: Earthscan/Routledge.

U.S. Department of Health and Human Services (HHS) (2010) *Health-related quality of life and well being. Healthy People 2020*, Washington, DC: U.S. Department of Health and Human Services. Retrieved from: http://www.healthypeople.gov/2020/about/QoLWBabout.aspx

U.S. Environmental Protection Agency Green Building Requirements and Policies (n.d.) Retrieved from: http://www.epa.gov/oaintrnt/projects/requirements.htm

USGBC (n.d.) Retrieved from: http://www.usgbc.org

Waxman, L., & Clemons, S. (2007) Student perceptions: Debunking television's portrayal of interior design. *Journal of Interior Design*, 32(2), pp. v–xi.

Wilson, B. (2008) The architectural Bat-signal: Exploring the relationship between justice and design. In B. Bell & K. Wakeford (eds) *Expanding architecture: Design as activism*. New York, NY: Metropolis Books, pp. 28–33.

Winchip, S. M. (2011) *Sustainable design for interior environments* (2nd ed.). New York, NY: Fairchild Books.

Jeff LOGSDON

CHAPTER 5

DESIGN THEORY TO PRACTICE AND THE DESIGN SCHOOL COLLECTIVE – BUILDING AN ESSENTIAL FRAMEWORK FOR EDUCATION AND PRACTICE IN THE UK – A LANDSCAPE ARCHITECTURE PERSPECTIVE

Introduction: Issues in Everyday Life

Life embedded in context and form is not in a static state. There are manifold issues. People live in unsure relationships with energy, form, space and each other, and are confronted by, for better or for worse, a continual state of change. Change transcends local and global scales – particularly where environmental issues arise from systems of flux. Theoretical and material environmental frameworks of life's open interlocking social and ecological systems are influenced by situations and conditions. In this context, people live with a perspective usually confining life to the inside of a parenthesis determined by personal references and experience (or lack of it), and education. Issues of importance to people are often bipolar and exacerbated by perception. These perceptions can sometimes be hidden from reality, but they generally hold at least a hint of common sense and truth – and can be steeped in actual realities and individual and collective references. In the context of the built environment, this affects people's willingness, desire and/or indifference to their surroundings.

However, the problems people see in their built environment are not only perceptual. They are real and, in many cases, physical. If we were to consider a list of global 'real and physical' design issues related to people's everyday life from a landscape-architecture perspective, the list would include, but would not be limited to: influences of climate change, changing technology, diminishing resources, pollution, water quality, energy generation, population dynamics, a fragile world and fragile economy. Issues of importance at smaller, working and operational scales could include: loss of habitat, functional aesthetics, waste disposal, mining reclamation, food production, transportation modes and systems, city edges and urban development.

Particularly in these latter contexts, because of the high value placed on 'the commons', there is constant economic pressure to appropriate public space.[1] Development pressure is a continual expression of appropriation that continues to return – whether it is Central Park in New York City, or Central Park in Chelmsford, Essex, where this paper will focus its attention. The issues to be dealt with by designers of the built environment, then, are oftentimes ubiquitous and evident in all societies. However, they are also specific to a group of local and regional design questions. These specific issues are frequently derived from larger scale situations – and they require both global and local thinking. They are real and embedded in the physical environment but are also perceptual and thus, to an extent, theoretical. They are invariably complex and layered, and therefore require responses from all design disciplines; they require a cross-disciplinary approach, whether it be from planners, architects, interior designers or, as we will discuss in more detail here, landscape architects.

Part 1: Design in Education and Practice and the Design School Collective – A Theory-to-practice Approach

Change in urban infrastructures, population density, social and psychological fatigue, and the seminal issues of loss of identity and 'placelessness' are symptomatic of modern life. The symptoms of this are diagnosed both in detail, through a microscope, and in contextually distant mosaics viewed from 30,000 feet. Landscape architecture – and design more generally – has the potential to respond to these issues. It can portray imaginative futures in phases of abstraction as well as the intimate realities of transparent and opaque relationships. It can also portray 'in-resolution' relationships between people and places, physical and ephemeral forms and space and time. It can impose order on the complex and changing nature of modern life.

In doing this, however, the range of issues to be dealt with is complex. Issues are interrelated, transcend single-discipline thinking and involve both questions of theory and practicality. For this reason, designers, and by extension design schools, have to respond to the socio-cultural and physical issues they are faced with through a very specific approach that links theory and practice. We will call it a *theory-to-practice approach*. We suggest that design, and its education, relies on an essential theory-to-practice approach that is open to an interdisciplinary spirit from each of its subject areas. Specifically, in education, it involves learning-by-doing, teamwork, self-reflection and learning-by-teaching as signature pedagogical concepts.[2]

These operate in numerous formats and approaches that create mutual learning environments: studios, lectures and seminars, active learning, collaborative learning and peer teaching. These formats and approaches are used to allow students to facilitate community learning and capacity building, while also facilitating their own growth.[3] The purpose behind this system[4] is to develop a relevant collaborative design programme that responds to complex interconnected socio-cultural and biophysical issues and conditions. These theoretical and practical issues are not always isolated to one place or one region, but are familiar, being often very similar to those of other societies, cultures and geographical locations. A theory-to-practice approach, then, not only involves theory and practice, and specific teaching techniques, but requires learning and experimenting in and out of global scales.

In a sense, this last point is a natural issue for design schools – they are, or should be (by necessity) world schools. So many design issues transcend scales in the form and dialogue of culture, climate, material and infrastructure that it cannot be otherwise. Donald Schön's research backs this up in that it reveals that the design-studio technique, the educator's concepts and the study of relationships between art, design and science that engage in the design process reappear in design-school education across the world.[5] John Maeda, President of Rhode Island School of Design (RISD) echoes the same point, writing that art and design are poised to transform our economy in the twenty-first century, like science and technology did in the last century: globally.[6] This sentiment is again repeated by Mohsen Mostafavi, Dean of Harvard Graduate School of Design (GSD), who speaks of the GSD as a 'world school' and thus one dealing with world issues.[7]

However, a 'world' school does not ignore its more local context. Project work, at what could be called an operational scale, brings the case closer to home. Here, the importance is that local projects will, in many respects, bring a reference to global situations even if the players, economies, spaces, histories and futures are situational. The pedestrian scale of detail comes to the point. At this scale, the situation, site and subject become a recognisable place negotiated as a design project. The detail, situation and dynamic of a site or place to be framed as a project allows design students and practitioners to begin to identify with a place, its people and its forms.

Theory and work become 'practice' when they are contingent, contextual and situated. In reference to landscape architecture, Meyer states that grounding in the immediate, the particular and the circumstantial is an attribute of *situational criticism*.[8] Landscape architectural theory and its relationship to projects 'invite practice' and, in Meyer's words, are situational and explicitly historical, contingent, pragmatic and ad hoc. The very idea of theory to practice is realised through these relationships of theory to the actualities and specifics of a place and the sensation of the 'ground'. Seen in this light, pedestrians are the first scale of the project and it proceeds through the observation of the immediate condition – and the sensory. It is from here, the specific and the local, that design thinking and impact move from the particular to a world place or site. Indeed, Burns and Kahn state that the site of design may be thought of in three distinct areas:

> The first most obvious one is the area of control, easy to trace in the property lines designating legal metes and bounds. The second, encompassing forces that act upon a plot without being confined to it, can be called the area of influence. Third is the area of effect – the domains impacted following design action. These three territories overlap despite their different geographies and temporalities.[9]

Beauregard, phrases it slightly differently:

> All sites exist first as places. Before places become objects of urban planning and design, they exist in personal experience.[10]

What this suggests is that a theory-to-practice approach to design, then, is both site specific and global. However, as already indicated, a school applying a theory-to-practice approach does not just understand and examine the relationship between the specific and the global, the small and the large; it acknowledges and responds to the complexity of the socio-cultural and physical problems designers have to deal with in order to construct better environments and, consequently, better lives for people. As a result, design schools have to be, and are by nature, interdisciplinary. Schools must work in systems with collaborative interdisciplinary relationships if they are to respond to what Mostafavi refers to as the 'notion of futures and the need for imagination'.[11]

To respond to this, the development of relationships between research, education and practice remains essential. Knowledge is advanced when new ideas and references to existing conditions and situations are interspersed and integral to all design disciplines and, indeed, non-design disciplines. Embedded in a complex theory-to-practice approach, then, is the notion that the physical sciences, art, engineering, business, sociology and psychology are appropriate design partners. Theory to practice thus becomes a multi-faceted approach aimed at creatively and holistically responding to the whole range of issues faced by the designers and users of the built environment. It is part of the fore thinking on a project and, indeed, the actual platform for defining a project. It facilitates the production of form from concepts and the development of ideas and the imagination – whether these emerge in relation to contextual realities that align with theory, or whether they come from an architecture, landscape architecture, urban design or art-and-design perspective. Actually, the integration of any discipline into design thinking and practice is plausible and relates to the explicit comprehension and advancement of design itself. Theory to practice facilitates and welcomes this.

Part 2: East of England – A Region of Design Issues

Having set out a theory-to-practice approach, its interdisciplinary base and its global – specific perspective, we will examine its potential application to the issues of importance to a specific place, Essex, in the East of England. The issues faced by Essex are similar to those spread across the UK – although generally urgent matters become more urgent where the population is urban and where the East of England is closely affiliated with London. The East of England still retains its countryside. It has a North Sea shore and a character that includes beautiful villages, rolling hills and an extensive coastline.

This is a region of diverse landscapes including the Fens, the Brecklands and coasts of Essex, Suffolk and Norfolk. There are many areas of high environmental value and a rich heritage of historic towns and villages.[12] The East of England's population of 5.4 million is distributed unevenly across the region. Density is the greatest in South Essex and Hertfordshire, where a quarter of the working population commute to jobs in London.[13] Density is lowest in the north. There, approximately one-third of the population lives in settlements of fewer than 10,000 people. In addition to the influence

Figure 1: Map of the United Kingdom locating the East of England and the County of Essex in red. Chelmsford and the Writtle School of Design are designated by the red star. London is located in the south-west corner of the map. An approximate centre of London (Charing Cross) is approximately 32 miles (51kilometers) from Chelmsford.

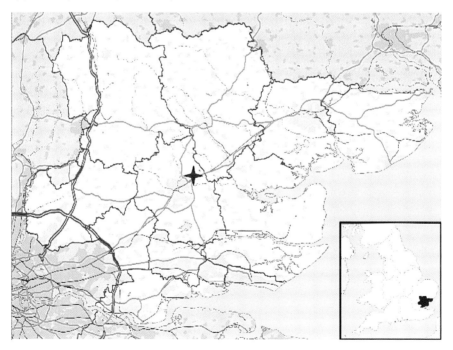

of London's population, there are a number of major sub-regional centres such as Southend, Ipswich, Cambridge, Norwich, Peterborough, Luton and Bedford, and an extensive hinterland of market towns and villages.

According to a 2003 Office of the Deputy Prime Minister report, the strategic challenges for the region include the key issues of:

- Addressing problems of high and rapidly rising house prices and their impact on the recruitment and retention of staff. Although particularly important in the vicinity of London and around Cambridge, it is an issue that spreads deeper into the region.

- Improving transport infrastructure – railways, roads, airports and ports to meet the needs of economic and population growth.

- Ensuring that the benefits of economic growth are spread across the region – particularly to those urban and rural communities facing problems of deprivation and peripherality.

- Addressing the development consequences of scarce water resources throughout the region and an increasing sea level for coastal and low-lying areas.

The priorities and details of importance when considering design and landscape architecture projects here are general to the region but also address the overall larger issues of the nation. However, more specific issues are set by local town and city governments, non-governmental organisations and citizen's action groups. The Royal Society for the encouragement of Arts, Manufactures and Commerce (RSA) is one of the active nongovernmental organisations that have looked at possible projects in the region. The Office of the Deputy Prime Minister is another. This latter body set the priorities in East of England development in their 2003 publication, *Sustainable Communities in the East of England – Building for the Future*. This publication states that a regional programme of action 'will maintain and create sustainable communities in the East of England'. It states that sustainable communities need to be created where people 'want to live' that must safeguard the countryside, be economically prosperous and have decent homes at a price people can afford. It states that these communities must enjoy a well-designed, accessible and pleasant living and working environment and be effectively and fairly governed with a strong sense of community. Although the programme of action does not attempt to cover all the issues of importance to communities in the region, it underlines actions required for addressing housing problems, effective planning and neighbourhood renewal schemes.[14] These issues are very clearly problems in the East of England, while at the same time being global issues – especially where urban populations are considered. They begin to specify projects and suggest issues that a design school, or particular design discipline, could – and should – acknowledge and tackle.

Part 3: The Response of Education – The Design School Collective

Design first comes in shades of a vernacular by building, as needed, in response to living and in a continued influence by itself. [15]

In the conceptual context just described, design projects are seen as filtered from local, regional and global scales – but not necessarily in this order. Given the specific geographical context, some of the particular local issues with regional implications to be addressed include: food production, mine reclamation, design of urban commons, and the redevelopment and reuse of urban rivers – all issues taken on by Writtle School of Design (WSD), based in Chelmsford, Essex. Like any design school, WSD thrives on issues and on collaboration – especially with public organisations. Its landscape-architecture programme is able to respond to the type of problem just outlined by developing design studios around these themes. In recent years it has done this by selecting one issue per year and getting public officials and citizens involved.

In the East of England, as in many areas across the UK, food production, the relationship to urban river systems, affordable housing and reclaiming areas are local issues that involve engagement in a spectrum of small and large scales. Food is part of health and part of supporting local economies. It is also a good measure of life quality, or the speed of one's life. 'Slow food' and 'slow space' are movements focused on regaining the qualities of everyday life, whereas 'fast food' is seen as the 'antichrist' from the perspective of organic and local food production. In the context of Essex, this becomes a very visible issue as towns in the East of England hold markets. Chelmsford, Essex, for example, holds a food market twice a week on Friday and Saturday. Writtle College is located next to Chelmsford and is fortunate to own and manage a farm estate which opens up the opportunity for advancing research, education, demonstration and support to local markets and production.

Markets and food production have been issues considered by the Chelmsford City Planning Department, Essex County Council, Writtle College and the region in general for some time.[16] As a result, it was possible to engage all these players with the school of design and its projects. One of these was intended to develop links between farmland on the Writtle College estate, local food production and markets, research activities in the college and an urban outreach programme. It was developed as part of the postgraduate landscape architecture programme's Urban Territory Studio and allowed the school to connect its educational program with practice in very direct ways.[17] In 2008–2009, issues of food production, the complexities surrounding food as a *system*, its connection with a 'way of life' and a specific urban situation were all explored within student design projects. The projects included both opportunities for research and design activities and engaged students, the public, local farmers and the local authorities. Although the projects developed here have not been built, they begin to address local food issues specific to the East of England and highlight issues that are, of course, directly related globally – food supply and quality, food sharing and cultural affiliations to food.

Figure 2: Masterplan for the 'Garden of Place Constructs in the Urban Territory' (GPCUT) (Courtesy of Writtle College, WSD, Postgraduate Landscape Architecture, 2007–2008).

Figure 3: Master plan – Design Proposal – Temporal Latency and the Didactic Landscape: campus design and reservoir reclamation (Design, photographs and rendering by Edward Flaxman MALA student, courtesy of Writtle College, WSD Postgraduate Landscape Architecture, 2008–2009).

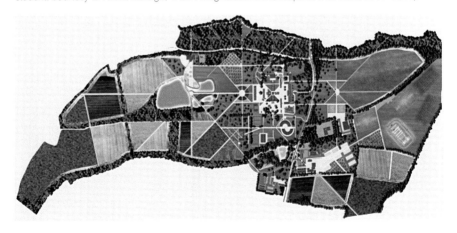

One design proposal to come from this was the 'Garden of Place Constructs in the Urban Territory' (Figure 2). In this example, the design of a 'Kitchen Garden' was proposed and seen as *a garden of production, meaning, learning, functional aesthetics and cultural expression*. The 'garden' was seen as a link within the urban territory via the market, and functioned as an extension of the college's programme structure by involving design, horticulture, sustainability and agriculture. In this sense, it captured perfectly the interdisciplinary ethos of the theory-to-practice approach. The design itself forms a parallel sinuosity with the river, installs itself by recognising the extent of the flood plain, and maintained and enhanced the ecological corridor through the site. There is a functional aesthetic to the organisation and use of its spaces that are stimulating and productive spaces to walk through, work in and observe. Abstraction within the design allows the space to expand and focus at the same time, revealing its artistic intentions and its theoretical base plane – again both aspects of the theory-to-practice approach. The project simply imbeds itself into the existing place and condition, while creating new links and maintaining old ones in a social network or ecological system for people in the contextual environment. Scale is taken into account by trajectories marked by lines that lead to the town centre and beyond. There is an aesthetic, functional and dynamic compliment between the main Writtle College campus and the project area directly across the road and in front of the College.

Another issue dealt with by the Urban Territories Design Studios was the question of mine reclamation. This too is another example of a local, regional and global issue addressed through the school's theory-to-practice approach. Mining reclamation has an interesting rural and urban relationship. Mining is characteristically unwanted in rural, residential or urban areas, but is necessary to build urban infrastructure. By following the radius of city growth outward on a map, one will find sand, and older gravel mining sites, located relatively close to the centre. Moving outward over time, newer ones will be found and thus nearly every map that shows a town or city will reveal a relationship to needs and land uses. The shadows on the map of mines or quarries become 'ghosts of past land use' as they are incorporated into the urban infrastructure and land uses of a region. Arbogast, Knepper and Langer suggest that former mines closer to the centre tend to merge into the urban system for the purposes of safety, recreation, art or other forms of development. [18] It is a need for new landform and land uses that comes out of the changing contextual necessities of urban spaces that invariably instigates the development of land-use alternatives, landscape modifications and changes to environmental quality.

The extraction or mining process always leaves something of a disaster behind it when complete. The hole in the ground caused by mining needs to find its way back contextually, aesthetically, functionally and ecologically into the system. This aggravates the issue to be dealt with and creates a complex set of questions to be raised by designers.[19] These issues were dealt with at WSD in another Urban Territory design project held on the Writtle College estate in the autumn of 2008. This time it was related directly to the mining process and the use of a mineral resource to build a new urban infrastructure (Figure 3).

Figure 4: Detailed plan – College Square – Broken Barriers: campus design and reservoir reclamation project (Design, photographs and rendering by Edward Flaxman MALA student, courtesy of Writtle College, WSD Postgraduate Landscape Architecture, 2008–2009).

This design proposal, entitled *Temporal Latency and the Didactic Landscape*, demonstrates connectivity, capacity and a functional aesthetic. The intention was to use landscape theory in relation to context, meaning, form, function, aesthetic and affect, and the use of concept and context with a social and didactic programme on a College Campus worked especially well in this case.[20] The project planned and designed the contextual relationships between the reservoir site itself and the remaining campus. It linked central campus, in-between areas and the reservoir site and transformed each of the spaces with an appropriate connecting aesthetic and function. The reservoir site extended through the central campus and was subject to additional studies and designs which came together as layers in the overall project.[21] The importance of the reclamation design project is that the site is appropriately and profoundly returned to the landscape system, and that the theories set forth became the practice or making of the project. The design successfully remakes the working site by transforming a major portion of the campus estate and opening up the remade landscape to educational, research and recreation uses and interpretive purposes (Figure 4).

Other issue-related projects carried out in the Urban Territories projects for WSD include: proposals for urban river systems; water and environmental quality projects; the development of historic sites; designs for listed buildings and gardens; urban integration projects to link scales from upstream to downstream; watershed projects and schemes to improve and adapt the transport system. The relationship between the urban river and the urban infrastructure necessitated at least visual access, urban river projects required a functional aesthetic while transportation projects dealt with intermodal forms of transportation including pedestrian, bicycle, automobile, tram and bus systems. These projects drew on and interpreted various existing theories, texts and government directives. A sample includes: *Sustainable Urban transport: Four Innovative Directions* by Goldman and Gorham (2006);[22] the Department of Transport publication, *Improving Local Transport* (October 2012);[23] *Home Zones: Reconciling People, Places and Transport* (2002) and *Urban Design: 'Why don't we do it in the road? – Modifying traffic behavior through legible urban design'* (2004), both by Ben Hamilton-Baillie.[24] It also includes *The Mayor's Transport Strategy* (2010).[25]

Projects on the urban design of town squares were premised on the required placement in appropriate locations of various infrastructures and the creation of inclusive, contextual, welcoming and dramatic spaces. In this regard, the theoretical texts referenced included: *The Death and Life of Great American Cities*, *The Image of the City* and *A Pattern Language*.[26] These are all examples of the beginnings of an understanding of the social, economic, infrastructure, human dynamics and the design of cities and reflect the concepts of contextual and dynamic urban space. Other more recent texts of importance include *The Landscape Urbanism Reader* and *The City Reader*.[27] These texts reflect and propose ideas on landscape urbanism and offer provocative interdisciplinary approaches to planning and design. In the projects based on these ideas, a basic premise was the need to create spaces that act as places to pass-through, sit in, rest, observe and meet people.

Housing development in the East of England continues to focus on improving the existing housing stock and developing liveable, affordable communities that relate to the urban centre and the larger community. Reclaimed industrial sites are a target for city-centre urban housing and one such project in Chelmsford is the Marconi industrial complex. City, non-governmental and citizen action groups are all in favour of the residential and commercial reuse of the area and, in addressing these issues, Urban Territories studios looked at one of the many ways to improve Chelmsford and engage in issues of direct relevance today. Chelmsford is a dynamic and growing market city with a diverse population and excellent schools, and is known as a major commuter centre. As is typical, however, planning is driven by developers and, as a result, planning policies can be in conflict with other, less-commercial aims. Nevertheless, there is, in some cases, resistances to the usual course of business and the complimentary planning departments in Essex and Chelmsford are generally supportive of rethinking standard approaches. In addition, there are two universities in Chelmsford where planning and design programmes exploit the many opportunities for local projects, and thus offer alternative visions. In many regards, these are conditions that are applicable and transferable to the rest of the UK and Europe. Consequently, when we look at the opportunities of linking theory to practice in Chelmsford, we are potentially not just looking at the specific – we are examining the global. Similarly, we may be looking at the issues concerned through the prism of landscape architecture, but this done in the full knowledge of the role other disciplines play in the solutions proposed – and in the full knowledge of how their particular perspectives can creatively inform landscape-architecture solutions for the creation of a better living environment and a better quality of life.

Part 4: An Educational Ethos – The Design School Collective Underlining Form, Futures, Relevance and Potential

The legitimacy of form, the creative importance of research, the abstraction and challenge of experimentation, and the questioning of the common denominator all secure a place for the ethos of a school in world terms. Mohsen Mostafavi, Dean of Harvard GSD, applies the following quote as a way to describe the GSD's sensibility and approach to planning and design education. 'In every era the attempt must be made anew to wrest tradition away from a conformism that is about to overpower it.'[28] Here, Mostafavi reveals a belief in the resistance to immediate convention as an imperative for designers and educationalists – a resistance evident in the projects just described that can be the nexus between theory and practice. Seen in this light, such projects can be a place marked by tradition in which convention is rethought and remade as a way to progress.

With this in mind, design can be seen as remaking and reconstituting materials, phenomena and space in the creation of new forms, new dynamics and new futures. It is driven by critical issues and the hope of improving urban, rural and in-between places – places that are states of human relations with regard to form, living space (lived-in space) and *the commons*. Across the spectrum of design education, practice and new realms in research, truths and futures exist in a time and place reality. At the same time, however, truths and futures can be imagined in a creative and responsive discourse and design response. Design thinking across a design school's disciplines creates a collective framework for design education that is interdisciplinary, open ended and that seeks to foster new thinking. It is the essence and strength of a design school. Although they may differ in this from other discipline schools – and despite being relatively costly in comparison to those of other disciplines – schools of design tend to be influential and have the capacity to bring significant recognition to the institution. Design is often separate and misunderstood by other departments, and aspects of its functioning may appear more abstract than those of physics or economics, for example. However, a school of design has the potential to connect to the pulse of a community outside of the university – locally and internationally. As with Writtle School of Design, this begins by setting real projects that link public and private organisations and citizens – although these projects must be interdisciplinary if the true potential of a design school is to be fulfilled. However, projects must also be creative, inspirational, experimental and impose few limits. They should also initiate open-ended thinking.

Design pedagogy engenders new processes and procedures, and employs advanced learning and teaching techniques that are templates often aimed for by other departments.[29] Studios, in combination with lectures, seminars, site visits and an interdisciplinary working knowledge, form the dynamic state of design education. Studios develop an abstraction phase, use narrative and language, cause interaction between students and organisations, and interpret places and phenomena. Critiques by juries[30] and team learning experiences are routine procedures in design schools and foster creativity and critical thinking.

Higher education is often thought of as life in a bubble and, while this may be true at times, this perception is also relative.[31] Ideally, design education tries to be experimental, imaginative, creative and problem-solving – but at the same time, it has to prepare practitioners. The pedagogy is thus based on informing practice by implanting theoretical overarching design principles and ways of thinking that balance and promote practical application. The idea is to develop thinkers who revisit convention by invention and resist life's everyday conundrum of low common denominators, comfortable solutions, functional aesthetic malfunctions and less-than-compatible social and ecological systems.

To facilitate the open ended thinking necessary for this, education and institutions are sometimes seen as sanctuaries that follow Appleton's 'prospect refuge theory'[32] – a theory that enables simultaneous observation, shelter and engagement. It allows one to see and not be seen, or to see and comprehend before intervening – to live in the 'wild' at the 'biological' edge, and to learn and experience from a perch. The perch is an observation point that involves both engagement and perception. But the perch can also be interpreted as a sanctuary – a place where the work of learning and experience is carried out in a constructive and simpler 'guarded' environment. 'Guarded' here means the protection of academic freedoms, such as the freedom to explore ideas through experimentation, resistance and open dialogues. Design culture is a sensibility; a subject engaged in interpreting society; a state of being; a way of living; and a cross-cultural perception of a state of interaction in space and form, and with people. Education must be provided with no limits, except for some economic limits of space and time. Schools tend to have their own specialist design disciplines which are rather independent and accompanied by their own theoretical and practical intellectual capital. The inherent inspiration in each of a design school's subject areas has to be harnessed for the real productive and innovative thinking necessary in practice and theory. It is the premise of this paper that the best way to do this – the best way of facilitating designers capable of producing better environments – is to develop design as a linked local–global collective engaged in an open-ended theory-to-practice approach. The design collective, whether in education or in practice, must be steeped in practical and profound ideas.

Notes

[1]   The commons are understood as accessible systems, a collective and a shared ground, layered by physical and phenomenal places of scale. Design has the possibility to engage people in this sense – to comprehend situations and contexts, create and signify infrastructure, and influence dynamic spatial relationships.

[2]   Active learning has broad implications for engaging research in teaching and learning as well as for forms of design practice (Wagener and Gansemer-Topf, 2005, p. 199).

[3]   Demming and Swaffield, 2011, p. 194.

[4]   This refers to a theory-to-practice approach using, for example, active learning and community learning to ensure participatory engagement.

[5]   Schön, 1988.

[6]   See: Maeda, 2012.

[7]   Jensen, 2010.

[8]   Meyer, 1997, p. 70.

[9]   Burns and Kahn, 2005, p. xii.

[10]   Beauregard, 2005, p. 39.

[11]   An interview by Boris Jensen titled 'The Harvard Recipe: Interview with Mohsen Mostafavi' (Jensen, 2010).

[12]   In addition to reports by the Office of the Deputy Prime Minister, 2003, more data and information on the economy, environmental condition, demographics and trends in the East of England Region are available online and in publications by Insighteast: Economic intelligence for the East of England; Department for Environment, Food and Rural Affairs (Defra); reports from the former East of England Development Agency (EEDA); Office of National Statistics (ONS) and the Environment Agency, Anglia Region.

[13]   For fuller information, see: Office of National Statistics (ONS).

[14]   See: Office of the Deputy Prime Minister, 2003.

[15]   Jackson, 1984.

[16]   The summary of East Anglia progress on sustainable food procurement is reported in the Project Report to GO-East and DEFRA (East Anglia Food Link, 2007).

[17]   The Urban Territory Studio has been recognised as one of the major contributors to WSD's highly regarded postgraduate landscape-architecture programme. Recognition has come from the Landscape Institute in the 2009 full accreditation process and report, the re-validation documents with commendations from the University of Essex in 2011, and the highly supportive external examiner reports in consecutive years 2006 to 2012. The studio is commended for its innovative projects linking local and regional issues, integral design theory and practice application, by linking local community citizens and organisations to landscape-architecture education and practice.

[18]   Arbogast, Knepper & Langer, 2000.

[19]   Various Land Use Policy journal articles have been published that see reclamation as both a local and regional imperative that must be well planned and designed. The book, The Human Factor in Mining Reclamation, examines the urban demands and social implications of mining operations in developed and undeveloped areas (Arbogast, Knepper & Langer, 2000). Although this book is primarily concerned with the U.S., the critical issues are globally very similar in developed and developing regions.

[20]   'Affect' is present here in the dramatic change to the mining site and illustrates how people could now interact at different scales and in different ways within the designed landscape.

[21]   These layers were defined as: 'Topography – Layer One (Reservoir)', 'The Didactic – Landscape', 'Threads of Knowledge – Learning Corridor' and 'Cultural Initiative – Social Plots'.

[22]   Four Innovative Directions by Goldman and Gorham (2006) is policy oriented and presents a systems approach to transportation.

[23]   The Department of Transport publication Improving Local Transport (October 2012) sets progressive planning and design criteria for funding local infrastructure.

[24]   Both these texts demonstratively illustrate innovative multimodal means of transportation

and how to modify traffic behaviour through design.

[25] *The Mayor's Transport Strategy* (2010) introduces a significant process for partners to engage in progressive transportation measures (Greater London Authority, 'Mayor's Transport Strategy', London: GLA, 2010).

[26] Jacobs, Jane. *The Death and Life of Great American Cities* (1961); Kevin Lynch, *The Image of the City* (1960); Christopher Alexander, *A Pattern Language* (1977).

[27] *The Landscape Urbanism Reader* (2006), edited by Charles Waldheim, and *The City Reader* (Fourth Edition, 2007), edited by Richard LeGates and Frederic Stout.

[28] Walter Benjamin, 'Theses on the Philosophy of History', 1940.

[29] Design studio could be taken as an exemplar for university-based professional schools (Schön, 1988).

[30] Critique by jury refers to the presentations that follow a design project in which students explain their work to an invited panel of reviewers.

[31] Education is a life phase promoted to a necessary step in a continuum of learning and making. Each design discipline has its practical applications and its theoretical underpinning. Sometimes, recognising where theory and practice meet, or whether or not there is a balance, or even if there should be, is complex.

[32] Appleton, 1975.

Bibliography

Appleton, J. (1975) *The Experience of Landscape* (1996 ed.). New York: Wiley.

Arbogast, M. F., Knepper Jr., D. H., & Langer, W. H. (2000) *The Human Factor in Mining Reclamation*. U.S. Geological Survey Circular 1191, Denver: U.S. Geological Survey.

Baudrillard, J. (1988) 'Simulacra and Simulations', in *Selected Writings*, ed. Mark Poster. Stanford: Stanford University Press, p. 166.

Beauregard, R. A. (2005) in Burns, C. and Kahn, A. (2005) *Site Matters: Design concepts, histories, and strategies*. New York: Routledge, p. 39.

Bell, M., & Leong, S. T. (eds) (1998) *Slow Space*. New York: Monacelli Press.

Bloodworth, A.J., Scott, P.W., & McEvoy, F.M. (2009) 'Digging the backyard: Mining and quarrying in the UK and their impact on future land use'. *Land Use Policy*, 26 (2), December 2009, S317.

Burns, C., and Kahn, A. (2005) *Site Matters: Design concepts, histories, and strategies*. New York: Routledge, p. xii.

Corner, J. (ed.) (1999) *Recovering Landscape: Essays in contemporary landscape architecture*. New York: Princeton Architectural Press.

Cosgrove, D. (1998) *Social Formation and Symbolic Landscape* (first published London: Croom Helm, 1984). Madison: University of Wisconsin Press.

Dee, C. (2010)'Form, Utility, and the Aesthetics of Thrift in Design Education'. *Landscape Journal*, Council of Educators in Landscape Architecture (CELA), Wisconsin: The University of Wisconsin Press, 29, No.1.

Demming, E. M., and Swaffield, S. (2011) Landscape Architecture Research: Inquiry, strategy, design. Hoboken, NJ: John Wiley & Sons, p. 194.

Deleuze, G. (1988) *Spinoza: Practical Philosophy*. San Francisco: City Lights Books.

Department of Transport (2012) *Improving Local Transport: Department for Transport, Investing in local transport infrastructure*, October.

East Anglia Food Link (2007) 'Sustainable Food Procurement in the East of England' reported in the Project Report to GO-East and DEFRA, May.

Eckbo, G. (1950) *Landscape for Living*. New York: Dodge, pp. 57–60.

Eco, U. (1986) *Travels in Hyperreality*. New York: Harcourt Brace Jovanovich, p. 43.

Goldman, T., and Gorham, R. (2006) 'Sustainable urban transport: Four innovative directions'. *Technology in Society*, 28, p. 261.

Greater London Authority (2010) 'Mayor's Transport Strategy'. London: GLA.

Hamilton-Baillie, B. (2002) 'Home zones: reconciling people, places and transport'. Cambridge: Harvard Design School.

Hamilton-Baillie, B. (2004) 'Urban design: why don't we do it in the road? Modifying traffic behavior through legible urban design', *Journal of Urban Technology*, 11(1), p. 43.

Holl, S. (2000) *Parallax*. New York: Princeton Architectural Press.

Howett, C. (1987) 'Systems, Signs, and Sensibilities'. *Landscape Journal*, 6, no. 1, pp. 4–12.

Jackson, J. B. (1984) *Discovering the Vernacular Landscape*. New Haven: Yale University Press.

Jensen, B. B. (2010) 'The Harvard Recipe: Interview with Mohsen Mostafavi'. *Conditions Magazine*, 26 May 2010.

Kunstler, J. H. (1994) *Geography of Nowhere: Rise and decline of America's manmade landscape*. New York: Touchstone.

Kwon, Miwon (2002) *One Place after Another: Site-specific art and locational identity*. Cambridge, MA: MIT Press.

Lynch, K. (1996) *Image of the City*. Cambridge, MA: MIT Press.

Maeda, J. (2012) *How to design a Better world*. CNN Opinion, 16 December. Retrieved from: www.cnn.com/2012/12/16/opinion/maeda-good-design/index.html (accessed 3 January 2013)

Menin, S. (ed.) (2003) *Constructing Place: Mind and matter*. London: Routledge.

Meyer, E. (1997) 'The Expanded Field of Landscape Architecture', in G. F. Thompson and F. R. Steiner (eds), *Ecological Design and Planning*. New York: John Wiley, p. 70.

Office of the Deputy Prime Minister (2003) *Sustainable Communities in the East of England – Building for the future*. London: Office of the Deputy Prime Minister.

Schön, D. A. (1984) 'The Architectural Studio as an Exemplar of Education for Reflection-in-Action'. *Journal of Architectural Education*, Vol. 38, No. 1, Autumn, pp. 2–9.

Schön, D. A. (1988) 'Toward a Marriage of Artistry & Applied Science in the Architectural Design Studio'. *Journal of Architectural Education*, Vol. 41, No. 4, Summer, 4–10.

Swaffield, S. (ed.) (2002) *Theory in Landscape Architecture: A Reader*. Philadelphia: University of Pennsylvania Press, p. xii.

Tuan, Y.-F. (1990) *Topophilia: A study of environmental perception, attitudes, and values*. New York: Columbia University Press.

Wagener, M. and Gansemer-Topf, A. (2005) Learning by teaching others: A qualitative study exploring the benefits of peer teaching. *Landscape Journal*, 24 (2), p. 199.

Waldheim, C. (ed.) (2006) *The Landscape Urbanism Reader*. New York: Princeton Architectural Press.

Joel OLIVARES RUIZ

CHAPTER 6

NEW CHALLENGES FOR THE EDUCATION OF ARCHITECTURE IN MEXICO

Mexico: Comments on Society, Architecture and Education

The history of architecture and architectural education in Mexico is complex and varied. As a country, we have been subject to various forms of government and various levels of external interference in domestic affairs. Architecturally, and at the level of the city, this has obviously left its mark. Up until the early twentieth century, the neoclassical cities, planned according to the urban principles of the Spanish King Felipe II, and later those of Barron Haussmann under the French-backed government of Ferdinand Maximillian I, were still seen as an appropriate model. Despite the fact that this approach to urbanism represented a clear imperial tendency, the neoclassical cities were sufficiently well adapted to the Mexican terrain and climate to function relatively well.[1] Indeed, the level of adaptation was such that it is possible to talk of this architecture as the Mexican style of the period.

Perhaps the most iconic of the actual buildings constructed in these cities and their surroundings was the Hacienda, a building typology that would become intrinsically associated with Mexico.[2] The Haciendas were of considerable importance in Mexico as, up until the mid-nineteenth century, they were the driving force of the social and economic development of the country: sustaining rural industries by processing the very crops they produced and ensuring an adequate level of economic self-sufficiency for the country. At that point in its history, Mexico was predominantly rural with only 600,000 people living in cities, including Mexico City.

However, as a result of the Mexican Revolution, the first of the twentieth century, the Haciendas were shut down and the social and economic systems they fostered moved to the urban centres where, currently, 40 per cent[3] of the Mexican population lives in just 10 macro-cities.[4] The political, architectural and urban models applied during this period where, once again, alien to the country – although by no means negative in all their aspects. The most notable and important change during this period was the continued and ever more aggressive process of industrialisation and modernisation. Today, the phenomenon of uncontrolled urban growth, and the abandoning of the countryside that accompanies it, continues its seemingly irreversible trend and, in this regard, Mexico echoes the situation in numerous other countries in the region.[5]

Although the roots of Mexican urbanisation can be found in the early twentieth century revolution, the growth of Mexican cities passed through an even more aggressive period of expansion from the 1950s onwards. This followed the nationalisation and industrialisation policies of the *Partido Revolucionario Institucional* led by Manuel Ávila Camacho: a shift that also saw the full adaptation of the Modern Movement in architectural and urban design circles. Camacho's emphasis on modernisation through state ownership of industry, and thus the economy at large, saw the nationalisation of the petroleum industry and the creation of a parastatal economic model, including companies such as the *Federal Electricity Commission*, the telecommunications company *Telmex National Rail* and the *Bank of Mexico*, to mention some of the most important. However, the poor management of these industries and the economy in general in the second half of the twentieth century led the government to sell off these parastatal companies, leaving the country in a state of permanent economic crisis.

The History of Architectural Education in Mexico

The most recent period of urbanisation in Mexico can thus be associated with its worst period of economic instability and the retreat of government from the control of national industry and infrastructure. In terms of consequences for the built environment, this has resulted in minimal state involvement and funding and, as a consequence, an increase in self-build (both good and bad) which, more often than not, proceeds without professional advice. Consequently, no social-professional model has developed and architects do not aspire to one. Currently, only 5 per cent of building work in Mexico is under professional supervision.

This is, in one respect, quite surprising given that architectural education in Mexico has deep roots and is well established. Mexico was the first country in Latin America in which architecture was taught formally. In 1785, the first school of Fine Arts was founded at the San Carlos Academy in Mexico City. Classes in architecture, painting and sculpture were given and European architects like the Spaniard Manuel Tolsá and the Italian Adamo Boari both taught there. In 1910, the San Carlos Academy became part of the old Royal and Pontifical University of Mexico (Real y Pontificia Universidad de México) and in 1930 its School of Architecture was moved to the Faculty of Engineering.[6] The effect of this was immediate: the Mexican Art Deco Movement emerging as a direct result.[7]

In the 1950s, the National University of Mexico's *University City* was built. It involved the participation of lecturers and students from the School of Architecture and followed the model of a North American or European campus. It was to be a model replicated in the capital city of each of Mexico's 32 provincial states in the coming years, a school of architecture being established in every university. In this regard, the state of Veracruz is typical: there are three main centres of development, each with a university campus and a school of architecture. However, since the 1960s, the number of private schools has grown to the extent that there are currently over 200 across the country. Following the deregulated model that has established itself in Mexico, of these 200 schools only 96 are recognised by the Association of Architectural Education Institutions (ASINEA), the association that certifies the quality of education in both public and private schools in the country. Despite the existence of a formal educational system for architects in Mexico, then, both in practice and in education, deregulation is the norm and standards become impossible to uphold.

Equally as problematic, however, is the fact that this deregulated context makes it very difficult to implement any new tendencies across the country which may, in one way or another, be required if the country's problems of urban decay and rural abandonment are to be dealt with. Typical in this regard is the difficulty that people arguing for sustainable design have in getting heard. Mexican cities continue to represent multiple social, spatial and urban problems such as overcrowding, poor-quality housing and inefficient energy use. These represent a series of problems that many in Mexico have tried to address in isolated cases.[8] The sustainable model of development, generally accepted in many countries, would in the Mexican context allow for a reconsideration of the agro-economic and architectural practices of our ancestors and, possibly, lead us to consider their recuperation.

According to this model, rural areas could be inhabited and the excessive growth of housing estates and property development could be curbed. At the very least, urban areas would be turned into 'green' areas, making the environment of our cities more human and less chaotic.[9] When there are cities like Curitiba in Brazil as models, a city that has managed to reformulate its economic development plans to be sustainable while retaining Latin American characteristics, there is no reason why these possibly utopian goals cannot be applied in Mexico. In this context, architects clearly need to take on a role in the creative planning, design and construction of our cities. Currently, they are not in a position to do so and it will take time for the profession, and the education of its professionals, to be fully equipped for this task. Incorporating ideas of sustainability into the mainstream of Mexico's architectural profession and educational system is essential if this situation is to be turned around as soon as possible.

Producing Creative Problem-solvers

The incorporation of new ideas such as sustainability into architectural education in Mexico has been slow, in part, because the curriculum of Mexican architectural schools has not advanced and adapted in recent decades. The early Mexican schools came out of the School of Fine Arts; the second wave was born from schools of engineering; and the third generation was established in design institutes. The latter group inherited the model of the old Arts and Crafts Movement educational system and also modelled themselves on design institutes such as the German Bauhaus, the Mackintosh School in Scotland and Vhuthemas in Russia. Many of these Mexican schools follow rigid educational systems that not only fail to address fully the technical and practical issues of today's environment, but also fail to address the flexibility of skills and thinking required by today's designers.

This failure to address the flexibility of thinking necessary for today's architects is particularly evident if we consider approaches to fostering design creativity, which will be the focus of this paper. In what has become the 'traditional' form of architectural education in Mexico, strategies for the 'generation of ideas' have not been understood and, as a result, there is little experimentation in the creative side of the design process. Rather than focus on design as a 'process' through which multiple innovative design solutions are toyed with, developed and moulded, the architectural student in Mexico is often faced with a definitive question very early in the process: *how do you want to do it?* For many, then, the opportunity to experiment and allow initial ideas to evolve and change through open-ended creative processes is, consequently, lost.

This situation is related to the fact that, in Mexico, the majority of architectural tutors have had no formal training as educators and, as a result, often simply repeat the tropes of their own educational processes in the classroom or studio. In the context of Mexico, this often means taking on a position of power. Whether we call it leadership, orientation or tuition, it is a role that often contributes to the asking of decontextualised questions which often lead students to generate their own criteria for progressing with design. For example, in the first zoning exercises, when open-ended experimentation is both possible and fruitful, students can be asked '*what will the floor be made out of?*' Inevitably, they are taken by surprise and come to believe that they should think about such levels of detail in even the earliest stages of the design process. The most disastrous part of this tendency is not that it limits their creativity in the educational context, but that it establishes a mindset in which they assume they will have to make decisions about such details in practice without having to consider other factors that may come into play in real commissions, such as the budget, the desires of the client or the requirements of factors such as sustainable and ecological design imperatives.

In some schools, however, attempts are being made to develop new teaching methods which address these issues. In our case, at the Universidad Gestalt de Diseño in the state of Veracruz, there are attempts to use these new methods to educate young architects into thinking about architecture as something holistic and integrated; as a phenomenon that involves the creation of interesting forms, the resolution of social issues and the consideration of questions of structure and sustainability. It is not a one-dimensional issue but a complex, integrated one that requires an open, intuitive and inventive mind. It also requires new thinking on the educational templates we employ.

Alternative Approaches to Education in the Universidad Gestalt de Diseño – Veracruz, México

At the Universidad Gestalt de Diseño, Veracruz, we have attempted to develop models of teaching that i) release the creative potential of students, on the one hand, and ii) give those students the skills and mental agility necessary to rethink outmoded architectural conventions, on the other. We have thus developed a 'gestaltian' based system that stresses the importance of 'ideation' in architectural design; that sees 'creativity' as something that can be developed methodologically and systematically; that uses real and virtual models as testing instruments; and which uses a 'scientific attitude' in architectural design. It is a model that stems from asking a deceptively simple question: *where do ideas come from?*

In order to generate ideas, we have to define our field of study very carefully, establish a clear methodological process and create a working environment that enables collaboration. It might seem obvious, but most Mexican schools work in the opposite way: the field of study is either ambiguous or too wide, the methodological process is not taken into account and the work environment encourages individuality and destructive criticism. There is seen to be a lack of dignity in working in a workshop. As a result, there is a lack of original ideas coming from students and a tendency to refine the first proposal and explore no further. Above all, students are too often unable to present a rationale for their projects and instead rely on ambiguous and emotional language to explain their proposal, which they consider to be an 'aesthetic delight'.

These students have interpreted their main objective as producing aesthetic architecture and, as a result, they turn their attention to the architecture of magazines; they superficially copy.[10] In these cases, the students have failed to recognise that good design requires more ideas than any one person could have. As a result, students defend rudimentary proposals, have a tendency to copy and, often pressed by practical architectural considerations, seek to understand material and structural issues immediately; an approach that again pushes them into (contradictorily) adapting standard responses rather than experimenting with structural or material alternatives.[11]

One of the key ideas in the educational framework proposed by the Universidad Gestalt de Diseño is the notion of 'intuition': the ability to understand something immediately and directly, without applying any methodology or reasoning process. Intellectual intuition, the ability to recognise the nature of things and their different uses through the universalisation of concepts, is enabled through perceptive or *apperceptive* knowledge (sensitive perception).[12] Some psychological theories, including the Gestalt, the Cognitive and the Psychogenetic theories, define intuition as knowledge that is not formulated rationally. Because of this, the subject is not able to verbalise an explanation or justification of the process they used to reach that understanding. This is colloquially referred to as 'the sixth sense'.[13]

According to Maturana,[14] intuition is developed in the primitive areas of the brain, such as the cerebellum and the spinal cord. Additionally, Gigerenzer[15] argues that many mental processes involve a subconscious perception and a drawing of inferences that lead to the recognition of the result, but not the thought process. Unlike in cognitive theory, where perception is divided into the input of information in the memory, reasoning, creativity and constructive skills, Gestalt theories suggest that perception helps us to structure knowledge as concepts and the perceptual process is always the same. That is to say, what we call reasoning or conscious thought is nothing other than the process of intuitive perception.[16]

In relation to this, cognitivists suggest that intuition is no different to conscious problem solving. They believe that as the academic or professional level increases and experience is accumulated, intuition is usually expressed as an instinctive reaction of the subconscious mind, which selects the information stored in the long-term memory and activates it to overcome particular complications. This would suggest that the important function of intuition can be developed through training or, in our case, architectural education and practice.

A Methodology of Creativity and Architectural Design

Existing in parallel to the idea of intuition in architectural education is the notion of creativity: the cognitive ability to produce different alternatives to solve problems. Creativity is often seen as innate, as something that cannot be taught or learnt.[17] Despite this view, it is something that can definitely be encouraged or obstructed. When it is encouraged, creativity generates a different attitude, one which can be conceptual, constructive, deviant, flexible and synthesising. It is constructive as it seeks order in disorder, while considering various possibilities of how it could be. It is deviant because it doesn't accept the superficial first impressions of reality, but positively implies leaving behind preconceptions. It is flexible in that it does not limit itself to just one possibility and is synthesising in that it brings together different parts in new objects and concepts.

Given the freedom of their context, architecture students in Mexico should be naturally creative and, indeed, many are. However, it is difficult for these students to adapt to situations requiring systematic thought; technical issues related to physics and maths for example. These students prefer the immediacy of the initial idea to working on alternative solutions that try to resolve the technical contradictions of their given proposal. In these cases, the role of the tutor can be problematic, seemingly forcing students to face the limitations of reality at the cost of creativity. Furthermore, this often occurs in the critical and tense situation of the design crit.[18] The problem here is that, from a psychological perspective, negative pressure is seen to inhibit creativity and productive and constructive attitudes that can lead to the generation of ideas and the innovative resolution of contradictions and problems. It limits the possibility of intuition playing a decisive role in the design process.

Ideas of intuition and creativity, then, are complicated notions in the semi-practical and, at times, adversarial context of architectural design and instruction. This is exacerbated in the Mexican context due to a lack of accepted or clearly understood pedagogical methodologies. In particular, no methodology seems to be implemented that works with the practical application of the creative tendency. At the Universidad Gestalt de Diseño, we try to apply just such a methodology so as to ensure that students are given the opportunity to flourish both in the subjective and emotional realm of design, and in its practical sphere as well.

In 1960s, the 'discourse of methodology' in architecture was established, impelled largely by Christopher Alexander's research. This research was the starting point of a *scientific* discourse about architectonic analysis[19] and it ranges from quantitative analysis (expressed in flows to create mathematical models and graphs with the purpose of *visualising* points of conflict and prioritising the solutions) to psychosocial factors of space perception within *speech patterns*. Since the 1960s, a multiplicity of interpretations of methodological discourse has arisen in different architecture schools[20] and came to be reflected in the architectural theory which, at that time, was in the historic–axiological stage of the Modern Architecture Movement.[21]

Alexander's ideas, however, also included what we may call the *method of staking*: a social–methodological system that literally gives users a 'stake' in the design of projects in line with certain humanist theories.[22] In this method, the architect conceptualises architecture as an *interpreter–organizer* of its users.[23] Working together, the architect and user determine areas and how they relate to one another by literally testing the architectonic form in the environmental and participative conditions of the users. The user is given a voice in the decisions from the beginning of the project instead of being asked their opinion when the project is already finished; at which point, the client has usually already been pushed away from the most alluring part of the project by either the language of the architect or by the beautiful and unquestionable images used to present the project.

As a methodology applicable to architectural education, this model suggests that education too must facilitate the introduction of voices other than that of the tutor. This is an approach that can, at its best, ensure a more rounded and more 'creative' and complex approach to understanding architecture and its teaching. The most obvious way of achieving this at the educational level is through the involvement of external teachers, critics, specialists, clients and, perhaps, the public. However, it can also be done through the use of different teaching methods which can ensure a school continually examines its own techniques and encourages different forms of intuition and creativity in its students. What follows is an overview of some of these ideas as implemented in the Universidad Gestalt de Diseño, the ultimate aim of which is to develop techniques of learning that facilitate creativity, but which are also applicable to architecture's practical and scientific side.

Analytic and Synthetic Methods

Methods of analysis and/or design are usually considered 'analytic' because their purpose is to identify the parts that make up the object of study and their various functional relationships. However, from the Gestalt approach, the separation of these parts causes an immediate loss of the entity as a whole and, depending on the instruments used, many important functions that are beyond the boundaries of our perception can be missed. Alexander's analytic method allowed him to see the complexity of factors and relationships involved in architectural design, but it also distanced him somewhat from the experience.[24] Therefore, if we apply analytical methods to architectural education we separate its constituent parts; creativity is isolated from science, for example.

By contrast, the synthetic method is a rational process which tends to reconstruct a whole from the elements identified in the analysis. We could say that synthesis is a mental process, the main goal of which is the full comprehension of the nature of the things we already know, in each of its parts and particularities. In our context, it would lead to seeing architectural education as holistic. *Synthesis* means *reconstruction, putting the parts of a whole together again*, but doing this also implies an improvement; the creation of something new and not just an analytical process examining what already exists. It does not mean a purely mechanical reconstruction of a whole, since this would not allow us to advance our understanding. It implies reaching an understanding of nature of the whole, and identifying every aspect of the whole, as well as their basic relationships from a perspective of a new *totality*.

However, there is more to it than this. *Synthesis* can also be explained as the process in which a set of apparently isolated cases can be related to each other, leading to a theoretical hypothesis that combines many different elements. By contrast, according to Ramón Ruiz, *analytical* judgement is the fragmentation of a phenomenon into its simpler constituent parts.[25] It is a mental process in which the representation of totality of a phenomenon is divided. Synthetic judgement, then, consists of joining the heterogeneous elements of a phenomenon; in our case, a teaching framework for architecture that is based on the analysis of the existing situation but which also proposes something new. Crucially, however, this new approach must be fluid and whole.

Assuming that *analysis* is the equivalent of fragmentation and *synthesis* the equivalent of composition, it could be said that our proposal for the *synthetic* method of architectural education consists of structuring the object of study in its constitutive parts but, instead of *dissecting* these parts and losing the whole, recombining them. It is a creative and divergent method and one which is directly analogous to the factual and holistic discipline that is design itself. It is examined here through the prism of the use of iconographical theories applied across the divergent fields and areas of architectural design, from the practical to the creative.

Iconographic Models Methodology

We define an iconographic model as a schematic and interpretative instrument of the functions, natures and forms of a natural or artificial object. It serves the purpose of testing ideas, firstly by checking the understanding of the phenomenon and secondly by checking its system of relationships to visualise its phenomenological effects and extract new concepts. In architectural education this is often manifest literally in the 'model': the three-dimensional representation of an actual idea or form. These can be abstract, rhetorical or just a simple copy of a represented object. The etymological root of the word *model* is a) a measure, quantity or proportion, b) an example or prototype and c) something proportionate to something else. However, when we consider models, we should make a methodological differentiation between a *model* and a *maquette*, or scale model.

We use the word *maquette* when we understand that its purpose is to be an illustrated representation of a proposal. By contrast, a *model* is an instrument used for experimenting and verifying, something which in industrial design can also be referred to as a simulation model. It is common to build these kinds of models in the field of industrial design to test wind-tunnel resistance in the automotive industry, for example. It is also increasingly common in architecture, although the maquette still dominates.

When we speak about *models*, then, we understand they are circumscribed within the natural sciences. In mathematics, each problem is a 'model' of a sort, but it cannot be understood as such, because everything is abstract and nothing is 'natural'. In architecture, models or maquettes are usually used as representations on a figurative scale and, because of this, they tend to be made at the end of the design process when everything has been defined. However, models can be made as part of the creative process as well. In this sense they are 'produced in the moment' an idea is conceived and, if considered to be three-dimensional objects to be used for testing, are active tools to be used in the creative design process.

This is pretty well understood in basic terms but, at the Universidad Gestalt de Diseño, we have tried to challenge our basic understanding of physical models, firstly by envisioning them as 'iconographical representations' and secondly by applying these 'iconographical representations' to more than representations of finished designs, by using them as tools for demonstration on the one hand and creative formal experimentation on the other. For us, the iconographical model has many more uses and can serve to *synthesise* our understanding of design products and processes on both creative and practical/scientific levels.

Icon, Iconic, Iconographic

Before going into detail about our use of *iconographic modelling*, however, it is useful firstly to clarify our use of the terms *icon*, *iconic* and *iconographical*. An **icon** (from the Greek εἰκών, *eikon*) is an image that refers to a picture or representation of an object. According to the semiotics of Charles S. Peirce, an icon is the sign which substitutes an object through its significant representation or by analogy.[26] When we consider how icons communicate visually, however, a slightly different definition comes into play: if an image is 'representative' of a group, its features (which must by definition be simple, emblematic and familiar) are defined as *iconic*.

Of most relevance to us, however, is the etymological root of *iconography* that lies in *icon (Eikon) y Graphia*, which literally means *image description*. As a result, iconography is seen as the most adequate methodological tool for allowing us to catalogue works and authors according to their use of iconic elements; a method similar to historiography. Thus 'icon', as we use it, refers to the image; 'iconic' to the group of common characteristics shared by the group of images; and 'iconography' to our 'description and categorisation' of these icons and iconic characteristics. Although this may not be a universally accepted set of definitions, it allows us to develop an Iconographic Models Methodology in which theories of the icon and the iconic become integrated into creative architectural educational activities that are operative at both the practical and the aesthetic levels.

Iconographic models, then, at their most basic level, are descriptive representations of whatever is being studied: the movement of air in a particular building form; the structural forces at play in a given engineered object; or the effects of light produced by a certain arrangement of structural elements. They are not intended to be literal in either their own form nor in their application which, as we shall see, leads us to use them for practices far beyond their initial descriptive potential. This Iconographic Models Methodology belongs, operationally, to the synthetic approach described earlier: it is applicable across various strands of architectural education; it is intended to reinforce our understanding of the discipline's integrated heterogeneity; it allows us to analyse and, crucially, also 'create' and develop new and original ideas.

The Use of Iconographic Models in Architecture: An Example Starting with Structures

One of the simplest ways of explaining what we mean by iconographic models is through an example that reveals their applicability to questions of architectural structural principles and their teaching. A question that we sometimes ask students in first-year structures classes is: *why doesn't a horse fall over when it lifts one leg?* This may be answered simply through an explanation that it is due to the movement that the horse makes in its body to restore balance from four to three legs. However, the *physical* explanation is that the horse actually changes its centre of gravity (*centroid*) to zero when it is not moving (see Figure 1).

An iconographical model examining this may be abstracted as a table with four legs, the *centroid* being a weight bar (Figure 2). The table represents the phenomenological essence of the body of the horse: as a body resting on four supports. If we put a weight on the table, in relation to the width and height of the legs, it can be moved until the point corresponds to a centre of gravity that allows one support to be removed. By

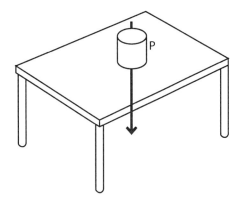

Figure 1

Figure 2

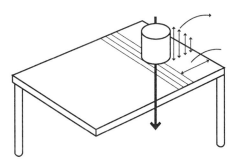

using a simple Iconographic Model such as this to examine the structural question, a simple but effective lesson can be taught (or described) that originates in the realm of equestrian studies but which is clearly applicable to architecture.

Another good example of the pedagogical descriptive possibilities of Iconographic Models in the context of architectural structures can be found in the topic of 'pressure', as often discussed in an early-level school class.[27] Pressure is defined as 'the force that is applied to an area'. It can be visually represented by a vector with its force acting on an area of the same size. It is represented algebraically by equation $P=F/A$. For example, 500 kg of weight over an area of 100 cm^2 is equal to a pressure of 5 kg per cm^2. The variables, in this case, are kilograms over different areas. In order to do this simple calculation, it is only necessary to remember the formula and the amounts in question. In this mathematical and conceptual 'model', the student learns to replace only the quantities in the formula, but does not necessarily understand the phenomenon of pressure.

This occurs even if it is represented diagrammatically, force being represented by a vector bar and area by a drawn square. However, if the student makes an abstracted *iconographic model* as they are encouraged to do at the Universidad Gestalt de Diseño, they are forced to think differently and to 'visualise' the structural forces in question. A typical simple example uses blocks of wood with different surface areas, but of identical weights, that are laid on a body of water. The correlation between surface area and pressure thus becomes evident through a simple model in a way that is impossible to explain through a mathematical formula, even a basic one as in this case. The principle behind both these examples is the same: the abstracted structural *iconographical* model allows the student to understand the principles at play in inventive and creative ways.

Uses of Iconographic Models in Architectural Education – A Sustainable Application

Clearly, the examples given thus far are very simple and rudimentary. However, the principles on display can be used to learn creatively about more complex phenomena and, as we shall see, lead to creative, unexpected and seemingly unconnected leaps in architectural design. The example we will discuss here is a series of models made by students and tutors to understand the Trombe wall. The Trombe wall has no real connection to the environmental conditions of our region in Mexico, which has a humid subtropical climate. As a result, a direct application of its passive heating model is difficult to find. Nevertheless, we consider an understanding and use of solar technology in architecture to be fundamental given that, in Mexico, there is currently so little comprehension of its importance or its possibilities. As a result, we thought it was necessary to experiment with it, to find ways of learning from it and, if possible, to discover creative ways of employing its lessons. We did this using our Iconographic Models Methodology.

In the examples seen here from undergraduate students, an iconographic model was made by recycling one-gallon paint cans and using them to create two particular spaces: **A**, a wall of water, and **B**, an empty space. A cone with glass was also used to represent the greenhouse effect, thermometers were installed to measure the temperature of the water and the empty space, a structure was installed to support the different parts and a hairdryer was used to heat the model (Figure 3). In another variation, cubes were used to create a similar differentiation between concomitant conditions and led to the same observations about air pressure, movement and temperature (Figure 4).

From models such as these, Year One students are introduced to such fundamental criteria as: the tendency for hot air to rise, the effects of natural convection and the possibility of using temperature difference to facilitate constant ventilation. After having understood the principles at play through our iconographic model, a design project can be set so that the lessons learnt can be applied.[28] In this case, the project set as criteria the requirement that excessive heat gain should be avoided in summer

Figure 3   Figure 4

(fundamental in the Mexican context) whilst, in winter, it should be taken advantage of by facilitating heating through solar radiation.[29]

Starting from these very basic premises, students applied the lessons they had learned about the formal and spatial properties required in Trombe-wall construction to their architectural projects. In some cases, this was done in purely technical terms; while in others it became equally a planning and formal exercise, as students developed alternative spatial layouts that met the technical criteria but which also allowed them to innovate spatially (Figure 5). At this stage of the creative process instigated through our use of iconographic models, many large-scale 'prototype-iconographic' models also get built at the school, thus ensuring that these experiments lead to a better understanding of the spatial effects produced and the practical requirements of large-scale construction (Figure 6).

Figure 5   Figure 6

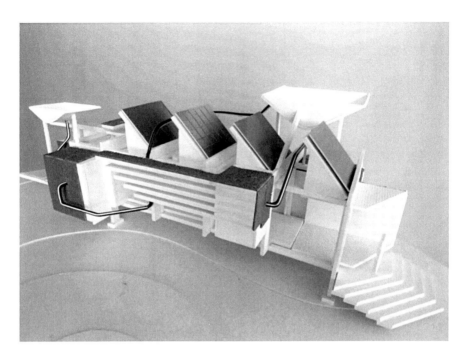

Figure 7

From here, these models inform more standard maquettes that illustrate design proposals and thus we see how our approach operates of multiple levels in a synthesised way: technical, formal, spatial and presentational (Figure 7). At this point then, we see clearly how the Iconographic Model approach clearly operates alongside standard, but still valuable and important, procedures and practices. Throughout, this is actually the focus, students being encouraged to consider problems 'synthetically': as a synthesis or fusion of practical and mental methods, processes and attitudes. It involves the recombination and reconfiguration of individual elements, ideas, practices and techniques from one aspect of architecture into a more holistic approach. The structural and technical model thus becomes integrated and inseparable from the creative and the formal model. The 'parts' are creatively synthesised.

Taking this 'synthesising' approach one stage further, a similar dual technical and creative approach was applied by one of the school's tutors, who subsequently developed more iconographic models of this type in the design and construction of a private project. Again, the iconographic model was used in practical and creative ways, and actually led to the construction of a real project that was both technically and formally innovative (Figures 8 and 9). In these scenarios, the architectural model becomes part of the initial exploration phase and serves as a theoretical and practical antecedent, creating, in this case, houses that are not predetermined by an established repertoire of given forms.[30]

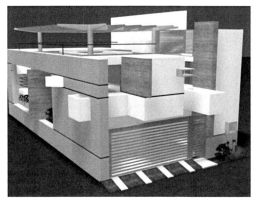

Figure 8 :   Figure 9

Conclusion

The approach outlined here in the context of the Department of Architecture is repeated in the Department of Graphic Design and the Department of Fashion at the school which, in their own ways, focus on similar issues of alternative thinking that combines the technical and the creative in a synthesised model of practice and teaching. In the specific architectural case, this is an approach to education that challenges accepted and established practices in the Mexican context. It seeks, primarily but not exclusively, to work through what we define as an *Iconographic Models Methodology* so as to use 'models' in a way that corresponds to our gestalt ideas and the notion of synthesis. It intends to offer a framework for creative experimentation, on the one hand, and an intuitive approach to the teaching of technical issues, on the other: both issues of little concern in the existing context of architectural education and practice in Mexico.

In the examples we have mentioned here, these experiments have been limited to questions of structures and a very specific aspect of sustainable design. In many ways, Mexico is not unique in its need to address these issues at the level of practice; but it is perhaps more 'unique' than it should be in adopting new pedagogical methods and addressing the issue of climate change and architecture's role in it. It is our contention, however, that the Iconographic Models Method and its broader context of synthesised design thought are not limited to these issues. In our school we apply these approaches to fashion and graphic design. However, they may well also be applicable to the other great issue facing countries like Mexico: urban design in congested cities.

This belief in its potential applicability at the urban level is a natural extension of our *synthetic* (Gestaltian) philosophy; a philosophy that sees all aspects of architectural education as linked and part of a holistic discipline that is fully integrated and mutually influencing. Consequently, the potential applicability of the educational model we propose to other fields is a key issue to raise. If applied beyond our doors to any great degree, it could represent a significant new model for architectural practice and pedagogy in our country. It would be a remodelling of thought that sees structures as interdependent with creativity and form making; that sees design as an intuitive process and architecture as something that can be *generated* and not just copied. Despite only being applied at this point in the limited way permitted by questions of scale and influence, our approach is one that tries to address the issues, problems and potentials of architectural practice in Mexico on a much broader scale.

It is our hope that educational experimentations like ours will, if applied nationally, help a future generation of Mexican architects respond creatively to the architectural and urban context that awaits them. Armed with a new methodology of design and thinking, it is to be hoped that this generation of architects will be able to operate in a way that is free from the need to mimic or apply standard responses to specific issues. It is our intention to facilitate students' ability to adapt creatively to the changing technical, ecological and social factors they will invariably encounter as Mexico moves forward into the next century. Just as Mexico's economic, cultural and architectural past has been rich, varied and at times contradictory, it is likely that the future will be too. Our intention is to implement a teaching model that encourages students to consider the multiple and varied aspects of their profession. They will need to if they are to respond to the problems they will face.

Notes

[1]   For an overview of the architecture of Mexico during this period, see: Gonzales Cortázar, F. (1976) *La Arquitectura Mexicana del Siglo XX*. Consejo Nacional de la Cultura y las Artes. México; Bojórquez Martínez, Y. (2011) *Modernización y nacionalismo de la Arquitectura Mexicana en cinco voces: 1925–1980*. México City: Universidad Autónoma de Aguascalientes.

[2]   The most significant contribution to our understanding of the Hacienda as a Mexican style of architecture can be found in: Cambrezy, L., & Lascuraín, B. (1992) *Crónicas de un territorio fraccionado, de la hacienda al ejido*. México City: Ediciones Larousse S.A.

[3]   These figures can be found in the National Institute of Geographical Statistics (INEGI, Instituto Nacional de Estadística Geografía e Informática). Retrieved from: <http://www.inegi.org.mx/lib/error.aspx?aspxerrorpath=/movil/mexicocifras/mexicoCifras.aspxhttp://www.inegi.org.mx/lib/error.aspx?aspxerrorpath=/movil/mexicocifras/mexicoCifras.aspx> (accessed 20th March 2010)

[4]   Some of these cities include: Mexico City, Distrito Federal, 8,720,916 inhabitants; Ecatepec de Morelos, Estado de México, 1,688,258 inhabitants; Guadalajara, Jalisco, 1,600,940 inhabitants; Puebla, Puebla, 1,485,941 inhabitants. A full list is available at the National Institute of Geographical Statistics website (ibid.).

[5]   This increase in population in other Central and South American cities is dealt with in works such as: Segre, R. (1996) *América latina en su arquitectura*. México City: Siglo veintiuno editores; Lopéz Rangel, R., & Segre, R. (eds) (1986) Tendencias Arquitectónicas y Caos Urbano en América Latina. México City: Gustavo Gili.

[6] The history of these schools is detailed in Bernhard, E. B. (ed.) (1994) Diseño. Historia, técnica y práctica del diseño industrial. Barcelona: Gustavo Gili.

[7] The most exhaustive documentation available on Mexican Art Nouveau and its relationship with the educational system of the time can be found in: Instituto Nacional de Bellas Artes, México City (1982) Apuntes para la historia y crítica de la arquitectura mexicana del siglo XX: 1900–1980. Vol.1 and Vol. 2. Cuadernos de arquitectura y conservación del patrimonio artístico. México City: Instituto Nacional de Bellas Artes.

[8] Two of the most notable architects in Mexico with regard issues of sustainability are Danilo Veras and Javier Senosiain.

[9] For information on sustainable architecture and urbanism in Mexico, see: Valerdi Nochebuena, M. C., & Sosa Oliver, J. (2008) Crítica al Urbanismo y su Arquitectura. México City: Fomento Editorial.

[10] This tendency has been identified in numerous visits to schools across Mexico and in the ten-year life of the Universidad Gestalt de Diseño, Veracruz, México.

[11] Detailed studies on the nature of architectural education have been carried out internationally. One of the most insightful is: Jones, J.C. (ed.) (1978) Metodos de Diseño. Barcelona: Gustavo Gili.

[12] In the Gestalt psychology of perception, 'Apperceptive Distinction' refers to an 'irrational system of perception' .See: Metzger, W., & Giunti, B. (eds) (1984) I fondamenti della psicología della Gestalt. Firenze. Rome.

[13] For an explanation of these ideas, see: Thompson, R. F. (ed.) (1996) Fundamentos de la Psicologia Fisiológica. México City: Trillas.

[14] The Chilean biologists Humberto Maturana and Francisco Varela proposed the theory of brain evolution. They proposed that the evolutionary development of the brain from a genetic point of view is stimulated by knowledge such as autopoiesis (the ability of systems to produce themselves).

[15] Gerd Gigerenzer, the American cognitive psychologist, studies Intuition.

[16] We can find clear examples of this in sports. When competing, athletes do not think or reason about the movements, situations and strategies they have put into practice in training sessions. On the contrary, they perform through intuition. Athletes learn to decode situations and adjust the strategies they have internalised, so as to deal with the different situations they confront.

[17] For descriptions/definitions of creativity as used in this text, see: Hofstadter, D. R. (1982) Gödel, Escher, Bach: Una Eterna Trenza Dorada. México City: Consejo Nacional de ciencia y tecnología.

[18] For a specific description of the design crit (and the design tutorial in more positive terms) see: Webber, M. (1984) El Político y el Científico. Madrid: Alianza Editorial S.A.

[19] In using his work here, we put special emphasis on his study of the Project Design stage; something that was until that point ignored by art and architectural critics, who had traditionally analysed the finished work but had not considered the architectonic language used in the design process.

[20] One variation important to the arguments put forward here is found in: Olivares-Acosta, A. (2001) Koszul Algebras from Combinatorics and their Products and Invariant Ideals. Glasgow: University of Glasgow.

[21] In this context, we suggest that Alexander's work in this area can be interpreted as an attempt to construe Architecture within the Neoclassical values, the ethics of the Arts and Crafts Movement, as well as the social approach of the Modern Architecture Movement.

[22] Here, we refer to humanist theories of 'psychology' in line with the work of Carl Ransom Rogers. The work of Rogers has three characteristics of relevance to this context. The first is his emphasis on subjectivity; the second, in his work related to Phenomenology and Existentialism, particularly, notions of the 'self', 'existence' and 'being'; the third, and most important, is his rejection of 'motivational' explanations of psychoanalytical theory and thus his definition of 'conduct' as indeterminable and people as 'free'. These ideas are explained in: Rogers, C. R. (1975) *El Proceso de Convertirse en Persona*. Buenos Aires: Paidós.

[23] This was most famously implemented by Alexander at Oregon University where, together with a group of collaborators, he was employed to develop design proposals for the campus in collaboration with various users. It was documented in: Alexander, C. (1975) *The Oregon Experiment*. Oregon: Center for Environmental Structure.

[24] This scientific bias that separates the architect from experience is evident in Alexander's establishment of an algorithmic system and trees of schematic functions as evident in his early writings: Alexander, C. (1964) *Notes on the Synthesis of Form*. Cambridge, MA: Harvard University Press; Alexander, C. (1965) A City is Not a Tree. Lund: Lund University. It is also evident in Alexander, C. (1977) *A Pattern Language: Towns, Buildings, Construction*. Oxford: Oxford University Press. However, in this case, he creates a series of 'patterns' based on a more phenomenological and humanist understanding of spatial relations which are presented as templates for design.

[25] Ruiz, R. *Historia y Evolución del Pensamiento Científico*. Retrieved from: http://www.monografias.com/trabajos-pdf/historia-pensamiento-cientifico/historia-pensamiento-cientifico.shtml (accessed 10 January 2012)

[26] For a description of the work of Pierce, see: *Charles S. Peirce: The Essential Writings*. Moore, E. C., & Baird, R. M. (eds) (1998) Prometheus Books, London.

[27] This example is based on a *Model of Physics* created in 1982 by students in their first year of secondary school, at Las Hayas School in Xalapa, Veracruz.

[28] In this case, the lessons were also applied by the teachers in their practice as architects: in particular, in the project, Vivienda Bioclimática (Veracruz, Mexico; Architect: Enrique Sanchez Pugliesse, 1999).

[29] These are basic principles of this type of design and can be found in numerous standard text books of ecological design. Material available on ecological design in the context of Mexico is more limited. See: Vanden Broeck, F. (2000) El Diseño de la Naturaleza o la Naturaleza del Diseño. México City: Editorial Universidad Metropolitana Azcapotzalco.

[30] Enrique Sánchez Pugliesses describes it as an approach that avoids 'compositional architecture' and produces designs that have 'determined their own forms as an outcome of considering the house as an Inhabitable Organism'. Enrique Sánchez Pugliesses. Interview with Dr. Joel Olivares Ruiz, Universidad Gestalt de Diseño, Xalapa, Mexico, September 2012.

Bibliography

Alexander, C. (1964) *Notes on the Synthesis of Form*. Cambridge, MA: Harvard University Press.

Alexander, C. (1974) *A City is Not a Tree*. (1965) Lund: Lund University.

Alexander, C. (1975) *The Oregon Experiment*. Oregon: The Center for Environmental Structure.

Alexander, C. (1977) *A Pattern Language: Towns, Buildings, Construction*. Oxford: Oxford University Press.

Bûrdek, B. E. (1994) Diseño. Historia, técnica y práctica del diseño industrial. Barcelona: Gustavo Gili.

Bojórquez Martínez, Y. (2011) Modernización de la Arquitectura Mexicana en cinco voces: 1925–1980. México City: Universidad Autónoma de Aguascalientes.

Cambrezy, L., & Lascuraín, B. (1992) Crónicas de un territorio fraccionado, de la hacienda al ejido. México City: Larousse.

Gonzales Cortázar, F. (1976) La Arquitectura Mexicana del Siglo XX. Consejo Nacional de la Cultura y las Artes. México.

INBA – Fine Arts national institute (1982) Apuntes para la historia y crítica de la arquitectura mexicana del siglo XX: 1900–1980. Vol.1 and Vol. 2. Cuadernos de arquitectura y conservación del patrimonio artístico. México City: Instituto Nacional de Bellas Artes.

INEGI – National Institute of Geographical Statistics (2010) (INEGI, Instituto Nacional de Estadística Geografía e Informática). Retrieved from: http://www.inegi.org.mx/lib/error.aspx?aspxerrorpath=/movil/mexicocifras/mexicoCifras.aspx

Jones, J. C. (1978) Metodos de Diseño. Barcelona: Gustavo Gili.

Lopéz Rangel, R., & Segre, R. (1986) Tendencias Arquitectónicas y Caos Urbano en América Latina. México City: Gustavo Gili.

Metzger, W., & Barbéra, G. (1984) I fondamenti della psicología della Gestalt. Firenze. Rome.

Moore, E. C., & Baird, R. M. (eds) (1998) *Charles S. Peirce: The Essential Writings*. London: Prometheus Books.

Olivares-Acosta, A. (2001) Koszul Algebras from Combinatorics and their Products and Invariant Ideals. Glasgow: University of Glasgow.

Rogers, C. R. (1975) El Proceso de Convertirse en Persona. Buenos Aires: Paidós.

Ruiz, R. (2006) Historia y Evolución del Pensamiento Científico. México: UNAM (Universidad Nacional autónoma de México).

Valerdi Nochebuena, M. C., & Sosa Oliver, J. (2008) Crítica al Urbanismo y su Arquitectura. México City: Fomento Editorial.

Vanden Broeck, F. (2000) El Diseño de la Naturaleza o la Naturaleza del Diseño. México City: Editorial Universidad Metropolitana Azcapotzalco.

Puay-peng HO

CHAPTER 7

WALKING THE TIGHT ROPE OF ARCHITECTURAL EDUCATION IN HONG KONG – BALANCING PEDAGOGY AND PRACTICE

Introduction

Hong Kong has an architectural culture that is cosmopolitan. It is also a culture situated in a region where urbanisation is progressing at an unprecedented rate (Figure 1). In the last weeks of 2011, more than half of China's population lived in the cities. This compared to just 13 per cent in 1953, and 36 per cent in 2000.[1] Such rapid urbanisation in recent years has created a host of issues for urban planners and architects to deal with.[2] Speed and quantity of construction are privileged over the design and quality of the architecture built. The demands placed by this on innovation and research in the built environment, from the scale of a small building to extensive urban design and master planning, are extreme. The challenges faced by architects and planners are enormous.[3]

One of those challenges is, of course, sustainable development. Sustainability is an issue increasingly embraced by Hong Kong society and this is reflected in all aspects of the built environment. It is seen in the setting up of government agencies and the emergence of local pressure groups pushing the sustainability agenda, and is evident in the renewal and updating of green building standards.[4] Most important in this regard is the fact that the legislative framework and building regulations of Hong Kong are tightening their standards to enforce lower energy usage.[5]

However, two other major issues raised by this unprecedented growth in urban environments include the creation of effective, functional and appropriate urban environments and the preservation of the region's existing architectural heritage. In direct response to this, the Hong Kong Institute of Urban Design (HKIUD) was established in 2009 and aims to ensure effective, controlled and sustainable urban expansion. Similarly, the Hong Kong Institute of Architecture Conservationists (HKICON) was founded in the same year and aims to address the pressures on the existing heritage of the region in this climate of ever stronger pressures to develop and redevelop.[6]

However, technical issues of planning, sustainability and preservation are not the whole story. Hong Kong is a melting pot of communities, cultures and activities that coexist in a tight, rich and intense setting; a setting created in an incremental way with buildings being constructed and torn down, and places and spaces being refurbished and replaced on a continuous cycle. Woven into this changing and dense urban fabric, then, are human activities driven by people from all walks of life, with varying backgrounds, conflicting aspirations and different perspectives on the physical environment. Their experience, their stories, their memories and their sense of place, are totally entwined in the urban landscape and, indeed, can be considered as the very factors that make these places come alive.[7]

Such issues are particularly relevant in Hong Kong, where the urban centre has the highest population density in the world. In all the hustle and bustle, how can people read the urban landscape that they traverse? Is there a place for history, culture and memory in their interpretation of the city? What vagaries lie in these varied readings? Such are the questions for architects and urban designers concerned with working with the personal experience of the people of Hong Kong in its complex and intensely concentrated urban fabric.

All of these concerns can, perhaps, be distilled into four issues: sustainability, urban design, heritage and liveability. They all overlap and thus all contribute to making the situation faced by designers in the region even more complex and contradictory. How do we design in a context that is this intense and still meet the emotional, functional and ecological needs of inhabitants and businesses? How do we do this whilst also preserving the region's architectural heritage? These issues facing the architectural practitioners of Hong Kong are, invariably, reflected in the educational context, in which the design curriculum is evolving in order to embrace developments and advanced research in these areas.

Educating Architects: The Case of the Chinese University of Hong Kong

In Hong Kong, as in other parts of Asia, students enter an undergraduate architectural programme at a very young age. Teaching design to young students who have relatively little experience of life within this economic and design culture is challenging. Architecture is often thought of as the physical embodiment of life and the appreciation of humanistic values, but it is also a technical discipline that, today, is more and more focused on technology and the green agenda. Finding a balance between practice, pedagogy and other academic and humanistic pursuits is, in itself, a fine art.

How can architectural education effectively impact young learners in a way that will result in them understanding forms of living? How can educators best prepare students to become competent and responsive catalysts of positive change? How can we balance the requirements of humanist agendas with those of technology and function? These questions are particularly pertinent to the Hong Kong context with its rapid urbanisation, its exclusively economic growth model of development, its concomitant side-lining of questions of social and cultural wellbeing, and the identity issues that come from a century of colonial rule. These are all issues that make it necessary to expose students to a range of values and ideas so that they may be better placed to operate in the global realm of contemporary architecture while respecting the local characteristics of the region.

In a sense, this necessity for a wide exposure to issues and ideas is inherent in architecture, as it is a field that deals with a wide range of questions. It has different sub-areas of specialisation and expertise, both in practice and research. Consequently, it is necessary for any architecture school to be equally broad in scope. Internationally and in East Asia, established faculties or schools of design tend to group together various departments such as architecture, urban design, planning, landscape architecture, building technology, conservation, interior design, industrial design and so forth. This is a separated model that respects discipline boundaries and reflects the increased specialisation seen in the 1980s and '90s.[8]

At the Chinese University of Hong Kong, however, the School of Architecture is organised differently. There are no sharp disciplinary divides within the school and the aim is to create a level platform upon which colleagues with specialised but different expertise work across boundaries. While this matrix curriculum and school may not be new internationally, it is distinct in the Asian context and is considered particularly suited to the nature of developments in the region today.

Currently, all teachers at the school are registered architects or have received architectural education to a substantial degree. However, in addition, each teacher has one or several specialisations in different sub-areas. These specialised areas include design, design theory, history, building technology, urban design, architectural practice, digital design and so on. Teachers at the School are encouraged to be interdisciplinary and to engage and collaborate with professionals from different disciplines, both within and outside the School – in teaching, research and practice.

This integrative approach allows for the flow of ideas across different specialisations and is seen as simulating the actual professional field. It is a cross-disciplinary approach that is reflected in the school's overall structure which, while having individual domains that offer independent programmes such as a master's degree in Architecture or Urban Design, allows students to take courses across these domains. It is a model

LIVERPOOL JOHN MOORES UNIVERSITY
LEARNING SERVICES

Figure 1: Victoria Harbour, Hong Kong.

Figure 2: Blue House Revitalization, Wanchai.

that has created unique patterns of knowledge acquisition and has enhanced the learning of each and every student. Furthermore, it has not only encouraged thinking across discipline boundaries but other types of boundary as well.

As with other international institutions in today's globalised world, the School of Architecture at the Chinese University of Hong Kong has seen a significant increase in students from non-traditional admission streams outside the local area in recent years. Many of these students are international and a spirit of diversity and exchange is thus fostered and underlined by increased international collaboration and the promotion of summer study programmes. Diversity and collaboration across disciplines are, then, only one of the emerging trends towards diversity in the architectural education of the school and the region more generally.[9]

It is believed that this approach will not only help the architecture school to establish itself, but also facilitate the exposure of students to a wide range of issues in the design of the built environment. The increased diversity of the student body has encouraged more peer exchanges, while international collaborations have encouraged the consideration of design and planning from multiple perspectives. This is considered particularly important for the graduate programmes, as the development of the capacity to think critically at this stage is essential.

Undergraduate Architecture Curriculum

The intentions of an architectural education programme can perhaps be best understood through its curriculum design. At the Chinese University of Hong Kong, for example, this is evident in its recent focus on the study of the historic and existing urban fabric that reflect recent changes in the city. The development of the city has entered a new phase in recent years – the idea of the wholesale destruction of urban fabric being replaced by an approach that seeks to balance development with conservation. Profit maximisation is no longer the ultimate goal and, instead, the most important criterion for urban renewal is increasingly seen to be the maintenance of the community spirit and the sense of place.[10] This is evident in recent projects by the Urban Renewal Authority and the Development Bureau, such as the Blue House in Wanchai (Figure 2).[11]

Alongside these changes there is a growing tendency for the public to demand direct participation in the processes of planning, urban renewal and the conservation of the historic fabric in Hong Kong.[12] The education provided at the school seeks to respond to this too by instilling an understanding of these changing requirements in students from day one. The aim of the school is to reflect the conditions of practice in the region while not losing sight of the fact that a region like Hong Kong operates and exists in an international context.

This local and global perspective of the school also seeks to balance the knowledge and requirements of the profession and the community in other ways too. Students are taught to consider the personal users of their projects, but are also exposed to research and theory and, of course, the technical requirements of design and construction. The aim is to ensure that they better understand how research can be translated into practice, how this has to be balanced with the needs and desires of their clients, and how they need to be equipped for the requirements of the professional world.

This current approach is actually only one of a number that, over the last twenty years, have informed the teaching pedagogies of the University. Today, the curriculum and the teaching agenda are designed according to four main learning fields through which students are led in their undergraduate studies. The undergraduate curriculum, as the first part of a two-degree sequence in professional architectural education, is designed to provide a basis for education in general, and preparation for professional work as an architect in particular. The core of studies consists of design studios, but these are supplemented by courses offered in the humanities, technology, professional practice and design computation. Students are encouraged to enrich their core of studies in architecture by exploring lateral relationships with other subjects and disciplines, as well as through independent study and experience of other cultures.

At undergraduate level, these studies are structured over six semesters that develop knowledge in sequence.[13] The first undergraduate (U1) studio is about breaking down preconceptions and introducing basic skills in presentation, form making and conceptualisation.[14] It is considered to function as a foundation course. It begins with an enquiry into form, space and context, and develops these basic concepts with specific exercises. The intention is to provide students with basic skills, give them hands-on experiences and aid in their creative thinking.

The studio pedagogy takes a progressive approach that leads the student from an examination of personal space to 'in-between' space, 'constructed' space, 'compositional' space and finally towards an 'integral' space. These five steps are designed to correlate to subsequent studios in the senior years, preparing students for the different aspects of their studies.[15] The subsequent four studios study issues of tectonics, habitation, technology and urban design and allow students to acquire design skills either by focusing on specific aspects of architecture or by addressing various factors that influence architectural form.

These issues are examined through studio projects and 'form making' activities in which students are required to demonstrate an understanding of structure, construction systems and materials.[16] For example, the exploration of architectural space done in U2 studio through a series of cumulative exercises is intended to cultivate a method of working through which spatial concepts are arrived at through working with different types of modelling, materials and a consideration of habitation.

Drawing and model-making skills are taught in a similarly integrated way that leads students from an introduction to basic concepts, to the development of sophisticated skills. Students are introduced to three basic types of space: continuous space, enveloped space and modulated space. They explore these issues through basic element types such as slab, block and stick. These are integrated into three projects:

a shelter, a studio and a pavilion. Each project consists of precisely defined exercises on a particular design issue.[17] The objectives are varied. Firstly, to help students understand basic design issues through keywords such as space, form, use, site, material and construction. Secondly, to develop a method of working that takes them from conception to realisation; and thirdly, to use model-making and graphic techniques to study, explore, articulate and present design ideas.

In linking architectural space to human activity, the approach of the U3 studio is to assemble and study 'archetypal activities' such as entry, gathering, worship, exchange, work and contemplation. It develops these ideas into more complex narratives involving the experience of space and its uses.[18] The studio helps facilitate the learner's appreciation of both the ordinary programmatic, and the symbolic, dimensions of every space associated with human activity. Indeed, the students develop projects that are intended to orchestrate events (the programme) in the service of the occasions (the symbolic). In doing so, they reinvent the relationship between events, spaces and symbols which, in architectural terms, is often designated in various ways: servant and served space; ground and figure; fabric and monument; function and expression; abstract space and event space, and so forth.

In examining the role of building technologies in architectural design, the U4 studio is structured to engage design in ways that relate to architectural theories, design technologies, critical innovations and pragmatic processes. The learning experience provides a context for understanding the forces of nature and their impact on the design of buildings. The studio employs a systematic approach that begins with identifying real or perceived potentials latent in the physical environment and develops them as an architectural strategy. Lastly, it evaluates performance through either simulation or physical testing with the aim of developing sustainable design proposals and solutions.[19]

The subject of the U5 studio is the idea of relating a building to its context. At the scale of a building, design is seen to exploit the unique quality of a site, inform the placement of buildings and shape the inside–outside relationship. At the contextual scale, the design approach of this studio considers architecture as a part of the city and contributes to the making of public places.[20] In traditional societies, this architectural response is obvious – a house forming a part of a village, several houses forming a village square, and a village fitting seamlessly into the rural context. However, with the increasing demand for individuality, the larger scale of cities and the rapid urbanisation seen in Asian today, this fundamental requirement of architecture is often ignored. As a result, it is more important than ever to address it in the educational context.

The final U6 studio of the undergraduate programme concentrates on bringing the four aforementioned fields of architecture together through a comprehensive project. Topics of study vary but students are expected to demonstrate a more advanced degree of mastery in all aspects of architecture through this exercise.[21] This includes detailed design and the presentation of a 1:20 sectional model or drawing that demonstrates an investigation and understanding of the building system at a higher degree of resolution (Figure 3).

Figure 3: Section and Interior Image of Ho Tsz Wai exploring light and spatiality in the design of in Year 3 studio, 2012, studio teacher: Patrick Hwang.

Figure 4: Museum of Memory, designing with former Italian barracks, Tianjin, David Chow, MArch 1 studio, 2012. Modern intervention in historical neighbourhoods for urban regeneration, studio teacher: Puay-peng Ho.

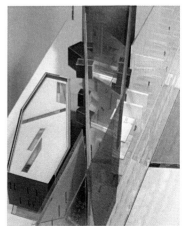

To complement the creative and practical learning framework set up through the studios, elective courses are offered to investigate particular fields of architecture which may include design, the humanities, technology and/or computation. Each specific elective is designed to allow students to gain in-depth knowledge in the relevant field. While such an approach may be common place and general in focus in the West, here in Asia it is a pedagogic approach that is unique and designed to address issues specific to the region.[22]

Graduate Architecture Curriculum

The School of Architecture regards the Master of Architecture (MArch) programme as a form of professional education. As with the undergraduate programme it is centred on the studio, but more focused and detailed projects are carried out. The advanced studios and independent design explorations contribute, from different perspectives, to clusters of the schools' research agendas and have a strong focus on emerging issues in Asian cities.

Their projects are rooted in an understanding of human experience as rich and varied, and they examine architecture and cities in a historical context – from antiquity to the twenty-first century. They are also concerned with various new aspects of urban realities such as density, urban memory, sustainability, mobility, capital influx, technology, politics and migration. These focused research-led studios are small in size, typically with a teacher–student ratio of 1 to 10. Some focus on urban design issues while others concentrate on energy efficient design and sustainability. Others centre on heritage and conservation.

The sharp focus of these studios allows students and teachers to explore different solutions to the architectural issues relevant to the Asian region and create new strategies in architectural design. With regard to professional competence, students are expected to demonstrate an appropriately complex and detailed command of skills in space planning, an awareness of regulatory requirements, detailed knowledge of construction and building technology, and considerable awareness of contemporary issues such as sustainability and construction economics.

In the second year of the MArch course, students have the freedom to explore different issues relating to architecture, the built environment, building technology and urbanism. Within the clusters of relevant thesis topics, advisors and students formulate research and study issues and relate these to architectural design. The final design theses to emerge are exhibited in public.

In addition to the MArch programme, there are three other specialised professional programmes offered at the School of Architecture at the Chinese University: the MSc in Sustainable and Environmental Design (SED); an MSc in Urban Design (UD); and an MSc in Architectural Conservation and Design (ACD). The SED programme has assembled a group of teachers who are internationally renowned and who share and teach theory in the practice of climate responsive design with both a global and local perspectives.

The sites of investigation for the UD programme are Hong Kong and the wider Pearl River Delta, and the programme focuses on issues of urban development crucial to the region. Examples include questions of liveability, density and the environment. The main objective is to teach the skills necessary for the creation of sustainable communities that offer quality living environments. In contrast to this, the ACD programme places its emphasis on an understanding and conserving of historic neighbourhoods and, in this sense, reflects another crucial issue in the region at this juncture (Figure 4).

Academic-led Research in Hong Kong and China

Embedded within this structured, responsive and forward-looking curriculum, then, research and teaching at the school are leading the way in the issues of most importance in the region at the moment: the conceptualisation of the urban fabrics, the study of built heritage, the development of conservation strategy and the promotion of public participation in the design and planning processes. However, it should also be noted that the technical aspects of building in tight urban conditions such as those in Hong Kong are also addressed. One example is the study of wind movement and heat-island effects that have also become two of the more specific and highly important research contributions of the School in recent years.[23]

Both these specific and more general developments arise from the potential and capacity of the cross-disciplinary teaching and research at the school. It is foreseen that the continued promotion of this approach will give rise to the establishment of more research centres and units in the coming years that will continue to address the specific issues of importance to the region. These centres, or units, are likely to focus on research issues that are found at the boundary of each sub-area or discipline concerned. However, in order to sustain their long-term operation and viability, they will also have to develop income-generating projects, consultancies and other commissioned projects.[24]

In addition, given the geographical location of Hong Kong, these projects will also have to keep looking across the old border. The urbanisation process that started a decade ago in China continues with even greater fervour today and will continue to be the focus of much design research and output.[25] As a growing percentage of Chinese people move to cities, the questions that must be asked by the region's design schools include: what kind of urban environments are most conducive for their living experience? What is, or should be, the model of a Chinese city?[26] How can the current homogeneity of the urban landscape in China be avoided?

As more and more building projects for Hong Kong architects are located in China, these questions will become increasingly important. How can the architects educated in Hong Kong contribute to the betterment of the urban design and district planning of Chinese cities? Given that the planning models of the West, and those developed in Hong Kong, may not be perfect solutions for China, due to the different cultural and societal contexts, further research is much called for. It is essential that a range of suitable models for modern living that respect the cultural strata of these cities be identified and developed soon.

Although there may not be a consensus on questions such as these, it is highly likely that some of the answers lie in respect for terrain, climate and local cultural specificities, rather than global, regional or indeed national issues.[27] It was on this premise that the recent Hung Shui Kiu New Town research project was carried out by staff and students in the school. Located in the north-west region of Hong Kong, the project investigated a possible model for a new town and housing development appropriate to the region. It involved the Institute of Urban Design, government agencies, various scholars and a workshop attended by academics from Harvard Graduate School of Design and the Bartlett School of Architecture.

The aim of the project was to explore development models and interdisciplinary methodologies for research, and it led to a design studio headed by professors Colin Fournier, Hendrik Tieben and Sujata Govada. This engaged students in exploring design proposals that inverted certain characteristics of the standard design approach in China. Large-scale regional and urban planning is common in China, but the involvement of different specialists with expertise and interests in creative approaches to social, environmental, liveability and transportation issues is not. This project attempted to implement just such an approach (Figure 5).

Another contested public issue of relevance to architectural research and teaching in the region is heritage and the conservation of historical buildings. Buzzwords and slogans that have become common in Hong Kong over the recent period include 'the collective memory' and 'the preservation of local culture and community'. The level of scrutiny under which heritage projects have come in recent years, be it from community advocacy or the media, is unprecedented in the history of Hong Kong. The same scenario can also be seen in China. While considerable urban heritage was lost in the rush to redevelop city centres, there are still grass-root movements attempting to conserve old urban districts, such as the Hutong of Beijing.

This aspect of architectural practice, much neglected in the past, has rightly gained centre stage recently. In response, the research and teaching of architecture faculty and students in the region has changed. In addition to required courses, for example, the School of Architecture at the Chinese University has run a graduate-level studio for the last four years. Specifically, this studio addresses issues faced both in Hong Kong and China in terms of heritage conservation and the revitalisation of historic neighbourhoods.

Students taking the studio must go through an introductory course running in parallel with the studio on the basic theory and practices of architectural conservation. The studio itself studies sites in Hong Kong, Tianjin and Beijing. In 2010, it looked at a block of industrial buildings in Tokwawan, Hong Kong, located next to the former Kai Tak Airport and the future Kai Tak sports hub. Although the existing buildings of the zone are not considered architecturally important, students were given the chance to

Figure 5: The conference organised by Hendrik Tieben for exploring the paradigms for regional planning and new-town development in Hong Kong and China.

Figure 6: A study of the existing buildings of the Oriental Cotton Mill Factory in Tokwawan and its transformation into a Fashion Academy by Chen Yue. MArch 1 studio, 2011, studio teacher: Puay-peng Ho.

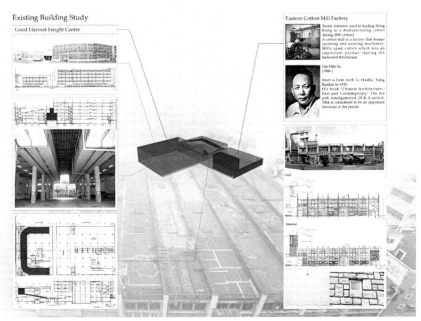

assess the buildings and propose strategies for preservation, demolition and adaptive reuse. They formulated conservation strategies, postulated compatible future uses and designed new additions to complement the historic fabrics that were to be conserved. Such issues are common to many historic centres in China, and the region in general, whilst it continues to undergo rapid urbanisation. Addressing them in the educational context has to be a priority (Figure 6).

The need to develop 'green architecture', one of the other issues facing architects with an unprecedented sense of urgency in Hong Kong today, is also one addressed at graduate level. How can the building industry and the design professions respond to accelerating climate change and rocketing energy costs? Is there any scope for sustainable architecture in a small compact metropolis such as Hong Kong or the developing societies of China? Teaching design against the backdrop of these questions requires that researchers, teachers and students must take into account the use of cutting-edge research to inform planning policy, housing design and urban design proposals.

One specific example addressed by the school has been the study of wind and ventilation effects in crowded city centres such as that of Hong Kong.[28] With a high-rise and high-density urban morphology, Hong Kong and other large cities in China would be well served by such detailed environmental assessments before the implementation of planning guidelines – something that is not the case at the moment. This type of research is integrated into the teaching at the School, particularly in the U6 undergraduate studio where students consider all issues relating to a building's design – including the sustainability of materials, construction techniques and systems, and the climatic responses and effects of all aspects of a given architectural project. This emphasis is also reflected in other studios where, for example, students have looked at the design of a neighbourhood in the Pearl River Delta in such a way as to address the specific issues of urban ventilation and heat-island effects it would have to deal with (Figure 7).

Conclusion

As indicated in the introduction, the region of southern China is undergoing a massive process of urbanisation and, despite changes being evident, the speed and quantity of construction is still too often seen as more important than the quality of the architecture built. This rapid urbanisation has produced a host of issues for urban planners and architects to deal with, and the need for effective design and research at all scales of the built environment is unprecedented. In this context of changing interests and expectations in the development of architecture and architectural design, however, it is important to keep sight of the main objective of education: to foster critical thinking and creativity in students.

William Moggridge, father of the laptop, coined the term 'T-shaped people' to refer to individuals who have deep knowledge in one area of expertise, while maintaining a broad range of interests in other areas.[29] The ideal curriculum design of an architecture

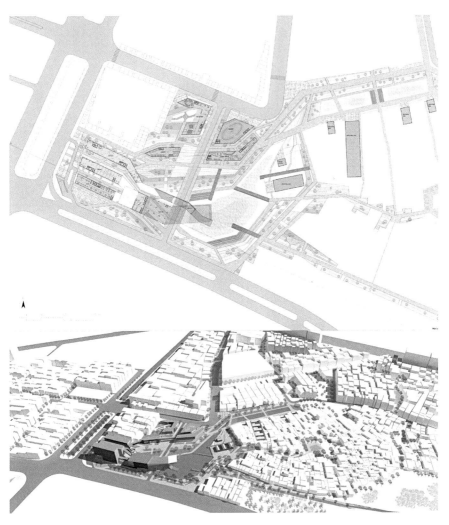

Figure 7: Investigating new Chinese urbanism, Feng Wenfang looked at the infamous Houjie, in Dongguan, known as the first Mega region in Pearl River Delta. MArch 1 studio, 2012, studio teacher: Doreen Liu.

programme, in this context, should allow students to deepen their knowledge of an aspect of architecture that appeals to them, while having the opportunity to be exposed to a broad horizon of issues. The design of programmes at the School of Architecture of the Chinese University aims to realise this curriculum structure so as to engender depth of knowledge and breadth of interest.

This, we would argue, reflects the professional world, in which there is a mix of individuals pursuing different professional objectives with differing degrees of knowledge and skills. However, it also reflects the nature of the design and architectural project today which, in a place like Hong Kong, has to address and respond to complex and often conflicting issues such as the conservation agenda, the creation of a rich, varied and healthy urban environment and so forth.

Although the phenomenal speed of developments in this region of the world is producing major changes to architecture's mode of practice, this fundamental characteristic is unlikely to change in the foreseeable future. That means students will require multiple skills and will need to negotiate with multiple players in their articulation of architectural form and space. They will have to navigate complex societal, environmental and technological contexts that, although evolving, will still call for competence, diversity of knowledge and an open and creative mind. There might be different degrees of importance attached to different aspects of designing the built environment in the future, but the need for lateral connectivity and synthesis will remain an imperative.

The specific challenges facing the building profession in this region might be different from those in other regions but, with regard to the need for open and creative thinking, they are broadly similar. Designing the ideal architectural education system in Hong Kong, then, is similar in many regards to other parts of the world, and is about laying a good foundation for the acquisition, synthesis and negotiation of various design parameters. However, architectural education is also about a breadth of knowledge and a depth of understanding, learning universal principles and applying them in specific local contexts. In the context of Hong Kong today, this means a specific application of universal knowledge to local questions of urban design, conservation, sustainability and liveability.

Notes

[1]   See the summary in University of Southern California (2012, March 27). Retrieved from: http://www.uschina.usc.edu/article@usct?infographic_chinas_census_data_18065.aspx

[2]   See report in the *Economist* (2012, Jan 18). Retrieved from: http://www.economist.com/blogs/graphicdetail/2012/01/daily-chart-6; and *China Daily* (2011, April 29). Retrieved from: http://www.chinadaily.com.cn/photo/2011-04/29/content_12416971.htm

[3]   One of the early analyses on the rise of urbanisation in East Asia can be seen in Rowe, P. G. (2005) *East Asia Modern: Shaping the Contemporary City.* London: Reaktion Books. Another comprehensive report can be seen in Liauw, L. (guest ed.) (2008, September/October) New urban China. *Architectural Design* 5(78). Liauw was an associate professor at the School of Architecture, the Chinese University of Hong Kong. For more recent developments, see Rowe, P. G. (2011) *Emergent Architectural Territories in East Asian Cities.* Basel: Birkhäuser.

[4]   The Hong Kong standard for green building, the Hong Kong BEAM Plus, is at the forefront of moves in this direction.

[5]   See also Roberts, B., & Kanaley, T. (eds) (2006) *Urbanization and Sustainability in Asia.* Manila: Asian Development Bank, pp. 117–150. In this document, the issues facing urbanisation in China and the government attempts at sustainable developments are outlined.

[6]   See the websites of the new organisations at: http://www.hkiud.org/ and http://www. hkicon.org

[7]   There is an increasing number of literature in Chinese on different districts of Hong Kong written and published by local historians, resident groups and amateur researchers. One more formal attempt is Hase, P. H. (ed.) (1999) *In the Heart of the Metropolis: Yaumatei and its People*. Hong Kong: Joint Publishing (H.K.) Co. Ltd.

[8]   See publications by the schools around the region, such as Caryl, C. (2012) *Building the Dragon City: History of the Faculty of Architecture at the University of Hong Kong*. Hong Kong: Hong Kong University Press; Chee, L. (ed.) (2011) *NUS design 2011*. Singapore: Department of Architecture, National University of Singapore; and the annals from Departments of Architecture, National Cheng Kung University, Tongji University, Tianjin University, Tsinghua University and Southeast University.

[9]   See discussions of various forms of interdisciplinary and collaborative studio models across Asia and the world in Chiu, M.-L. (ed.) (2006) *Re-imaging Architectural Design Studios*. Taipei: Archidata Co. Ltd.

[10] The Urban Renewal Authority in Hong Kong chose in recent years to classify their projects under 'redevelopment' and 'rehabilitation'. For rehabilitation projects, the one important strategy to keeping the spirit of existing urban centres is rehabilitation and heritage preservation and revitalisation. See their website: http://www.ura.org.hk/en/ projects/heritage-preservation-and-revitalisation.aspx

[11] St. James' Settlement, a local NGO, negotiated with URA and the Housing Society to launch the Blue House as a bottom-up conservation community project. Details of the process can be seen in Lam, L. (2007, June) Proposing community heritage preservation model through the Blue House project. Retrieved from: http://courses. washington.edu/quanzhou/pacrim/papers/HKHS-BlueHouse-130607-lowres-English.pdf

[12] The most publicised public participation project initiated by URA is titled 'Central Oasis' and involves the conversion of a 1939 central market into a community hub in the middle of the urban centre in Hong Kong. Retrieved from: http://www.centraloasis.org.hk/eng/ home.aspx

[13] See Chung, T. (ed.) (2012) *Black Book 2012–13*. Hong Kong: School of Architecture, CUHK, p. 15. The description of the studios can also be found in this annual publication.

[14] The studio had been formulated by, and its pedagogy published, in Gu, D., & Bertin, V. (2010) *Introduction to Architectural Design*. Beijing: China Architecture and Building Press.

[15] This is similar to the approach adopted in some schools that take design as 'a particular form of synthetic intellectual inquiry and as a process for the production of concepts'. Hight, C. (2012) One steps towards an ecology of design. In Hensel, M. U. (ed.) *Design Innovation for the |Built Environment*. Oxon: Routledge, p. 21. See also earlier discussions in Schön, D. A. (1985) *The Design Studio: An Exploration of its Tradition and Potentials*. London: RIBA Publications.

[16] The studio references methodology and theory seen in: Gu & Bertin, op. cit.; and von Meiss, P. (1990) *Elements of Architecture – From Form to Place*. London and New York: Van Nostrand Reinhold.

[17] See pedagogy and examples of works in: Gu, D., & Bertin, V. (2011) *Space, Tectonics*

and Design. Beijing: China Architecture and Building Press.

[18] References used in the studio include: Pallasma, J. (1996) *The Eyes of the Skin: Architecture and the Senses.* London: Academy Edition; Zumthor, P. (2006) *Thinking Architecture.* Basel and Boston: Birhäuser; and Tschumi, B. (1994) *The Manhattan Transcripts.* London: Academy Editions.

[19] Many of the ideas contained in Spiridonidis & Voyatzaki's *Architectural Design and Construction Education* resonate with the studio pedagogy. See: Spiridonidis, C., & Voyatzaki, M. (2009) *Architectural Design and Construction Education: Experimentation Towards Integration.* Proceedings of ENHSA-EAAE Architectural Design Teachers' and Construction Teachers' Networks, particularly Session 3.2 Integration of environmental Issues, and Session 4.1 Integrating the Teaching of Structures.

[20] See materials referenced in the studio, including: Rowe, C., & Koetter, F. (1978) *Collage City.* Cambridge: MIT Press; Tschumi, B. (1990) *Questions of Space: Lectures on Architecture.* London: Architectural Association; and Wall, A. (1999) Programming the Urban Surface. In Corner, J. (ed.) *Recovering Landscape – Essays in Contemporary Landscape Architecture.* New York: Princeton University Press, pp. 233–251.

[21] Reference is again drawn to Spiridonidis & Voyatzaki (2009, op. cit.), in which many examples of integrative design studio are listed.

[22] See Chiu's *Re-imaging Architectural Design Studios,* in which many authors describe the particular approaches to the design studio based on the regional social and professional contexts. Chiu, M.-L. (ed.) (2006) *Re-imaging Architectural Design Studios,* Taipei: Archidata Co. Ltd.

[23] See publications of faculty members in Tsou, J.-Y., et al. (eds) (2011) *Proceedings of the 9th China Urban Housing Conference – Low Carbon Green City and the Harmonious Habitat Society.* Beijing: China Architecture and Building Press; and Ren, C., & Ng, E. (eds) (2012) *Urban Climate Map – An Information Tool for Sustainable Urban Planning.* Beijing: China Architecture and Building Press.

[24] Through this model, these research units will contribute to enhancing knowledge transfer between academia, businesses, government bodies and the community at large. See the debates on design research (particularly in the first three chapters) in: Hensel, M. U. (ed.) (2012) *Design Innovation for the Built Environment – Research by Design and the Renovation of Practice.* London and New York: Routledge.

[25] This can be seen in the fast pace of urbanisation in China. It is also projected that by 2050, 80 per cent of the population will live in the city. See Staniford, S. (2012, December 5) China urbanisation in context. Retrieved from: http://earlywarn.blogspot.hk/2012/12/chinese-urbanization-in-context.html. Also see: Hulshof, M., & Roggeveen, D. (2011) *How the City Moved to Mr Sun – China's New Megacities.* Amsterdam: SUN Martied de Vletter for a closer look at the social conditions facing different cities in China and their urban development.

[26] See Wong's 'Planning between reliability and flexibility – Contemporary urban development in China' (in Roseman, J., Qu, L., & Sepúlveda, D. (eds) (2009) *The New Urban Question – Urbanism Beyond Neo-liberalism.* Rotterdam: IFoU, pp. 321–333) for discussions on many issues facing the rapid urbanisation in China.

[27] See Liauw (2008), particularly the article by Wang, 'The "people's city"' (pp. 44–47).

[28] See many articles in Ng, E. (ed.) (2010) *Designing High-density Cities for Social and Environmental Sustainability*. London & Sterling, VA: Earthscan. For example: Ng, 'Designing for urban ventilation', pp. 119–136; Allard, F., et al., 'Natural ventilation in high-density cities', pp. 137–162; and Ng, J., 'Microclimate in public housing: An environmental approach to community development', pp. 309–320.

[29] See a version of the term in: http://www.metropolismag.com/story/20101020/bill-moggridge

Bibliography

Caryl, C. (2012) *Building the Dragon City: History of the Faculty of Architecture at the University of Hong Kong*. Hong Kong: Hong Kong University Press.

Chiu, M.-L. (ed.) (2006) *Re-imaging Architectural Design Studios*. Taipei: Archidata Co. Ltd.

Chung, T. (ed.) (2012) *Black Book 2012–13*. Hong Kong: School of Architecture, CUHK.

Gu, D., & Bertin, V. (2010) *Introduction to Architectural Design*. Beijing: China Architecture and Building Press.

Gu, D., & Bertin, V. (2011) *Space, Tectonics and Design*. Beijing: China Architecture and Building Press.

Hase, P. H. (ed.) (1999) *In the Heart of the Metropolis: Yaumatei and its People*. Hong Kong: Joint Publishing (H.K.) Co. Ltd.

Hensel, M. U. (ed.) (2012) *Design Innovation for the Built Environment – Research by Design and the Renovation of Practice*. London and New York: Routledge.

Hight C. (2012) One steps towards an ecology of design. In Hensel, M. U. (ed.) (2012) *Design Innovation for the Built Environment – Research by Design and the Renovation of Practice*. London and New York: Routledge.

Hulshof, M., & Roggeveen, D. (2011) *How the City Moved to Mr Sun – China's New Megacities*. Amsterdam: SUN Martied de Vletter.

Lam, L. (2007, June) Proposing community heritage preservation model through the Blue House project. Retrieved from: http://courses.washington.edu/quanzhou/pacrim/papers/HKHS-BlueHouse-130607-lowres-English.pdf

Liauw, L. (guest ed.) (2008, September–October) New urban China. *Architectural Design* 5(78).

von Meiss, P. (1990) *Elements of Architecture – From Form to Place*. London and New York: Van Nostrand Reinhold.

Pallasma, J. (1996) *The Eyes of the Skin: Architecture and the Senses*. London: Academy Edition.

Ng, E. (ed.) (2010) *Designing High-density Cities for Social and Environmental Sustainability*. London & Sterling, VA: Earthscan.

Ren, C., & Ng, E. (eds) (2012) *Urban Climate Map – An Information Tool for Sustainable Urban Planning*. Beijing: China Architecture and Building Press.

Roberts, B., & Kanaley, T. (eds) (2006) *Urbanization and Sustainability in Asia*. Manila: Asian Development Bank.

Rowe, C., & Koetter, F. (1978) *Collage city*. Cambridge: MIT Press.

Rowe, P. G. (2005) *East Asia Modern: Shaping the Contemporary City*. London: Reaktion Books.

Rowe, P. G. (2011) *Emergent Architectural Territories in East Asian Cities*. Basel: Birkhäuser.

Schön, D. A. (1985) *The Design Studio: An Exploration of its Tradition and Potentials*. London: RIBA Publications.

Spiridonidis, C., & Voyatzaki, M. (2009) *Architectural Design and Construction Education: Experimentation towards Integration*. Proceedings of ENHSA-EAAE Architectural Design Teachers' and Construction Teachers' Networks.

Staniford, S. (2012, December 5) China urbanization in context. Retrieved from http://earlywarn.blogspot.hk/2012/12/chinese-urbanization-in-context.html.

Tschumi, B. (1990) *Questions of Space: Lectures on Architecture*. London: Architectural Association.

Tschumi, B. (1994) *The Manhattan Transcripts*. London: Academy Editions.

Tsou, J.-Y., et al. (eds) (2011) *Proceedings of the 9th China Urban Housing Conference – Low Carbon Green City and the Harmonious Habitat Society*. Beijing: China Architecture and Building Press.

Wall, A. (1999) Programming the urban surface. In Corner, J. (ed.) *Recovering Landscape – Essays in Contemporary Landscape Architecture*. New York: Princeton University Press, pp. 233–251.

Wong, C.Y. (2009) Planning between reliability and flexibility – Contemporary urban development in China. In Roseman, J., Lei, Q., & Sepúlveda, D. (eds) *The New Urban Question – Urbanism Beyond Neo-liberalism*. Rotterdam: IFoU, pp. 321–333.

Zumthor, P. (2006) *Thinking Architecture*. Basel and Boston: Birhäuser.

Helka-Liisa HENTILÄ

CHAPTER 8

A GOOD LIVING ENVIRONMENT AND SUSTAINABLE COMMUNITIES AS GOALS – CHALLENGES AND TRENDS IN FINNISH LAND-USE PLANNING

Land Use and Land-use Planning in Finland

In Finland, 80 per cent of people live in cities or urban areas and one-fifth of the population – a little over a million people – live in Helsinki and its surrounding counties. Other Finnish cities are considered mid-sized or small when measured by population, with Oulu (Finland's sixth largest city – and the site of the projects discussed later) having approximately 143,000 inhabitants.[1] Major urbanisation did not take place until after the Second World War when the rapidly growing paper and mechanical engineering industries, as well as the need to house 400,000 evacuees from the Finnish Karelian regions, became key factors in reorganising the demographic make-up of the country. Despite this process of industrialisation led by mechanical and paper manufacturers, Finland remained predominantly rural until the early 1970s, at which point the number of urban inhabitants exceeded the number of rural inhabitants for the first time.[2] This was intensified in the coming years with a third of all developed urban land in the country being created between 1980 and 2000.[3]

In an international comparison, Finland's urban structure would be considered dispersed and fragmented. For instance, although Finland and Sweden have more or less the same urban population to total population ratios, the density of urban areas is much higher in Sweden.[4] Despite this dispersed spread of urban areas in Finland, however, only about 10 per cent of Finnish land has been developed.[5] Consequently, we can consider Finland to be sparsely populated and 'thinly' built.[6] Control over this situation is in the hands of the government that sets national laws and development guidelines.[7]

The core planning law in Finland is the Land Use and Building Act[8] whose stated objective is the 'promotion of good living environments, the sustainable development of communities, and the construction of high quality building.'[9] Despite these stated objectives, and recent moves towards a more transparent and 'communicative' approach,[10] the planning system is very hierarchical and dictates national objectives for regional land us, general national and regional zoning laws and town planning generally.[11] Furthermore, it still emphasises a view of town planning that sees it as primarily a question of physical design and construction, and thus sometimes fails to take into account the changing social patterns and issues that can affect the built environment in indirect, but fundamental, ways.[12]

In addition to these characteristics, the Finnish planning system also focuses primarily on urban and suburban issues, despite the fact that the country has enormous swathes of rural land that could potentially be developed or is already in need of development. Indeed, 90 per cent of the country is rural: 76 per cent of this rural land is forest and thus the site of related forestry industries; the remainder of this is the site of almost all the nation's domestic food production and other significant industries, such as mining. Thus, when considering the challenges faced by architects, planners and landscape designers in Finland, it is necessary to consider the urban alongside the suburban, but also to pay particular attention to the rural. In what follows, these issues will be examined from a strategic planning perspective and, subsequently, examples of how they are informing architecture, planning and design education in the country will be described.

Part One: The Growth of the Suburb and the Problem of Sprawl

After the Second World War, increased industrialisation led to a growth in Finnish cities and also the birth of the country's first suburbs. At its heart, land-use planning at the time focused on growth and the solving of the housing shortage. The planning system generally followed the principles laid out by the Modern Movement, which led to the creation of suburbs characterised by separated functional zones, an emphasis on new transportation, isolated 'green areas' and the proliferation of high-rise apartment buildings. In the case of suburbia, however, this last point was superseded in the 1990s onwards by the construction of functional single-family dwellings – a characteristic that led to suburbia's ever-greater sprawl.

Figure 1: Kaakkuri suburb, Oulu. Photo: Helka-Liisa Hentilä.

Suburban planning was greatly affected by Otto-Iivari Meurman's 1947 book, *Principles of Town Planning* (*Asemakaavaoppi*). Meurman was Finland's first Professor of Town Planning and his ideas on 'decentralisation' became the central design principle in the practice and education of the period.[13] These ideas were a development of the 'organic decentralisation' notion introduced in Finland through Eliel Saarinen's 1918 publication of the planning scheme *Pro Helsingfors*.[14] Meurman had worked in Saarinen's office and, in his memoirs, describes the influence that Ebeneser Howard's *Garden City* and Camillo Sitte's urban planning ideas had on his work. As a result, although Finnish planning has modernist characteristics, it can also be said to have roots in the design tradition of 'international decentralisation'.[15]

Large suburban developments based on these decentralised concepts are still being planned and built in Finland today, although it is now accepted that they are problematic and in need of reconsideration.[16] The physical and functional structure of these areas can be defined as 'thin' – mixed use and densely built areas are limited to city centres. Indeed, such is the dominance of suburbia in Finland that the Sociologist Pasi Mäenpää claims directly that, 'urbanity is simply something that we don't have'. [17] He nuances this by identifying that the relationship between Finns and suburban and urban development is characterised by what he calls 'almost-urbanity'.[18] Finland, then, is a country with a mixed and nuanced relationship with the city in which, in recent years, suburban sprawl has become a problem increasingly recognised by both designers and, indeed, government (Figure 1).

The primary preventive strategy being proposed against urban sprawl is *complementary building* which, amongst other things, involves the construction of additional buildings in urban and existing old suburban areas to ameliorate the need for new ones. In addition to new buildings, however, *complementary building* often involves repairing or upgrading the technical infrastructure of existing urban/suburban plans through improved road and rail systems, for example. Consequently, in terms of its operational objectives, it is easy to identify certain similarities with new urbanism or neo-traditional town planning, albeit without the historical pastiche that has generally accompanied these initiatives.[19]

The objectives of *complementary building*, then, are quite pragmatic and its implementations follow in the stylistic footsteps of modernism.[20] It is a strategy that has most notably been applied in old suburbs and along railroad lines in the Helsinki metropolitan area, although it has also been used in other growing cities more recently. [21] It remains problematic, however, because the low-rise, lower-density recent suburbs still attract many Finns. Residential housing in the new suburbs on the outskirts of growing cities continues to be highly sought after and these developments have been used to attract new residents from urban areas in municipalities across the country – municipalities with both growing and shrinking populations.[22]

To understand why this is so, it is necessary to consider a few of the social issues that are too often overlooked in the 'object-focused' planning system we have today. For example, increased mobility can be seen as the main factor facilitating the continued growth of the suburbs. According to an EU-funded project which examined urban sprawl, *Urbs Pandens*,[23] households are no longer dependent on a specific place for work and home. People can live further from urban centres when a suitable home is found, so long as their workplace, schools, services and activities are within a 'tolerable' driving distance. To this, however, one also has to add the question of finance. From the home buyer's point of view, the attraction of living outside urban areas is primarily cost: the price per square meter for a home outside a city is considerably less than that of a comparable home in the city.

This is of course tied up with the fact that, for families, owning one's own home means acquiring equity by paying off their mortgage which, as in other parts of the world, is seen as a long-term financial investment. With more affordable new suburban housing, it also becomes possible to purchase, amongst other things, a second car, thus compounding the problems of sprawl and decentralisation. Living in a single-family dwelling is also seen as facilitating greater autonomy and, in addition, suburbia has been presented as a child-friendly and safe environment.

Although families are seen to benefit from this style of living, amongst those that also prosper from this new form of living arrangement are: landowners who sell former agricultural and forestry areas for building; real-estate businesses; the construction industry; raw-material suppliers; the numerous manufacturers of domestic products for residential housing; and the automobile industry. In addition, public institutions can be seen as profiting by the way they either increase or decrease the demand, and thus value, of the land they own.

Within the complex web of business and economic transactions that underlie the development of new suburbs there is of course one big loser: nature. Decentralised planning produces more emissions, consumes more land, homogenises biodiversity and decreases the possibilities for agricultural production near cities. Moreover, the built environment becomes more homogenous, particularly when the quality of planning and design decisions is poor and the use of the same templates is continually repeated. The negatives for the inhabitants are also obvious, if not always clearly expressed by those promoting this type of development. They include long commutes to work; great distances to public services such as hospitals; poor public transportation; almost total reliance on the car; high building and infrastructure maintenance costs; increased traffic; and a resultant increase in pollution.[24]

These are all standard consequences of new suburban development which, above all else, exacerbates a global problem of climate change through CO_2 emissions. The role of the car in this is fundamental and is exacerbated by the fact that, today, it is seen as both a necessity and a status symbol. An increased number of cars creates the need to build more roads, results in longer travel distances, increases pollution and makes alternative forms of clean transportation, such as walking and bicycling, less comfortable, less safe and less popular. [25] Given that in Finland, areas with a low population density do not sustain a public transportation system, with the exception of the Helsinki city centre, driving is often more convenient and faster than other modes of transportation.[26] To deal with this scenario, various cities and suburbs in Finland have begun experimenting with *complementary building* and a zone-based approach to planning that profiles different areas according to the main mode of transportation – whether that be pedestrian, public transportation or private motor vehicles.[27] One example is Kuopio, a city that has grown sufficiently in recent years to allow for the implementation of a functional and sustainable public transportation system.[28]

Despite isolated successes such as this, however, people still drive cars because it is easy and comfortable. As long as driving remains the fastest and most comfortable mode of transport, it will be difficult to change this. We cannot tackle urban sprawl without an integrated public transport system which, in addition to being integrated, reliable and effective, has to be comfortable. Despite the problems, however, this is particularly important in a country like Finland, where the climate is often not conducive to discouraging the use of the car. There are examples of effective systems across Finland. There is also a growing emphasis on making cities walkable and encouraging the use of bicycles. In the city of Oulu, for example, the local administration has invested in a comprehensive bicycle network and now almost 20 per cent of people move around the city on bicycles. The country average is 12 per cent and in the Helsinki metropolitan area it is 11 per cent.[29]

However, transport is only one of the ways in which the cities of Finland are attempting to respond to the need to prevent further urban and suburban sprawl. Higher density development is key, as is the effective provision of services, the control of house prices and the creation of more attractive urban areas. Tied into this last point is the 'introduction of nature' into urban and suburban developments, so that people's desire to live near the country can also be addressed, at least to some degree. *Complementary building* is a central component of this overarching set of initiatives and is, perhaps, one of the more original aspects of Finland's response to the global problem of suburban sprawl.

Complementary Building as a Tool Against Sprawl

Finnish *complementary building* differs from most foreign examples, in that abroad it is normally applied in city centres which have already declined, in part, due to suburbanisation. In Finland, however, the target areas for the implementation of *complementary building* initiatives have been the older suburbs. Today, we can see efforts to enliven and develop these suburbs by refocusing on their original ideas of providing local services such as the kindergarten, the local school, the branch library, the local health centre, the shopping mall and so forth. We can also see examples of the promotion of public transport systems and the introduction of new 'green areas' into the suburban matrix. This has proved difficult, however, given that modern life styles, as reflected by the more recent decentralised suburban model, have changed significantly.

Current residents of these older suburbs fear losing their views and green areas and, although *complementary building* offers new benefits such as the introduction of new services, opposition to new proposals from existing residents is often vigorous. This is particularly the case because the focus of new *complementary building* is on high-density developments which go against the more contemporary suburban ethos. Curiously, this also produces a certain reticence from new potential residents who desire to live in suburbia for its new single-family-dwelling model.

In addressing what can be done, several issues can and should be considered. A central challenge in planning *complementary building* is to design quality and attractive high-density housing that is, in some ways, comparable to the existent single-family houses. Several things that increase the appeal of single-family housing are: adequate storage and functional utility rooms; adaptability to personal needs; private exterior spaces; closeness to nature; and perceived safety. In addition, smooth everyday logistics play a role for families purchasing massive amounts of consumer retail products each year that need to be transported from the stores to homes by the car. A garage and a ground-floor entrance thus become basic aspects of daily life that are desirable. If *complementary building* initiatives are to be a success, these 'everyday' issues have to be dealt with successfully.

Furthermore, Finns value the feeling of living close to nature and this too has traditionally been one of the great draws of the old and new suburbs.[30] Quite how much nature is enough to create the feeling of closeness to it, however, is an open question: a two-hectare property, a half a hectare property close to a forest, or a few trees and a view of the blue sky? Could a more or less symbolic act, like an impressive, engineered drain water system, be sufficient to satisfy people's needs for being close to nature? These questions have to be asked if alternative solutions are to be found. It does seem that today young families moving to new single-family housing areas are no longer satisfied with the unmaintained natural forests that are a central part of the nature of existing suburban areas.[31] They want maintained parks and green areas – something that could potentially be turned into an advantage in attempts to redevelop existing suburban areas along new 'complementary' lines.

Another related solution that has to be examined is the possibility of urban gardening, which has been promoted and successfully implemented in other countries.[32] Indeed, in Helsinki, temporary and communal urban gardens have been established, and other variations such as rooftop, balcony and façade gardening could also be tried. Despite the fact that the desire to produce healthy local foods and a greener urban environment exists, and is easily promoted as a 'hobby close to home', it has yet to be exploited in any major Finnish complementary building initiative.[33] Naturally, the Finnish climate sets many limits on this type of urban/suburban experience – the soil, climate and the growing season all severely limiting its possibilities.[34] Nevertheless, possibilities do exists and should be explored.

Other ways of addressing inhabitant behaviours and expectations with regard to the shared public spaces of suburbia include adding various sports environments. For example, BMX biking, skating and climbing areas can form part of exterior spaces and offer new possibilities for local teenagers.[35] Communal urban acts and events such as these have the potential to shape urban and suburban spaces into types of 'indie spaces', where NIMBYs are replaced by YIMBYs ('Yes, in my backyard'). From the viewpoint of planning, this means accepting and supporting a certain 'incompleteness' to existing public spaces, not totally predetermining and controlling functions but encouraging diversity.[36]

Without being implemented alongside additional ideas such as these, complementary building initiatives can appear isolated and thus be more likely to be resisted.[37] This may be ameliorated by applying the 'compensation principle' through which, for example, a neighbourhood forest might be removed in a complementary building development as long as it is replaced with a different area suitable for recreation. Clearly then, the issues to be dealt with in addressing the suburban condition in Finland are various. They involve considering infrastructure and planning approaches, understanding social trends and personal aspirations, developing new living patterns, responding to changing economic conditions, and much more.

Design Education and the Question of Sprawl

Given the complexity of the issues involved on the ground, it is inevitable that a design education program that seeks to respond to Finland's suburban sprawl must embed this complexity into its structure. This is certainly the case of the University of Oulu's Department of Architecture, where projects are often set that reflect the need for Finnish design professionals to rethink their approach to design and the design process. One such example is discussed here in which the possibility of using complementary building, in the so-called Oulu forest suburbs of 1960 and '70s, was set as the theme.

The Kaukovainio suburb is located three km southeast of Oulu city centre and was part of the 1952 City of Oulu master plan by the architects Otto-Iivari Meurman and Aarne Ervi. The plan for the Kaukovainio suburb adopted Meurman's ideas of organic decentralisation and the detailed zoning dates from the year 1965. It was the work of the architect Pentti Ahola. The main structural element of the plan is a central forest zone that gathers services together: a small shopping mall, a lower-level primary school and a kindergarten. Housing is grouped around the green heart, car traffic is directed around the outermost circle, smaller green strips are used as buffer zones and the majority of its building stock was built between 1965 and 1974. In 1975 the number of residents was above 8,000, but nowadays the number of residents is approximately 5,000 – many of them senior citizens. The shopping mall is half empty and much of the building stock is in need of significant repair. There are also a number of social problems associated with the suburb that have given it a negative image in recent years. The overall challenge for any new design proposal is to re-establish the vitality of the suburb.

Although complementary building alone is not able to solve all the problems, it was proposed as a possible model. As a result, the theoretic grounding for the Master's student project documented here was based on an understanding of the aims and strategies of complementary building, as well as a discussion of the theoretical framework of participatory planning and the role of residents in complementary planning processes. In this case, it led to an analysis that included the mapping of resident opinions on the introduction of complementary building in their home suburb – something that contributed to their overwhelmingly favourable response at the end of the project.[38]

This approach mirrors a more participatory design ethos considered more and more important today to solve the problems of public perception described earlier. Here, it led to the development of a design that included many positive proposals from, and for, new and existing residents. The main principles of the project include, firstly, the assembling of public activities and thus people and life in public spaces; and secondly, the strengthening of the edge border between built structures and forest. These features create a greater sense of physical integration and a sense of community, they maintain the physical characteristics and experienced identity of the suburb and, in addition, prevent further sprawl.

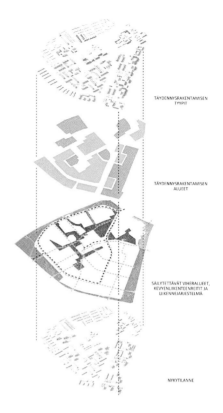

Figure 2: Kaukovainio suburb. Design Proposal
Photo, project and images by Jaana Keränen.

The plan also involves identifying underused parking lots or buffer zones that are suitable for new housing; the introduction of new senior housing into the core; the creation of edges between half-private housing yards and public green areas; and the extension of existing buildings. For example, the design proposes extending existing three-storey blocks of flats through the addition of one or two more storeys. This increases density whilst also allowing for the technical renovation of the existing flats and yards – which becomes economically feasible for developers since their profits come from the sale of the newer properties (Figure 2).

The project includes many initiatives that could potentially be rolled out and used in other suburbs across Finland and is thus an example of the use of the educational project as a general case study. Its focus on the implementation of complementary building in a suburban context addresses very specific and real issues in Finland and explores a model that potentially offers flexibility to Finnish planners as they move forward; the complementary approach being centred around adaptation rather than new completely whole and new developments. Furthermore, it is also an example of a more inclusive and consultation-led design process and thus functions on various levels as an example of how education in Finland can, and is, responding to the needs of the country in terms of planning and development.

Part Two: On Rural Planning – New Driving Forces

The fact that Finland is applying *complementary building* initiatives, normally considered as responses to urban issues, in suburban areas reflects the Finnish case of unusually large-scale suburban development in comparison to its urban areas. That said, however, the amount of urban and suburban development in Finland is still dwarfed by the amount of rural land the country possesses. Apart from Finland being the northernmost country in the European Union, it is also the most rural, with 90 per cent of its land area classified as countryside – and 76 per cent of this being forest. [39] Ironically, however, the focal point of land-use planning has been, and still is, on urban planning – despite the fact that cities would not exist without developments in agriculture and that they cannot survive without the produce it supplies.[40] Today, rural land-use planning is not recognised as a field requiring specific expertise, although this may have to change quickly if we are both to protect and effectively use rural environments and their natural resources.[41]

This is a particularly relevant question at the moment as living conditions in the warmer areas of the earth worsen and pressures on their natural resources grow. For northern countries, this situation both poses new challenges and opens new opportunities in utilising their own resources and developing new ones. In addition, the continued melting of the northern polar ice cap could, in time, have consequences for global trade by moving the maritime transport system in the direction of Hammerfest, Murmansk and Arkhangelsk.[42] This in turn would create new regional pressures and opportunities for different industries in countries like Finland, with industries like forestry, mining and nature tourism being perhaps the most directly and obviously affected. If such global changes were to lead to an increase in the manufacturing and service industries in northern countries, it would of course exacerbate the need for the sustainable maintenance and planning of renewable and non-renewable natural resources.[43]

Such concerns are not purely hypothetical. They are based on current trends and developments. The increase in global demand for raw materials for example, has already increased the level of mineral mining in Finland to such an extent that it is now the European leader in this field. Several dozen large mineral prospecting and mining projects are underway in rural regions including, most notably, the Suhanko palladium project in Ranua, the Sokli apatite project in Savukoski and the Kevitsa nickel project in Sodankylä.[44] Other mines have also been opened recently, such as the Suurkuusikko gold mine in Kittilä, the Sotkamo nickel mine in Talvivaara, and the Ilomantsi gold mine in Pampalo.[45] A good basic infrastructure of roads, railroads, power supply and harbours, together with a stable society and an educated population, make Finland a very attractive prospect for such mining companies[46] (Figure 3).

From the viewpoint of land-use planning, the challenge is that the location of mines cannot be determined by commonly used criteria such as proximity to current industries or existing transportation infrastructures. The location of a possible mine is established only after the long multi-phased research process required in mineral prospecting and, as a result, such projects are full of uncertainties about profitability, size, location and scheduling. Integrating new mining projects into the existing terrain and existing infrastructures requires detailed collaboration at the level of land-use planning, with regular communication between all parties involved. It is a type of rural development that underlines the need for a concerted and coordinated rural land-use planning system which accommodates not only the mining industry, but also economic and social sectors of the country such as tourism and farming.[47]

The locations of new mines do not necessarily result in further fragmentation of the suburban structure, however, since most employees are willing to commute from established urban and suburban regions. Consequently, new mining villages that are separate from the general urban/suburban structure are not required (although they do augment car use in the areas affected). Furthermore, many rural areas have vacant buildings left over from the earlier boom years of the welfare state with, for example, empty schools being common in these areas. Not only can these buildings be remodelled to function as bases for the mining industry, there are many seasonal vacation rental houses that could be used year round by mining employees.[48] These issues are already coming to the fore in some areas where the boom in mining has resulted in a shortage of housing and increased prices. For example, in Sodankylä, a town in Lapland with only 9,000 inhabitants, the rents for small apartments are as high as those in Helsinki city centre.[49]

In dealing with the development of the mining industry in these rural areas, it is also important to remember that most mining ventures do not result in the establishment of mines and, even when they do, they do not produce immediate profits. The probability of finding enough resources to justify development in any single site investigation can be as low as 0.1 per cent and the lead-in times for development are often measured in years. This is not always understood by the local press, public and municipalities who occasionally have unrealistic expectations of fast and positive development, and similarly extreme concerns about environmental damage. This is undoubtedly of fundamental importance, and ways need to be found to integrate mining with the other economic interests of the areas such as tourism and reindeer herding, to name but two.[50]

Another feature of the mining industry to keep in mind is that it is based on the exploitation of limited resources. Every mine will eventually reach the end of its life and so it is important for planners to create a plan for the entire life span of these projects, including demolition, re-use and the repair of the landscape.[51] The same applies to the towns and villages that grow as a result of the mining boom which, afterwards, will need to be planned to prevent the desertion of building stock and the complete dismantling of the community structure. Can entire communities be converted, moved or recycled?

What does convertibility or movability mean for rural structures, networks of services and building stock? What solutions enable a housing area built for the mining industry to be converted for tourism, for example? What planning tools and methods work best at the planning and implementation phases of projects, and which ones work best with global interests? How do these issues respond to the needs of local residents? Again, the questions and issues to be dealt with are multiple and varied.

The Changing Nature of Agriculture and Rural Patterns

If we consider a more traditionally rural industry, farming, a similarly complex set of factors come into play. Food consumption is estimated to triple by the year 2050 and urban gardening is capable of producing only a fraction of the food that is consumed in cities.[52] Consequently, rural environments will remain our primary food-production landscapes for some time to come.[53] However, current planning policies for rural areas focus on centralised agricultural production and lead to an increase in farm sizes, and the construction of ever-larger production facilities such as barns, dairies and slaughter houses.[54] The facilities designed to house the concomitant increase in farm animals and machinery are bordering on the scale (and the effects) of industrial buildings. However, they are not aesthetically appropriate to the traditional agricultural landscape.

In the light of all this, the planning of these areas and their production facilities is an urgent issue that requires the knowledge of qualified designers, as well as clear guidance with regard to the use of energy-efficient facilities. For example, new zoning guidelines and building regulations may be required to ensure that building sites are suitably located and that they are designed to produce as little environmental damage as possible. If implemented properly and vigorously, however, such 'restrictions' could open the door to the development of new agricultural buildings that are both energy efficient and architectonically of high quality. If an effective strategy were in place and backed up by investment, these restrictions could result in ideas that lead world industries.[55]

If we turn our attention to another emerging 'rural' issue in Finland, we see similar dynamics again in play. One of the possible consequences of further global warming is a shift in food production further north – a scenario that could bring a temporary work force to countries like Finland during the harvest season. Indeed, berry picking is already an industry that uses foreign labour, with many Thai rice farmers flying to Finland every year to pick various wild berries (such as cloudberries, lingonberries and blueberries) at harvest time. Many workers also come from Russia and the Ukraine as part of an organised effort on the part of industry that sees these workers using village schools and other unused buildings as temporary accommodation. International buyers arrive each evening to purchase the berries picked each day at these sites; and what results is business that is truly international, from production through to consumption.

Another aspect of this new agricultural trend that may further signpost developments in the future is the international commerce around cep and matsutake mushrooms that are now exported to Italy and Japan.[56] In Finland, picking berries and mushrooms is

Figure 3: Road to Pampalo under-ground gold mine, Photo: Endomines Oy.

Figure 4:
Äkäslompolo.
Analysis Map.
Photo by
Anniina Valjus.

considered an 'everyman's' right and, as a result, the income is not taxed – clearly an important additional incentive that is fostering the development of this industry in the region.[57] At the moment, only a small fraction of the wild berries and mushrooms available are being harvested and, in this light, all of this can be seen as simply the tip of the iceberg with regard to what these natural resource-based industries could become. The vastness of these operations, however, has also triggered public discussion and, in some places, social conflict – there have been various reported incidents of clashes and tensions between guest workers and local residents.[58]

There is clear potential and need for a coherent and well-developed land-use planning system that responds to the needs and conditions of these and other scenarios in Finland's rural areas. However, as mentioned earlier, there is still an urban bias in Finland that is preventing this happening to the level it should. Furthermore, the rural planning system is perceived, by both local officials and rural residents, as too bureaucratic and as producing too few positive results.[59] For example, it has failed to guide the auspicious locating of residential housing areas, and its landscape management and planning regulations are not being implemented – in part because those responsible are not sufficiently trained in the regulatory processes and broader planning strategies involved.[60]

Ownership also plays a role in some of the problems and difficulties associated with rural planning: the anonymous owners of urban spaces are being replaced in rural areas by active landowners whose own livelihoods depend on the land use and natural resources under consideration. For planning to be a positive value-adding tool, rather than a dictatorial and often misguided ruling from above, it is crucial that the process implemented in these rural areas be open and interactive, and for those involved to become more specialised and knowledgeable. In order to balance successfully the sustainable development of industries that harvest natural resources and manage rural development and land use, more thorough knowledge, better tools for guidance and improved planning methods will be required in the future. The situation currently is unsatisfactory.

Design Education and Rural Development

Reflecting the potentially wide range of futures for Finnish rural areas, and the complex integrated needs of the differing sectors that operate within them, the educational context again has to adapt and re-orientate itself in response. This is of course essential so as to ensure that the appropriate technical and intellectual skills are taught, and that tomorrow's designers are aware of the varied issues that they will need to deal with. Reflecting this, the projects set in the University of Oulu's Department of Architecture also focus on the realities of rural development as well as the urban and suburban projects mentioned earlier.

One example of this is the pilot program arranged in the fall of 2012 by the Architecture Department in which students focused on interactive and strategic planning for rural land use in the context of a mining project. The project was set in the framework of the 15 ECTS Master's level municipal-planning course and centred on the village of Äkäslompolo located in municipality of Kolari, Western Lapland, 150 km north of the polar circle. The village has been permanently settled since the eighteenth century and, due to its beautiful location at the shore of lake Äkäslompolojärvi in the vicinity of seven fells, it has attracted tourists since 1930s.

As a result of this, tourism has become the main source of living for the villagers – although reindeer herding and forestry still play a noticeable economic role in the livelihood of the community. Nowadays the village is part of Ylläs, a major tourist area that attracts large numbers of both domestic and international visitors, especially in the winter.[61] Recently, it has been subject to a major planning proposal by the municipality that earmarked new zones for the enlargement of the existing cottage areas, the basic dwelling tourist unit of the region.

Whilst this was not controversial or problematic in itself, the plan failed to take account of the nearby Hannukainen iron-ore mine – a project commenced recently in response to rising raw material prices in the global market. Northland Resources S.A., the company leading the project, has announced that the construction of the mine will begin in 2014 and that it is intended to be fully functional sometime in 2015–2016.[62] The mining project will clearly have major land-use impacts in both its immediate vicinity and beyond. The industrial site itself will obviously be reconfigured massively, but so too will the surroundings through the construction of new infrastructures such as housing, service-industry provisions and the construction of a new road network, for example.

Although the exact location and size of the industrial site have yet to be definitively determined, whatever the final location, the range of impacts it will have will be broadly similar. The nearest village is Äkäslompolo and it is there that the most obvious effects for regional inhabitants will be felt. The village is basic and has a school and good (but partly seasonal) services. Not only has the municipality failed to consider the effects of this mining project on the broader region and the tourist potential of the area, it has failed to consider the more specific impact it could have on this village.

It was in this context that the studio project of the Municipal Planning Course was set. The task of the students was to draft a land-use vision for the village that would cover the period from today to 2040. Implementing a model that would be highly recommendable for the Municipality, the project sought to estimate the impact of the mining project across an extended geographical area and over an extended period of time. As with the project described earlier, the design methodology applied was a participatory planning approach in which local stakeholders, including representatives of the municipality, villagers, the mining company and other key players, were all consulted.

In addition, it applied a strategic planning approach based on the 'scenario technique' – the envisaging of a range of consequences based on the consideration of different future circumstances. The first step was an examination that applied an integrative analysis framework that explores the study area from the perspectives of functions, structures, sensory environment and meanings. The aim of this is more appropriately to understand and create an 'identity profile' of the village.[63] The next step involved drafting three alternative scenarios, one of which was based on the idea that the mine would never be built;[64] the second on the idea that the mine would be in operation for a limited period of time; and the third on the idea that it would stay in operation for a long period of time and that the operation would expand. Once these scenarios were assessed and their impacts analysed, the last part of the pilot project involved the setting of strategic goals and the concretising of the actions needed. In the second scenario with a limited period of operation, the strategic goals identified included structures being easily converted to other uses with tourism being envisaged as the most likely (Figure 4).

Although the project was based on predicting long-term major effects, the immediate term and the smaller scale were not overlooked. For example, one proposal put forward the idea of turning off the street lights at night so as to better see the northern lights – clearly an idea of potential benefit to locals and the tourist industry in the area. This idea emerged from one of the consultation meetings with local stakeholders and was realised almost immediately – even before the pilot project ended. A proposal that would require more time and investment was for a Pitkätörmä: a new small-scale housing area that would serve as a base for the mining workers, but which could be turned into a cottage area for tourists once the mine closed – or used for this purpose if no mine were ever built.

From the point of the view of the local stakeholders, the use of this 'strategic approach' to design, the consultation it involved and the end results of the project were all seen to be both positive and useful. From the students' point of view, a real-life setting was experienced for the first time in which their discussions with local people, and the chance to work in a multidisciplinary group, were highly appreciated.[65] From the teachers' point of view, the multifaceted approach was definitely rewarding, despite the extra resources needed for the preparation and practical arrangement of field trips and participatory events.[66] It is another clear example of how the educational context is being used in the university to explore the real issues faced by Finland and its planning system today.

Conclusion

It was argued at the beginning of this chapter that current global forces and the problem of a changing environment are not only challenging the hierarchical Finnish land-use planning system and its policies, but demanding that it adapt. In many ways, the system is adapting; but not all the changes are proving sufficient or indeed beneficial. For example, as a result of trials in regional self-government[67] and the merger of municipalities, it has become more common for the research behind land-use planning decisions to be outsourced to expert consultants. Municipal officials are thus left in the position of coordinators rather than investigators. This requires that they have good knowledge of procurement legislation and public administration and ensures that they focus on certain aspects of public consultation such as the public display of plans, but it does not help them better understand the details of the issues at play.

To an extent, this is tied in to the public administration's recent attempts to move away from a hierarchal structure towards a more cooperative and responsive structure, where possibilities for democratic participation are made available through means other than legislation.[68] The Land Use and Building Act's objective for an open and interactive planning process is perhaps the most obvious example. Despite such changes, however, there are still many failings in the system and many municipality planning commissions suffer from limited resources in both personnel and finances which only exacerbates the disconnect between planners and the realities on the ground.

Another problem that emerges from this new system is the bureaucracy associated with public-administrative planning work. The organisation of municipality government structures is often cumbersome and often causes delays in the planning process – a situation made worse by the additional layers of engagement imposed by multiplying the players involved.[69] Another failing is the slowness with which the system has adapted to modern technologies. In the architecture and the building industries, information modelling today enables data collection, illustrative presentations and performance simulations throughout the life span of buildings and structures. Although similar techniques have been developed for land-use research and the documentation of planning and urban structures,[70] a base map and a notational system still persists in the Finnish planning system.

Many of these established tools, practices and characteristics have contributed to the failure of the planning system to guide physical change in a way that would result in a clearly better living environment – urban sprawl continues today, for example. It could be argued that they have also contributed to the failure of rural planning to rise further up the planning agenda, something that will be essential if the demand for natural resources in the north grows. Both these issues need new thinking and a new approach at government level – as well as in education where new designers and planners have to be made aware of the issues likely to face the country in the future.

Common to both the types of student project discussed earlier was just this application of a new type of thinking towards planning and development in suburban and rural Finland. However, if such projects are to be implemented, it is necessary for a similar reconsideration of thinking and premises to occur at the national planning level. Without reconfigurations at this level, ideas such as the ones discussed here will not have the opportunity to emerge and meet the current needs of the country. What needs to be done to turn the current planning system into one that applies a strategic approach is not yet clear. On the one hand, some contend that increased social and cultural flux requires flexible tools that facilitate quick reactions to changes in the planned environment. In other words, that less official planning and guidance are required. On the other had however, there are voices calling for a clear central and overarching planning system to be implemented – more official planning and guidance.

The key to solving this conundrum may lie in understanding the nature of land-use planning practices. The timeline in land-use planning is typically long, even as long as 25 years in some cases. A long timeline makes predicting both changes in the functional environment and the development of internal factors of land-use projects more difficult. It also makes it necessary to plan for the long term, however. Over such an extended period, it is perhaps inevitable that not only physical conditions and requirements change, but also social thinking, attitudes and preferences too. A broad range of uncertainties are always present in both land-use planning and commercial enterprises but so too are long-term goals and objectives.[71] According to urban planning theorist Jean Hillier, our view of planning should shift from 'steering the city' to 'strategic navigation'. In short, a broad outline of goals should be set that is capable of adapting as conditions change.[72]

With this postulation, Hillier proposes a model that, in many ways, seeks a balance between less control and more control. It is certainly the model underlying the educational projects discussed earlier. In addition to their focus on public participation and the implementation of new ideas, both the suburban and rural projects discussed were premised on flexibility within an overall planning structure. In the case of the Kaukovainio suburb, the complementary building approach is itself a flexible and adaptive system; whilst in the case of Äkäslompolo village and its surrounding areas, it involved the explicit inscription into the project of uncertainty and design adaptability. All of these approaches, it is argued here, will be key to Finnish practitioners and educationalists as they develop new techniques and theories to respond to the needs for long-term planning and an uncertain future.

Notes

[1] Retrieved from: http://www.stat.fi/tup/suoluk/suoluk_vaesto_en.html
[2] See, for example: Nikula, R. (1984) *Architecture and Landscape: The Building of Finland*. Keuruu: Otava, and Jutikkala, E. (1984) Urbanisoituminen. In *Suomen kaupunkilaitoksen historia 3*. Vantaa: Suomen kaupunkiliitto, p. 15.
[3] Retrieved from: http://www.environment.fi/default.asp?contentid=302209&lan=fi&clan=fi
[4] Retrieved from: http://www.ymparisto.fi/download.asp?contentid=98312&lan=fi
[5] 'Development' here refers to the construction of towns and cities, roads, harbours, airports and other similar features of the built environment.
[6] Retrieved from: http://www.ymparisto.fi/default.asp?node=109&lan=FI
[7] Newman and Thornley (1996) have classified European planning into five categories: British, Napoleonic, Germanic, Scandinavian and East European. The grouping of the planning systems is based on *legal families* and on *administrative families,* in which the limitations of the liability between the national, regional and local levels are examined. Denmark, Finland, Norway and Sweden are classified as Scandinavian. The planning systems are relatively similar because of the tri-partition into national, regional and local levels. In Finland, the planning system is regarded as a hierarchical system but

in Denmark and Sweden the hierarchy is not stressed. Local self-government is seen as one of the cornerstones of the Scandinavian constitution. In all of the countries, the role of the local land-use planning level is the most influential. (Newman, P., & Thornley, A. (1996) *Urban Planning in Europe: International Competition, National Systems and Planning Projects*. London: Routledge, pp. 34–35.)

[8] Unofficial translation of the Land Use and Building Act, see: http://www.finlex.fi/en/laki/kaannokset/1999/en19990132.pdf

[9] Retrieved from: http://www.ymparisto.fi/default.asp?contentid=323527&lan=fi&clan=fi

[10] Different phases in urban planning theory – see, for example: Taylor, N. (2003/2008) *Urban Planning Theory since 1945*. London: Sage.

[11] The national objectives for land use set guidelines for nationally important land-use issues. The Finnish Council of State decides on the objectives for land use. A regional scheme defines a region's development goals. It includes the regional development program and the regional plan. The regional plan gives the national objectives for land use a concrete form, as well as also presenting the land-use principles and proposing necessary areas for the development of the region. The regional plan is approved by the Ministry of Environment. The local master plan is the official tool for municipal level general planning. The purpose of the local master plan is to guide the development of the urban structure and to coordinate different functions. The local master plan is created and approved by the municipality. A local master plan gives guidelines to a local detailed plan, which in turn guides building. A local detailed plan is also created and approved by the municipality. Retrieved from: http://www.finlex.fi/en/laki/kaannokset/1999/en19990132.pdf

[12] This might be due to the fact that Finnish land-use planning is generally created by architects. There is no distinct educational program for land-use planning. Finnish urban planners are described in an article by Kangasoja, J., Mälkki, M., Puustinen, S., Hirvonen, J., & Mäntysalo, R. (2011) Architectural Education as a basis for Planning Work – the Pros and Cons of Professional Enculturation. *The Journal for Education in the Built Environment* 2010: 2, pp. 25–38.

[13] Meurman, O.-I. (1947) *Asemakaavaoppi*. Helsinki: Otava.

[14] See, for example: Mikkola, K. (1984) The roots of Eliel Saarinen's town plans. In M. Komonen (ed.), *Saarinen in Finland*. Helsinki: Suomen rakennustaiteen museo, pp. 88–118.

[15] Meurman, O.-I., & Huovinen, M. (1989) *Mörrin muistelmia*. Juva: WSOY, pp. 87–103.

[16] See, for example, http://oulu.ouka.fi/tekninen/hiukkavaara/ and http://www.tampere.fi/vuores.html

[17] Mäenpää, P. (2011) *Helsinki takaisin jaloilleen*. Helsinki: Gaudeamus, p. 23.

[18] Ibid., pp. 37, 44.

[19] For new urbanism, see, for example: Katz, P. (ed.) (1994) *New Urbanism: Towards an Architecture of Community*. New York: McGraw-Hill.

[20] Alatalo, E. (ed.) (2012) *Hurmaava lähiö. Energiatehokas lähiökorjaaminen -hankkeen loppujulkaisu*. Tampere: Tampereen teknillinen yliopisto, Arkkitehtuurin laitos. Retrieved from: http://www.ara.fi/download.asp?contentid=25784&lan=fi

[21] http://www.ymparisto.fi/download.asp?contentid=98312&lan=fi

[22] See, for example: Hentilä, H.-L., Mäntysalo, R., & Soudunsaari, L. (eds) (2006) *Ekosukat. Ekotehokkuus Supistuvissa ja Kasvavissa Taajamissa: Muuttuvan yhdyskuntarakenteen fyysinen, sosiaalinen ja ekologinen kestävyys. Loppuraportti.* Oulu: Oulun yliopisto, arkkitehtuurin osasto, B27.

[23] http://www.ff.uni-lj.si/oddelki/geo/publikacije/dela/files/Dela_27/06_pichler.pdf

[24] Finnish research of the phenomenon began in the mid-2000s. For Finnish-speaking readers, a comprehensive introduction to the related research is offered by a report by Kuoppa, J., & Mäntysalo, R. (eds) (2010) *Kestävä yhdyskuntarakenne ja elinympäristö. Ympäristöklusterin neljännen ohjelmakauden tuloksia.* Espoo: Aalto-yliopisto, Teknillinen korkeakoulu, Yhdyskuntasuunnittelun tutkimus- ja koulutuskeskuksen julkaisuja B97. Retrieved from: http://lib.tkk.fi/Reports/2010/isbn9789526032351.pdf. The recognised variables and effects are largely the same as in international urban sprawl-related research. See, for example: Freilich, R.H., Sitkowski, R.J., & Mennillo, S.D. (2010) *From Sprawl to Sustainability. Smart Growth, New Urbanism, Green Development and Renewable Energy.* USA: ABA Publishing.

[25] Jane Jacobs wrote about the domination of cars in urban planning as early as 1961 in her classic work *Death and Life of Great American Cities.* Jacobs, J. (1989/1961) *Death and Life of Great American Cities.* New York: Vintage Books. Finland is only now awaking to the subject, and researchers are both defining the phenomenon of car dependency and seeking alternatives to it. See, for example: Kanninen, V., Kontio, P., Mäntysalo, R., & Ristimäki, M. (2010) *Autoriippuvainen yhdyskunta ja sen vaihtoehdot.* Espoo: Yhdyskuntasuunnittelun koulutuskeskuksen julkaisuja B101, Retrieved from: http://lib.tkk. fi/Reports/2010/isbn9789526035352.pdf

[26] Joensuu, T. (2011) *Joukkoliikenteen ja maankäytön integrointi kaupunkiseuduilla.* Helsinki: Liikenneviraston tutkimuksia ja selvityksiä 27. Retrieved from: http://www2. liikennevirasto.fi/julkaisut/pdf3/lts_2011-27_joukkoliikenteen_ja_web.pdf

[27] A physicist and system analyst, Cesare Marchetti, developed the three-way division while researching the development of cities and people's movability. His conclusion was that in different eras the daily travelling time for man is approximately one hour. The radius of mobility varies greatly according to the different methods of transportation. See, for example: http://www.cesaremarchetti.org/archive/electronic/basic_instincts.pdf

[28] See, for example: http://www.ymparisto.fi/download.asp?contentid=135516&lan=fi

[29] Oulu residents ride bicycles year round: having studded winter tires and good maintenance of bicycle paths in the winter along with the excellent trail network contributes to successful winter bicycling. See http://www.poljin.fi/tilastoja/tilastot_ kotimaa/

[30] Strandell, A. (2011) *Asukasbarometri.* Helsinki: Suomen ympäristö 31. Retrieved from: http://www.ymparisto.fi/download.asp?contentid=133932&lan=fi; and http://www.ymparisto.fi/download.asp?contentid=133934&lan=fi

[31] Simonen, M. (2006) Kaupungin läheinen maaseutu asuinpaikkana. Limingan Tupokseen muuttaneiden näkemykset asuinalueestaan. In M. Mönkkönen, & R. Mäntysalo (eds), *EkoSuKaT-projektin väliraportteja 4. Limingan Tupos.* Oulu: Oulun yliopisto, Arkkitehtuurin osasto, Yhdyskuntasuunnittelun laboratorio, Julkaisu C 100, p. 31–32.

[32] One can argue that while striving for a sustainable city, Western countries have in a way

reinvented the possibility of cultivating and producing food in a city. In developing cities, urban agriculture is still a necessity – not just a fun hobby for hipsters. See, for example: Freeman, D.B. (1991) *A City of Farmers: Informal Urban Agriculture in the Open Spaces of Nairobi, Kenya.* Toronto: McGill-Queen's University Press.

[33] Urban gardening in Finland is practised mainly in traditional allotment garden areas. The situation was different after the Second World War: single-family housing lots were sized to allow for growing potatoes and other vegetables. Interest in urban gardening is growing. See, for example: Paavilainen, K. (2010, April 28) Kaupunkiviljely asuinympäristössä. Maankäyttösuunnitelma Helsingin Kuninkaantammeen. Diplomityö, Oulun yliopisto, arkkitehtuurin osasto, 71 p. + Annexes 1–6.

[34] Donald, B. (2012/2010) Food Systems Planning and Sustainable Cities and Regions. In A. Blay-Palmer, *Imagining Sustainable Food Systems. Theory and Practice* (Farnham: Ashgate, pp. 115–133.

[35] Hentilä, H.-L., & Luoma, S. (2009) *Arkiliikunta murroksessa. Nousevat lajit Oulussa.* Oulu: Oulun yliopisto, arkkitehtuurin osasto, C127. Retrieved from: http://herkules.oulu.fi/isbn9789514292620/isbn9789514292620.pdf

[36] Jane Jacobs was far-sighted in dealing with the thematics of citizen empowerment in her classic work from 1961. Jacobs, J. (1989/1961), op. cit.

[37] Peltonen, L., Hirvonen, J., Manninen, R., Linjama, H., & Savikko, R. (2006) *Maankäytön konfliktit ja niiden ratkaisumahdollisuudet. Suomalaisen nykytilan kartoitus.* Helsinki: Ympäristöministeriö, Suomen ympäristö 12. Retrieved from: http://www.ymparisto.fi/download.asp?contentid=55270&lan=fi

[38] This was in stark contrast to the first complementary building proposals put forward for the suburb by the City of Oulu planners. These designs proposed new housing in a spot identified by the residents as an important green zone. This created mistrust towards the whole idea of complementary building and was definitely not a good way to open up the official planning process.

[39] Malinen, P., et al. (2006) *Suomen maaseututyypit.* Vammala: Maa- ja metsätalousministeriö, 7.

[40] Rural areas can be categorised into three different types: sparsely populated rural areas, rural heartland areas and rural areas close to urban areas. See Malinen, P., et al. (2006) op. cit. The division is based on the inner differences and development prospects of rural areas, and it attempts to recognise the common difficulties and challenges of the same types of areas. Based on this structure, common solutions and development strategies can be found for similar areas. Sparsely populated rural areas exist mainly in Eastern and Northern Finland and are threatened by the cycle of poor development: young people move away, the amount of elderly people increases, services disappear and thus the economic capacity of the municipalities diminishes. Sustainable land-use planning principles are often compromised when attempting to attract new residents and industries.

[41] Some light can be shed on the rural planning questions' secondary importance through an illustrative definition, according to which 'rural planning deals with areas that are not yet urban'. Caves, R. W. (ed.) (2005) *Encyclopedia of the City.* London and New York: Routledge, p. 480. Rural areas are left with a secondary position also in theories

on global development: they are seen as declining areas outside of fibres and knots. See, for example Castells, M. (1996–1998) *The Information Age: Economy, Society and Culture*, Vol. I–III. Oxford: Blackwell.

[42] See, for example: Smith, L. (2011) *T. Uusi pohjoinen – maailma vuonna 2050*. Porvoo: Tähtitieteellinen yhdistys Ursa ry.

[43] The tightening competition for natural resources has created an industry called Marine (or Maritime) Spatial Planning (MSP). Developing this industry is also supported by the EU. A transnational research and development project that piloted one possible tool was carried out in the Bothnian Sea area recently. Seaways, fishing grounds, reserves and other natural sites as well as areas for energy production were recognised as integral factors in planning offshore areas. Maritime transport in the Bothnian Sea is predicted to grow rapidly as mining production increases. Icy conditions during the winter are a challenge of their own: ice breakers are still needed in aiding maritime transport, even if the climate is warming. Renewable forms of energy, such as tidal and wind energy are estimated to increase their share in energy production. Locating large wind farms presents a landscaping and environmental challenge. Furthermore, sea-sand excavation is also growing. See Backer, H., & Frias, M. (2012) *Planning the Bothnian Sea. Key findings of Plan Bothnia Project*. Turku: Finepress.

[44] In addition to demand, legislative changes are also a factor. The functional environment of the Finnish and Swedish mining industries changed completely when the previously closed and government-regulated markets opened up to multinational operators in 1994 as a result of changes in mining legislature due to the EEA arrangements. Since then several international mining companies have started mining prospecting and the related geological research in Finland. See Lindborg, T. (1996) *Suomalaisen kaivosklusterin rakennemuutos*. Oulu: Oulun yliopisto.

[45] See, for example: Uusitalo, M. (ed.) (2012) *Kaivosteollisuus. Toimialaraportti.* TEM, 2012/2. Retrieved from: http://www.temtoimialapalvelu.fi/files/1589/Kaivosteollisuus2012_web.pdf

[46] Hentilä, H.-L. & Ihatsu, E. (eds) (2009) *Kasvun ja supistumisen ohjauskeinot ja elinympäristön laatu – tapauksena pohjoisen Suomen kaivoskunnat*. Oulu: Oulun yliopisto, arkkitehtuurin osasto, C124. Retrieved from: http://herkules.oulu.fi/isbn9789514291340/isbn9789514291340.pdf

[47] Ibid.

[48] Ibid.

[49] See, for example: http://yle.fi/uutiset/kaivoskunnissa_asuntopulaa/6028616, and http://yle.fi/uutiset/sodankylassa_huippuhinnat_asuntomarkkinoilla/6346181.

[50] The joint cooperative research project of the Universities of Lapland and Oulu as well as Finnish Forest Research Institute (Metla) 'Different Land Use Activities and Local Communities in Mining Projects (DILACOMI)' (2011–2013) outlines sustainable methods for the mining industry. The project's website is: http://www.ulapland.fi/?deptid=21176

[51] Hentilä, H.-L. & Ihatsu, E. (eds) (2009) op. cit.

[52] Levitte, Y. (2012/2010) Thinking about Labour in Alternative Food Systems. In A. Blay-Palmer, *Imagining Sustainable Food Systems. Theory and Practice*. Farnham: Ashgate, p. 72.

[53] The area of strong primary production, or rural heartland area, is located in Southern and Western Finland. There are concentrations of primary production in the rural heartland areas with pig farming, fur farming, green-house cultivation and poultry farming. Several mid-sized centres as well as industry concentrations are located in the vicinity of rural heartland areas. Community centres have diverse functions and most villages are lively. See Malinen, P., et al. (2006) op. cit.

[54] See, for example: http://www.stat.fi/tup/suoluk/suoluk_maatalous_en.html

[55] It should be noted that the EU already regulates such buildings. Therefore national legislature has very little effect on it at the moment.

[56] See, for example: Rantanen, P., & Valkonen, J. (2011, December 15) Ulkomaiset metsämarjanpoimijat Suomessa. Retrieved from: http://formin.finland.fi/public/download.aspx?ID=88464&GUID={33EAB400-3CF7-4B9D-9AB3-84C5EE8FE8D8}

[57] In the summer of 2012 the Finnish Central Union of Agricultural Producers and Forest Owners (MTK) took the initiative both to limit everyman's rights and to tax the income received from berry picking. The Finnish media dismissed the initiative completely. See, for example: http://yle.fi/uutiset/reviiriajattelu_ei_pade_metsassa/6229534; and http://www.hs.fi/paakirjoitus/artikkeli/Marjastusoikeudesta+ei+pid%C3%A4+tinki%C3%A4/1329104444486

[58] See, for example: http://yle.fi/uutiset/marjanpoimijoiden_toiminta_tyrmistyttaa_-_veivat_varpuja_kansallispuistosta/6240006

[59] In the prior Land Use and Building Act, the rural planning forms were different from those of town and densely built areas. The current law from the year 2000 no longer differentiates between them. Jääskeläinen, L., & Syrjänen, O. (2010) Maankäyttö- ja rakennuslaki selityksineen. Helsinki: Rakennustieto.

[60] The (MASUKE)-research project (2010–12) of the Department of Architecture at the University of Oulu, 'Rural View in Land Use Planning: Assessing and Developing of Planning Methods', funded by the Ministry of Agriculture and Forestry, researched the practices of rural land-use planning and developed new practices. See Rönkkö, E., Hentilä, H.-L., & Illikainen, H. (2012) Maaseutunäkökulma maankäytön suunnittelussa: suunnittelumenetelmien arviointi ja kehittäminen. Oulu: Oulun yliopisto, arkkitehtuurin osasto. Retrieved from: http://herkules.oulu.fi/isbn9789514299346/isbn9789514299346.pdf

[61] See: http://www.yllas.fi/en

[62] http://www.hannukaisenkaivos.fi/index.html

[63] The analysis framework is based on the results presented in the doctoral thesis of Emilia Rönkkö. See: Rönkkö, E. (2012) Kulttuuriympäristöselvitykset. Tieto, taito ja ymmärrys maaseudun maankäytön suunnittelussa. Oulu: Oulun yliopisto, arkkitehtuurin osasto. Retrieved from: http://herkules.oulu.fi/isbn9789514298158/isbn9789514298158.pdf

[64] This is seen as a likely scenario given that market prices are likely to sink again at some point in the future.

[65] There were nine students of architecture and three students of geography in the groups.

[66] The author was in charge of the course. The assisting teacher was M.Sc. (Arch.) Leena Soudunsaari.

[67] Trials in Regional self-government have been carried out in Kainuu and are planned

in Päijät-Häme, for example. Various other initiatives have been carried out around the country. See: Prättälä, K. (2010) Kohti kunnallishallinnon uutta rakennetta. In T. Tuominen (ed.), *Avoin, tehokas ja riippumaton*. Helsinki: Edita, p. 136.

[68] Kulla, H. (2010) Hierarkiasta verkostoihin, in T. Tuominen (ed.), op. cit., pp. 93–94.

[69] One of the root causes of this is the dual-government system of civil-servant management and a political management system operating in tandem. In this system, personnel often feel incapable of influencing the planning process and this diminishes the capability of utilising the creative potential and commitment of personnel.

[70] See, for example: Nuojua, J., Soudunsaari, L., & Hentilä, H.-L. (2010, November 29 – December 3) Boosting Web-based public participation in urban planning with a group of key stakeholders. Proceedings of the 11th Annual Conference on Participatory Design 2010: Participation, the Challenge, Sydney, Australia.
Also, see Joutsiniemi, A. (2010) *Becoming Metapolis – A Configurational Approach*. Tampereen teknillinen yliopisto. The dissertation introduces a dynamic modelling tool of the interactive link between transport and land use.

[71] Hentilä, H.-L. (2010) Näkökulmana toimintaympäristön muutos. In *Asiantuntija-arviot Itä-Uudenmaan ja Uudenmaan maakuntakaavan rakennemalleista*. Helsinki: Uudenmaan liiton julkaisuja E 112, pp. 9–18. Retrieved from: http://www.uudenmaanliitto.fi/files/3430/Asiantuntija-arviot_Uudenmaan_ja_Ita-Uudenmaan_rakennemalleista_2035.pdf

[72] Hillier, J. (2008, September 18–19) Are we there yet? From 'steering the city' to strategic navigation and further theoretical becoming., YTK 40 years anniversary, Key Note Lecture.

Bibliography

Alatalo, E. (ed.) (2012) *Hurmaava lähiö. Energiatehokas lähiökorjaaminen -hankkeen loppujulkaisu*. Tampere: Tampereen teknillinen yliopisto, Arkkitehtuurin laitos. Retrieved from: http://www.ara.fi/download.asp?contentid=25784&lan=fi

Backer, H., & Frias, M. (2012) *Planning the Bothnian Sea: Key findings of Plan Bothnia Project*. Turku: Finepress.

Castells, M. (1996–1998) *The Information Age: Economy, Society and Culture*, Vol. I-III. Oxford: Blackwell.

Caves, R.W. (ed.) (2005) *Encyclopedia of the City*. London and New York: Routledge, p. 480.

Donald, B. (2012/2010) Food Systems Planning and Sustainable Cities and Regions. In A. Blay-Palmer, *Imagining Sustainable Food Systems. Theory and Practice*. Farnham: Ashgate, pp. 115–133.

Freeman, D.B. (1991) *A City of Farmers: Informal Urban Agriculture in the Open Spaces of Nairobi, Kenya*. Toronto: McGill-Queen's University Press.

Freilich, R.H., Sitkowski, R.J., & Mennillo, S.D. (2010) *From Sprawl to Sustainability. Smart Growth, New Urbanism, Green Development and Renewable Energy*. USA: ABA Publishing.

Hentilä, H.-L. (2010) Näkökulmana toimintaympäristön muutos. In *Asiantuntija-arviot Itä-Uudenmaan ja Uudenmaan maakuntakaavan rakennemalleista*. Helsinki: Uudenmaan liiton julkaisuja E 112, pp. 9–18. Retrieved from: http://www.uudenmaanliitto.fi/files/3430/

Asiantuntija-arviot_Uudenmaan_ja_Ita-Uudenmaan_rakennemalleista_2035.pdf

Hentilä, H.-L., & Ihatsu, E. (eds) (2009) *Kasvun ja supistumisen ohjauskeinot ja elinympäristön laatu – tapauksena pohjoisen Suomen kaivoskunnat.* Oulu: Oulun yliopisto, arkkitehtuurin osasto, C124. Retrieved from: http://herkules.oulu.fi/isbn9789514291340/isbn9789514291340.pdf

Hentilä, H.-L., & Luoma, S. (2009) *Arkiliikunta murroksessa. Nousevat lajit Oulussa.* Oulu: Oulun yliopisto, arkkitehtuurin osasto, C127. Retrieved from: http://herkules.oulu.fi/isbn9789514292620/isbn9789514292620.pdf

Hentilä, H.-L., Mäntysalo, R., & Soudunsaari, L. (eds) (2006) *Ekosukat. Ekotehokkuus Supistuvissa ja Kasvavissa Taajamissa: Muuttuvan yhdyskuntarakenteen fyysinen, sosiaalinen ja ekologinen kestävyys. Loppuraportti.* Oulu: Oulun yliopisto, arkkitehtuurin osasto, B27.

Hillier, J. (2008, September 18–19) Are we there yet? From 'steering the city' to strategic navigation and further theoretical becoming. YTK 40 years anniversary, Key Note Lecture.

Jääskeläinen, L., & Syrjänen, O. (2010) *Maankäyttö- ja rakennuslaki selityksineen.* Helsinki: Rakennustieto.

Jacobs, J. (1989/1961) *Death and Life of Great American Cities.* New York: Vintage Books.

Joensuu, T. (2011) *Joukkoliikenteen ja maankäytön integrointi kaupunkiseuduilla.* Helsinki: Liikenneviraston tutkimuksia ja selvityksiä 27. Retrieved from: http://www2.liikennevirasto.fi/julkaisut/pdf3/lts_2011-27_joukkoliikenteen_ja_web.pdf

Joutsiniemi, A. (2010) *Becoming Metapolis – A Configurational Approach.* Tampereen teknillinen yliopisto.

Kangasoja, J., Mälkki, M., Puustinen, S., Hirvonen, J., & Mäntysalo, R. (2011) Architectural Education as a Basis for Planning Work – The Pros and Cons of Professional Enculturation. *Journal for Education in the Built Environment* 2010: 2, pp. 25–38.

Kanninen, V., Kontio, P., Mäntysalo, R., & Ristimäki, M. (2010) *Autoriippuvainen yhdyskunta ja sen vaihtoehdot.* Espoo: Yhdyskuntasuunnittelun koulutuskeskuksen julkaisuja B101. Retrieved from: http://lib.tkk.fi/Reports/2010/isbn9789526035352.pdf

Katz, P. (ed.) (1994) *New Urbanism: Towards an Architecture of Community.* New York: McGraw-Hill.

Kulla, H. (2010) Hierarkiasta verkostoihin. In T. Tuominen (ed.) op. cit., pp. 93–94.

Kuoppa, J., & Mäntysalo, R. (eds) (2010) *Kestävä yhdyskuntarakenne ja elinympäristö.* Ympäristöklusterin neljännen ohjelmakauden tuloksia. Espoo: Aalto-yliopisto, Teknillinen korkeakoulu, Yhdyskuntasuunnittelun tutkimus- ja koulutuskeskuksen julkaisuja B97. Retrieved from: http://lib.tkk.fi/Reports/2010/isbn9789526032351.pdf

Levitte, Y. (2012/2010) Thinking about Labour in Alternative Food Systems. In A. Blay-Palmer, *Imagining Sustainable Food Systems. Theory and Practice.* Farnham: Ashgate, p. 72.

Lindborg, T. (1996) *Suomalaisen kaivosklusterin rakennemuutos.* Oulu: Oulun yliopisto.

Malinen, P., et al. (2006) *Suomen maaseututyypit.* Vammala: Maa- ja metsätalousministeriö, p. 7.

Meurman, O.-I. (1947) *Asemakaavaoppi.* Helsinki: Otava.

Meurman, O.-I., & Huovinen, M. (1989) *Mörrin muistelmia.* Juva: WSOY, pp. 87–103.

Mikkola, K. (1984) The roots of Eliel Saarinen's town plans. In M. Komonen (ed.), *Saarinen in*

Finland. Helsinki: Suomen rakennustaiteen museo, pp. 88–118.

Mäenpää, P. (2011) *Helsinki takaisin jaloilleen*. Helsinki: Gaudeamus, p. 23.

Newman, P., & Thornley, A. (1996) *Urban Planning in Europe: International Competition, National Systems and Planning Projects*. London: Routledge, pp. 34–35.

Nikula, R. (1984) *Architecture and Landscape: The Building of Finland*. Keuruu: Otava, and Jutikkala, E. (1984) Urbanisoituminen. In *Suomen kaupunkilaitoksen historia 3*. Vantaa: Suomen kaupunkiliitto, p. 15.

Nuojua, J., Soudunsaari, L., & Hentilä, H.-L. (2010, November 29 – December 3) Boosting Web-based public participation in urban planning with a group of key stakeholders. Proceedings of the 11th Annual Conference on Participatory Design 2010: Participation, the Challenge, Sydney, Australia.

Paavilainen, K. (2010, April 28) Kaupunkiviljely asuinympäristössä. Maankäyttösuunnitelma Helsingin Kuninkaantammeen. Diplomityö, Oulun yliopisto, arkkitehtuurin osasto, 71 p. + Annexes 1–6.

Peltonen, L., Hirvonen, J., Manninen, R., Linjama, H., & Savikko, R. (2006) *Maankäytön konfliktit ja niiden ratkaisumahdollisuudet. Suomalaisen nykytilan kartoitus*. Helsinki: Ympäristöministeriö, Suomen ympäristö 12. Retrieved from: http://www.ymparisto.fi/download.asp?contentid=55270&lan=fi

Prättälä, K. (2010) Kohti kunnallishallinnon uutta rakennetta. In T. Tuominen (ed.), *Avoin, tehokas ja riippumaton*. Helsinki: Edita, p. 136.

Rantanen, P., & Valkonen, J. (2011, December 15) Ulkomaiset metsämarjanpoimijat Suomessa. Retrieved from: http://formin.finland.fi/public/download.aspx?ID=88464&GUID={33EAB400-3CF7-4B9D-9AB3-84C5EE8FE8D8}

Rönkkö, E. (2012) *Kulttuuriympäristöselvitykset. Tieto, taito ja ymmärrys maaseudun maankäytön suunnittelussa*. Oulu: Oulun yliopisto, arkkitehtuurin osasto. Retrieved from: http://herkules.oulu.fi/isbn9789514298158/isbn9789514298158.pdf

Rönkkö, E., Hentilä, H.-L., & Illikainen, H. (2012) *Maaseutunäkökulma maankäytön suunnittelussa: suunnittelumenetelmien arviointi ja kehittäminen*. Oulu: Oulun yliopisto, arkkitehtuurin osasto. Retrieved from: http://herkules.oulu.fi/isbn9789514299346/isbn9789514299346.pdf

Simonen, M. (2006) Kaupungin läheinen maaseutu asuinpaikkana. Limingan Tupokseen muuttaneiden näkemykset asuinalueestaan. In M. Mönkkönen & R. Mäntysalo (eds) (2006) *EkoSuKaT-projektin väliraportteja 4. Limingan Tupos*. Oulu: Oulun yliopisto, Arkkitehtuurin osasto, Yhdyskuntasuunnittelun laboratorio, Julkaisu C 100, pp. 31–32.

Smith, L. (2011) *T. Uusi pohjoinen – maailma vuonna 2050*. Porvoo: Tähtitieteellinen yhdistys Ursa ry.

Strandell, A. (2011) *Asukasbarometri*. Helsinki: Suomen ympäristö 31. Retrieved from: http://www.ymparisto.fi/download.asp?contentid=133932&lan=fi; and http://www.ymparisto.fi/download.asp?contentid=133934&lan=fi

Taylor, N. (2003/2008) *Urban Planning Theory since 1945*. London: Sage.

Uusitalo, M. (ed.) (2012) *Kaivosteollisuus. Toimialaraportti*. TEM, 2012/2. Retrieved from: http://www.temtoimialapalvelu.fi/files/1589/Kaivosteollisuus2012_web.pdf

Siddhartha MUKHERJEE,
Sat GHOSH,
Shreyas PANAMBUR

CHAPTER 9

THE ARCHITECTURAL HERITAGE OF SOUTH AND CENTRAL INDIA – A STUDY IN ENVIRONMENTAL DESIGN

Architectural and Cultural Heritage

South and Central India possess one of the World's most sophisticated historic cultures. That culture ebbed and flowed on its shores for millennia. It has a cultural energy whose effects resonate even today. It is evident in its monuments and buildings, and in its traditions that continue to be reinterpreted today. Its architectural roots stretch back to the Dravidian civilisation, which flourished over 3,500 years ago. Throughout its history, this architecture has been creatively adapted to the needs of its users and the characteristics of its climate and location. It has always, and still does, fulfil the needs and nourish the spirit of its people.

The sensitivity underlying its architecture and its traditions is also seen in the cities of the subcontinent. These cities, which were some world's first and most celebrated, survived the ravages of time and the changing conditions of political and cultural tides. In addition, they were sustainable for over two millennia. Much has been written about these first cities: Harappa, Mohenjodaro and, a city we will mention in more detail later, Lothal. They have their roots in the Indus Valley Civilisation and represent ancient cultures that tell us much that is of interest today from a cultural and spiritual perspective.

One aspect of these cities, and the architecture to be found in them, that has yet to be fully explored from a contemporary perspective, however, is what they can teach us about sustainable building practices. In order to understand the lessons we can take from these cities and buildings in this regard, it is necessary not only to examine the technical characteristics of their layout and construction but to understand the culture that led to the emergence of those characteristics. This dual approach is at the heart of various projects currently being undertaken in India and informs both practice and education. In these projects, various threads come together that help us better understand the complex relationships that can be found between culture, history, modern technology and contemporary ideas around sustainability. They are projects that look to the future, but have their roots in the past.

History and Tradition

In examining the lessons to be learnt from the history and traditions of Central and Southern India, we can examine both individual buildings and city layouts. Both reveal interesting ideas of importance. If we take the ancient city plan of Lothal, for example, we find that it was comprised of double- and single-storeyed buildings clustered around geometrical grids with three divisions: 'The Citadel', 'The Middle Town' and 'The Lower Town'.[1] The ancients took advantage of the cool ground temperatures in the summer months by building their residential quarters in the Lower Town and South Indian architecture even today conforms to this principle (Figure 1).

Traditionally, they believed that in a cosmological sense there are eight cardinal directions that radiate from a central or focal point. The mountain–sea and the sunrise–sunset axes were the most influential. This belief affected everything from the biggest spiritual plans for monuments to the characteristics of the everyday. For example, a Southern Indian must sleep with his head towards the rising sun so that the feet, which they believe to be unclean, do not point towards the east. Intrinsically then, spatial

Figure 1: Rectangular grid blocks and clustered foundations in the Vijayanagara kingdom (1336 AD – 1646 AD).

orientations correspond to spiritual axes, rather than the directional compasses.[2,3] However, these beliefs also produced an approach to orientation that was, more often than not, perfectly attuned with the climate – door openings to the south, for example, allowing the cool evening breeze to flow in during most seasons.

Around 3,500 years ago, then, the ancients already had a sensitive understanding of orientation, and by extension daylighting and solar gain, which matured subsequently during the Vedic period (circa 1700–1100 BC). However, they also had an intuitive grasp of good and sound construction and infrastructure: the rectangular clustering pattern of cities such as Lothal, for example, also maximised floor-space utilisation and accommodated a well-planned drainage system. In turn, this made the construction of buildings easier and more efficient and remains a characteristic evident today.[4]

These buildings took on many forms, but one typical system involved four pillars (*upamits*) against which beams were leant at an angle as props (*pratimits*). The upright pillars were connected by cross beams (*parimits*) resting upon them, the roof was formed of bamboo canes (*vamsa*) and the walls were filled up with grass bundles (*palada*).[5] (Figure 2) This particular system is not only functional in terms of its structure, however: it is very reminiscent of contemporary Eco-wall systems today – a self-automated, hydroponic living system that is effective environmentally.

When we add to this the fact that the orientation of these buildings often coincided with what would be considered good practice in contemporary ecological design, we see that 'functionalism' and 'environmental design' have roots in India that can be traced back centuries to a time when emphasis was placed on human life being in harmony with physical and metaphysical forces, and not just material objectives.[6] Other examples of this double-sided phenomenon include: the placing of doors and windows to optimise fenestration; the choice of appropriate construction sites and building materials; and the orientation of buildings to achieve maximum sunlight during winter whilst minimising the same during summer. This was an architecture unified with the spiritual Indian being but clearly in harmony with its environment.[7]

Descriptions of this architecture aren't only to be found in the Vedic period, however. Indirect references to it can also be found in Buddhist Literature. One example is the following extract from *Sthapatya Ved-Vastu Sastra*: 'the houses were all together, in a group, separated only by narrow lanes. Immediately adjoining was the sacred grove of trees of the primeval forest.' In this extract, the Buddha describes ancient architecture and goes on to outline it in more detail: 'I allow you abodes of five kinds – *Vihara* [Monasteries or Temples], *Ardhayoga* [buildings that were partly religious and partly residential], *Prasada* [residential buildings], *Harmya* [Palaces of multi-storeyed houses], and *Griha* [houses for the middle classes].'[8]

These 'five kinds of abode' were all typical of the region and have persisted over thousands of years. Each of them had the solid structural engineering concepts that are also found in the Dravidian buildings of the magnificent Central and Southern cities such as Lothal. Although we cannot argue that descriptions of them in the *Sthapatya Ved-Vastu Sastra* are based on an understanding of sustainability as we understand it technically today, their appearance in these texts does illustrate the deep-rooted history of these sustainable building approaches in the context of Southern and Central India and underline the argument that sustainability in the Indian context is not, and should not be, seen as a purely technological or contemporary phenomenon.

Energy Efficiency in the Materials and Constructions of the Past

Underlining our argument that, in addition to cultural and spiritual influences in the traditional cities and buildings of this region, a deep understanding of climate and site was also fundamental to the building practices of the ancients is the work of Antonin Raymond.[9] Raymond, a long-term resident French architect in India, has observed that: 'the first great principle that all great architecture teaches us, is to consider the local conditions as the one known basic factor from which to start, and to allow the structure to take the most logical shape dictated by these local conditions.'[10] These ideas underlay the architecture of both Buddhist and Dravidian origin and are key to the lessons we can learn today.

In the more southerly areas of India, where the hot equatorial sun is most intense, the site itself is often used for its 'architectural' properties: for example, a thick 'umbrella' of interlacing coconut fronds is often used to filter the sun, thus minimising heat. This technique is not only effective environmentally, but also emotively as these trees can sway gently in the breeze with soothing, cooling effects on both the skin and the mind. [11] It is a natural 'architectural' feature born from an understanding of climate and site. Tied into such adaptations of the site is an inherent understanding of the materials that Central and Southern Indians have been experimenting with for millennia: stones, pliable fabrics, clay from the Cauvery delta, and bales from palm and coconut fronds being typical examples.

The shell of a building using these materials functions as a barrier between the varying external environment, which can be uncomfortably hot or cold depending on the season and the time of day. However, although these building shells can still act as moderators of climate, it is now also common for artificial systems to be used during seasonal extremes. Traditionally, this was obviously not an option and ancient civilisations found a whole range of passive techniques to moderate the effects of the climate. The most common building materials for housing were mud, baked bricks, wood and reed, but stone was also used and was particularly effective as it has good thermal mass.[12]

Tamil villages in the Southern regions have some of the oldest mud built houses of the region and employ a combination of sun dried and baked bricks for their wall construction. These were treated with cow-dung slurry for its antiseptic properties, but also because this allows extra protection against the rains.[13] The floors of these

Figure 2: Use of traditional techniques: wood, thatch and mud in Andhra houses (circa 1990).

buildings are also made of rammed earth and finished with a red oxide coating; and a combination of cow dung and bamboo mats are placed under the thatched roof to prolong its life, which is often as long as 25 years. During the Dravidian period, these village dwellings would also often be arranged in a fenced commune and the coconut, palm-tree trunks and bamboo timbers used in their construction would often be elegantly styled.[14] The system is still in use today (Figure 2).

The ceilings of the more elaborate structures of the time and the region are marked by heavy wooden beams and wooden joists supporting terrace roofing. The walls were generally made of brick-on-edge masonry in a lime mortar.[15,16] This distinction was typical of Tamil houses where stark differences between the upper and lower classes of

Figure 3: Traditional construction: an indoor courtyard in a Tamil house (circa 1990).

Figure 4: Traditional construction: note the tall stooping roof in a typical Keralan house (circa 1990).

society were deliberately made explicit. These more expensive and permanent houses used Burmese teak for doors and windows, and the roof was made of tiles supported on wooden battens and beams which, in turn, were supported on flared columns. Cuddapah stone was used in the courtyard and terracotta tiles on interior floors – all of which helped maintain a cooler indoor temperature (Figure 3).[17]

Slightly further north in Kerala, there was a very different set of techniques being used, albeit ones that also responded intuitively to the climate and the site of their specific region. Here, there was a practice of building double-storeyed houses with sloping roofs. Their Southern counterparts used wood as the primary building material and were predominantly single-storied dwellings. However, despite these differences, they shared the long, steep roof structure intended to protect the house's walls against the heavy monsoon.[18] A cursory glance across a Keralan landscape shows how these sloping roofs have been uniformly adopted across the entire state and represent, perhaps, its most notable characteristic.[19] Again, it is still common today (Figure 4).

Unlike the cold northern climes where houses are built to shut the rains out, these houses seem to enhance its emotive effect. Indeed, much Tamil and Malayalam devotional literature has been written by bards brooding on the courtyards that accompany these houses in which it is not rare to find a peacock 'dancing to the crescendo of lashing rainfall, under a swirling montage of abstract cloud forms'. However, these houses and their courtyards are also functional, with their open, semi-covered and covered spaces having evolved to use both cool and shade to counter the heat of the tropics.[20]

These features are found in single dwellings but are also evident in buildings organised in the traditional 'cluster' arrangements typical of the region. Particularly representative of this characteristic are Brahmin houses that are arranged in narrow, long sets with each house connected by a common wall.[21,22] These Brahmin dwellings, again common today, are often built without interior courtyards but have open spaces at the

front and rear (Figure 6). In some variations on this, as in the case of farmer's houses, however, there is an inner courtyard which is used for drying grains and shelling pods. In all cases, there is a raised veranda or small seating area at the front of the house, called a *tinnai*, and the construction is generally brick walls with timber pillars, doors and windows, and a rammed-earth floor finished with a red oxide coating.

Adapting and Studying Traditional Practices in Modern High-tech Design

The purpose of outlining these techniques, and the deeper traditions that underlie them, is to develop a deeper understanding of how new sustainable technologies and practices can optimise the properties and characteristics of the materials, forms and construction techniques they employ. In the examples given thus far, we have mentioned spatial techniques such as the use of inner and outer courtyards, the employment of steep roofs, large overhangs and construction in stone, timber and mud. We have also mentioned the spiritual reasons behind some of these forms and techniques. Similarly, we have listed issues of city, building layout, overall planning and orientation. In part, each of these things is spiritual; but they are also partly practical and reveal an intuitive understanding of climate and site conditions.

All these techniques and characteristics have recently been found to offer useful templates and ideas to contemporary designers who have not only employed them but have begun to analyse them fully. Some designers have even begun to develop new construction techniques and practices that rework these older traditions in a modern guise. In the context of India, no individual or grouping has been more involved in this than the Auroville Earth Institute in Pondicherry – an idealised sustainable community devoted to an experiment in human unity set up by Mirra Alfassa in the 1960s.[23] Right from its inception, engineers, architects and artists from across the world have worked together at Auroville in the creation of building forms, construction techniques and high-technology systems. Extensive use of sustainable building fabrics and a heavy emphasis on aesthetics has resulted in buildings that are perfectly adapted to the local microclimate and are individual works of modern art in themselves (Figure 6).

Despite their modern appearance, however, the buildings at Auroville employ a deep understanding of traditional techniques and practices. For example, the surface area to volume ratio of many of their building is kept small, to minimise the entry of hot air from the outside. Simultaneously, they take advantage of solar gain, natural light and ventilation by avoiding deep-plan layouts.[24] Through a commingling of traditional intuitive building forms and practices, designs of unbounded artistic vision, and perfectly engineered construction parameters, these buildings become aesthetically elegant spaces based on tradition and sustainable techniques. They show that beauty, modernity and ecological designs rooted in tradition can become a new 'norm'.

Although it has high aspirations and spiritual origins, Auroville also engages in the nitty-gritty detail of sustainable construction in India. For example, it has been involved in working with Compressed Stabilised Earth Blocks (CSEB), now the most widely used earth technology worldwide. This traditional technique was developed in conjunction with modern scientific experimentation and technology that identified ways of stabilising soil and using the resultant bricks in conjunction with soil-cement mortar.

The Auroville Earth Institute has also been involved in developing a range of building fabrics that not only have low U-values but also utilise a minimum amount of cement, so as to be as environmentally friendly as possible.[25] Not all these materials and techniques have their origins here, of course; but they are used, monitored and improved through the experimentation and adaptation of their features that occurs at Auroville. The employment of straw bales is one example. A typical straw-bale building at Auroville is rendered on the outer skin to provide protection from the rain and plastered on the inside. The render, plaster and construction technique are adapted to

Figure 6: A Building in Auromodele (circa 1985).

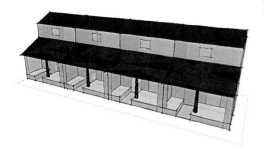

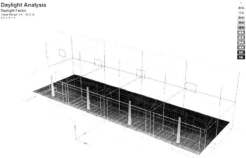

Figure 7: Ecotect reconstruction –
Tamil Brahmin houses.

Figure 8: Daylight analysis of residential
clusters.

the local conditions and ensure an eco-wall of low U-values appropriate to its specific location.

Whilst Auroville represents a largely privately financed initiative, it does have governmental support and can thus be seen as part of a broader attempt at government level to promote the development of new sustainable technologies based on traditional techniques. That philosophy is certainly at the heart of the project known as the 'Essence of Energy Efficiency in Past and Extant Forms: A fluid Mechanical Analysis'. This project, funded by the School of Mechanical and Building Sciences at Vellore Institute of Technology (VIT) University, attempts to analyse the vernacular architecture of the ancient constructions and planning arrangements found in the city of Lothal. This particular project uses contemporary modelling software such as *Autodesk*, *Ecotect* and *Analysis* to model and compute a whole range of variables that allow us to develop a better understanding of how these ancient buildings, and their planning systems, can best be used as models in contemporary projects.[26]

The Essence of Energy Efficiency project makes use of modern software as comprehensive concept-to-detail sustainable-building design tools. It has simulated Tamil buildings in the region so as to undertake a number of studies including daylight and thermal analysis; energy consumption investigations; heating and cooling load calculations; and analyses of building form, fabric and orientation – all of which help to reveal how these ancient buildings performed, and could perform today, in the context of their environment.[27] The intention is to apply the results in the design of modern buildings in the region. One specific example is the calculation of the amount of natural lighting that would be available inside these buildings so as to estimate the need for artificial lighting if they were to be used as models for contemporary buildings. The project has also given an account of building fabric performance to delineate active and passive zones vis-à-vis orientation and microclimate.

The first step of the project was to re-create a model of a single basic dwelling unit that was hypothetically orientated in various positions to better grasp its optimal site arrangement. Subsequently, models were made of 'clustered buildings' typical of the region's traditional housing. The relative performance of buildings with and without shared walls was thus compared. In the example shown here, typical Tamil Brahmin houses are studied in various orientations. They are double-storey 'cluster' houses and share walls with adjacent neighbours. They have a protruding roof which covers a small veranda leading into the house. This roof construction thus blocks out the harsh overhead sun in the afternoon while also allowing for the gentle lower-altitude sunlight to enter in the mornings and the evenings (Figures 7–8).

Following these studies, others were made to gain a full understanding of the houses' thermal performance and we were able to vary the use of wall materials so as to predict which will perform best in any later reconstructions using these spatial layouts. These studies revealed that contemporary conventional constructions, like plastered brick and concrete block, do not perform well in the hot summer months, with the indoor temperatures rising to 37.9 °C and 38.5 °C, respectively. However, when the effects of rammed-earth walls of 300mm and 500mm thickness (typical traditional techniques) were factored into the model, a predicted reduction of temperature to around 36.5 °C emerged.[28] An additional thermal comfort analysis showed that the daily hours during which the temperature could be kept in the comfortable band of 18–26 °C were at their greatest with rammed-earth construction.

When these studies focused on questions of orientation, a south-westerly preference was revealed in cities such as Lothal, as it provides the best possible balance between the need to provide warmth during the short winters and ensure cool temperatures during the long hot summers (Figure 9). In turn, these factors were balanced with questions of daylighting; and in the daylight analyses carried out as part of the project, we identified clearly demarcated active and passive zones in the dwellings. It was thus highlighted that the veranda technique reduces glare inside, whilst still allowing enough daylight to enter. This allows most of the interior to be a passive zone that requires no artificial lighting, thus requiring zero energy consumption.

	Coldest Day (Jan 1)		Hottest Day (June 20)	
Orientation	Inside Temp (°C)	Outside Temp (°C)	Inside Temp (°C)	Outside Temp (°C)
South	13.3	4.1	38.8	41.5
South west	13.4	4.1	36.0	41.5
West	13.5	4.1	36.2	41.5

Figure 9: Temperatures in Lothal dwellings varying with building orientation.

Together, all these studies allow designers to better understand the properties and benefits, as well as some of the restrictions and limitations, of traditional construction techniques in terms of materials, orientation, building form and spatial layout. Despite being technical in nature, the ideas being drawn out of these modern technical computer studies are related to much older Indian cultures – cultures in which intuitive decisions on orientation and clustering, for example, give us ideas we can perfect in today's sustainable architecture.

Sustainable Practice in Modern India – Practice and Education

Developing sustainable techniques and living arrangements such as the ones indicated by these studies of traditional buildings and town layouts is essential in India today. India is one of the most populous countries in the world, with over 1.2 billion people, 638,000 villages, more than 5,100 towns and over 380 urban agglomerations.[29] After a political leaning towards socialism for over 40 years during which the economy was centrally planned, sudden economic liberalisation and globalisation have recently accelerated massive urban growth; a phenomenon that has coincided with a general population explosion across the country. This has placed even greater strain on resources and meant an increased urgency for sustainable design, at both the level of the city and individual buildings.

At the level of the individual building, over the last century, a marked distinction has emerged between those of the developed and those of the developing world. Prior to technologies such as air conditioning and electric lighting, the passive conditioning and illumination of spaces was basically similar. In addition, our tolerance to the climate was also, by and large, similar. However, as these new technologies emerged, a generation seems to have emerged of people who cannot do without mechanical conditioning, heating or lighting. This is now the case not only in the 'developed' world, but also in the 'developing' world where, even in rural areas, it is now common to see an almost automatic increase in the use of mechanical/electrical equipment as income levels rise.

The Western consumption culture has also influenced new Indian cities with large shopping malls, clusters of residential apartments and tall unplanned building structures now marring the landscape of urban India. While many of these issues are now being addressed by green architects, town planners and other bodies at the decision-making level in India, the transition from the country's developing-nation status to that of a developed nation clearly comes at an environmental price. The energy demands for a non-OECD (Organization for Economic Cooperation and Development) nation like India are projected to increased by 60 per cent by the year 2040.[30] Inevitably, this means that sources of alternative energy must be put to use if major economic and environmental problems are to be avoided, particularly given that coal and oil reserves are limited.

In India, nowhere is a response to this need more evident than in the Central and Southern regions where much of the country's research into alternative sources of energy takes place. However, even though sustainability is now a global buzz word and India has seen many 'green buildings' constructed in recent years, it remains in its infancy. However, big steps are being taken. The Confederation of Indian Industries Green Building Centre (CII – GBC) in Hyderabad was the first building outside the US to be awarded the LEED (Leadership in Energy and Environmental Design) 'platinum' rating by the US Green Building Council. In addition, The Energy Conservation and Building Code (ECBC), The Energy and Resources Institute (TERI) GRIHA and the National Building Council (NBC) have all been set up in recent years and now provide national rating guidelines.

However, while these technological developments are all essential, it is important to remember that sustainability is not just a technical fix, and that technology has to respond to social and cultural needs as well as material requirements. In India, this means developing sustainable cities and sustainable facilities for the poor – most importantly, housing. This is certainly the basis of the proposal regarding sustainable housing developments put forward by the Nobel Laureate Amartya Sen. His 'Capabilty Approach' to homelessness focuses on housing according to an individual's capabilities and needs, and has been developed by Guillem Fernàndez Evangelista who suggests that: 'in terms of the family, the house not only provides shelter and allows for the home to be configured, but also relates to the care of the people that share it, along with their self-esteem, communication, identity, participation and, in effect, their fulfilment as people.'[31]

The technical approach outlined in these pages, then, is only part of the picture. The requirements of the Indian people and Indian cities go beyond material questions. As a result, we see in India today concerns for issues of social and urban development going hand-in-hand with concerns for more environmentally effective building practices. Again, we see the cultural and the technological being combined. Increasingly this dual approach is more and more embedded in practice; but it is in the educational context that it is most obvious.

The Council of Architecture (COA) develops the curriculum in India and prescribes the standards and quality of education that are followed by institutions all over the country. The All India Council for Technical Education (AICTE) and COA monitor educational institutes imparting professional education in the field of engineering and architecture respectively and, in particular, the COA emphasises the importance of viewing architecture as a 'social art' – as a discipline with roots in the Humanities, the Sciences, the Arts and Technology.

The COA expresses the importance of networking and associating with experts from allied fields, and reiterates the significance of integrated design – which is at the heart of adapting ancient architectural paradigms to the fast-growing urban Indian landscape. It also shows its concern towards a whole series of 'national priorities' in the fields of energy conservation, such as: ecology; environmental pollution; the protection and preservation of architectural heritage; low-cost housing; urban renewals; rural upliftment;

and economic development at local and district levels. It stipulates the curriculum content areas for the various stages of a design curriculum and stresses that architecture should be eclectic enough to respond to diverse needs.[32] As a result, it stipulates Climatology, Building Services and Architectural History as core subject areas.

Despite this overarching perspective, the modern curriculum in India has changed in recent years to reflect the increased importance of sustainable design and technologies. Consequently, special attention is given to the introduction of 'first principles' in energy- and water-efficient design, and an understanding of the Energy Conservation Building Code (ECBC).[33] Similarly, projects chosen in the field of energy-conscious designs are encouraged and easy access to the latest computational software is provided to students, as in the case projects such as the Essence of Energy Efficiency project; the Health and Wellness Centre, designed in IIT Kharagpur; and the Net Zero Energy Building Program, a project part-funded by the USAID/ECO-III initiative Energy Conservation and Commercialization.[34]

Such schemes and projects aim to provide architects, engineers and building-energy professionals with state of the art tools for research in sustainable architecture. Energy-simulation tools and reference materials on the principles of energy efficiency in buildings are provided to students and professionals for their research projects – as was the case with the Essence of Energy Efficiency project described earlier. It was also the case with the project, The Shape of Things to come in Indian Slums: Sustainable Kitchen Designs: an initiative aimed at containing carbon emissions that is run under the aegis of Vilgro, an agency that funds sustainable design projects impacting the lives of India's rural poor. One of the objectives of all these projects, and their overarching funding structures, is to make India a global and intellectual leader in the field of building physics and energy simulation by 2015.[35]

On the flip side of this technological bias is the Indian National Trust for Cultural Heritage (INTACH) which has 140 centres all over India. Its aims are to improve conservation and increase an awareness of cultural heritage, and it too has had an effect on the curriculums of Indian schools of architecture, planning and design.[36] They conduct workshops and exhibitions to increase awareness about issues related to conservation and aim to build a sense of pride in the richness of Indian architecture and culture. Towards this end they have, amongst many other events and activities, arranged and funded heritage walks and TV programs.

INTACH plays a major role in heritage conservation, reinventing historical and cultural buildings so as to preserve them for future generations. It believes that most of these buildings are 'beautiful and better adapted to the local climate than modern buildings' and, consequently, pushes for their preservation from both a cultural and an ecological standpoint. In this sense, the arguments put forward by INTACH resonate with those presented here: that sustainability is not just about modern technologies, but is something that is intrinsically linked to traditions that are operative at a cultural and a material level in India. That these issues are not only being discussed by practitioners, but now lie at the core of the Indian education system, is evident in projects mentioned here.

At various levels, then, it is obvious that in India serious attempts are being made to push the country to the forefront of world design in terms of new technologies; but this is being done in a way that does not leave the past behind. Indeed, in many ways, these new developments are embedded in the past. The focus may be technological, as in the case of the projects discussed in detail here, but it is not exclusively so. Thus, what we see in these projects is an attempt to bring many threads of sustainability together in the Indian context. These threads are deeply rooted culturally and socially, are engrained in our traditional architecture and should, as we move forward towards the future, be integrated into cutting-edge technological developments in both practice and education.

Notes

[1]   Panambur, S., et al. (2012) 'Energy efficiency in architectural designs in the Indus Valley Civilization: Lessons learnt for new designing', Reinventing Architecture and Interiors: the past, the present and the future, IE International Conference.

[2]   Khan, O. (1995) 'Indus Valley Civilization at Lothal', A Walk Through Lothal. Retrieved from: www.harappa.com (accessed 11 November 2011)

[3]   Danino, M. (2008) 'New Insights into Harappan Town Planning, Proportions and Units, With Special Reference to Dholavira'. *Man and Environment*, Vol. XXXIII, No. 1, 2008, pp. 66–79.

[4]   Steadman, P. (2006) 'Why are most buildings Rectangular?' *Architectural Research Quarterly*, Vol. 10, No. 2, 2006, pp. 119–130.

[5]   Das, K. S. (1944) *The Economic History of India*. Munshi Ram Manohar Lal, p. 143.

[6]   These traditional (and metaphysical) practices can be said to have embodied, in themselves, the idea of energy efficiency. See: Borden, M. (2003) 'Living with Vastu Energy', Vastu Overview [website]. Retrieved from: http://www.vastu-design.com/overview.php (accessed 15 March 2012)

[7]   South India is a region where the traditions of the past are still alive, and are maintained through a daily practice of religious rituals in temples. The pyramid-shaped *Koils*, which have intricately carved stones and statues, have used Vastu Shastra as a backbone for their design and construction. This form of temple architecture is one of the three styles found in the Vedas, which was pioneered by Maha Muni Mayan of the Sangam Era in Tamil Nadu. The city of Mammalapuram, built during the Pallava dynasty has its distinct style of architecture, which is born from the literature ascribed by Mayan. See: Omved Lifestyle (2010) 'Vastu: Its ancient literature', Vastu [website]. Retrieved from: http://www.omved.com/our-products/vastu (accessed 17 March 2012)

[8]   Niketan Anand Gaur (2002) *Sthapatya Ved-Vastu Sastra*. New Age Books.

[9]   If we take the case of Tamil Nadu, for example, we have a region where the tropical climate varies little between the winter and summer months, and the days and nights are roughly equal all the year round. The hottest months here can go above 40 degrees centigrade and its coastal regions are markedly humid. Here, nights tend to be cooler, and a much-welcome sea breeze fills in the hot afternoons. South India receives the retreating monsoons and Tamil Nadu's first showers wet the month of October,

continuing up to December. A more westerly Kerala remains pleasant for most part of the year. Although it is tropical, the temperature goes up to around 33 degrees centigrade. The monsoons here begin much earlier, by the month of June, when the humidity peaks to its maximum. Downpours spanning a few days are not unheard of. By October, the onset of winter has this smallest of the four Southern states in a much more pleasant climate, at around 20 degrees. Moving higher up brings us to Karnataka, which experiences the best of the climate among the Southern states. The hottest summer days here peak at 35 degrees centigrade and the crack of monsoon showers can be first felt around June, which is also the commencement of the dominant climate of the year. Finally, the last easterly state is Andhra Pradesh, which has the maximum variation in temperature, with the hottest summer regions tipping at 42 degrees centigrade and falling down to 10 degrees centigrade in the winters, which are colder over the plateau regions. Andhra Pradesh is often hit by cyclones crossing the Bay of Bengal, which has impacted the local architecture tremendously.

[10]   Raymond, A. (2011) *Golconde*. Pondicherry: Sri Aurobindo Book Distribution Agency.
[11]   South Indians believe there is a life force in coconut and an entire culture has grown out of the availability of coconut and palm, which are used as a material and method of construction in architecture and engineering, furniture and furnishings.
[12]   Thermal mass allows the stone to absorb the outside temperature during the day, thus keeping the internal temperature down. The collected heat is radiated outwards at night once the outside temperature falls. Mofidi, S.M. (2007) 'Passive Architectural Cooling Principles for Arid Climates'. *Paper presented at the 2nd PALENC Conference and 28th AIVC Conference on Building Low Energy Cooling and Advanced Ventilation Technologies in the 21st Century. September 2007.* Crete Island, Greece.
[13]   Ghosh, S., et al. (2009) 'Building fabric characteristics in traditional & modern architectural forms in DakshinaChitra', ICAMB School of Mechanical and Building Sciences, VIT University, Vellore.
[14]   Temporary buildings (*Kuccha* houses) were made of mud, wood and grass while the permanent buildings (*Pukka* houses) were made of stone and burnt brick.
[15]   GardenVisit (9 November 1998) 'Kuccha and Pakka', Indian Garden and Buildings [website]. Retrieved from: http://www.gardenvisit.com/history_theory/garden_landscape_design_articles/west_asia/indian_garden_hindu_buddhist> (accessed 28 March 2012)
[16]   Pondicherry Past and Present (10 February 2000) 'French Buildings', Domestic Architecture [website].
[17]   The culture of Tamil Nadu speaks of multifarious art forms and styles, and merchants often employed masons specialising in decorative use of lime plaster to adorn their walls, depicting stories sprawling across ceilings and rooms. This became a common feature of Tamil houses in later years. Dakshinachitra (20 August 2004) 'Merchant's House from Chettinad, Tamilnadu', Tamilnadu [website]. Retrieved from: http://dakshinachitra.net/scripts/tn-merchanthouse.asp (accessed 1 April 2012)
[18]   Water here is plentiful and every house has its own well, while many have stone-lined agricultural tanks often used for bathing. A traditional feature of these houses is the granary and special storage spaces, underlining the importance of agriculture in Kerala.

See: Prokerala (2005) 'Kerala Climate', Kerala [website]. Retrieved from: http://www.prokerala.com/kerala/climate.htm (accessed 19 March 2012)

[19] Calicut houses are characterised by pitched roofs, wooden ceilings and windows (see Figure 4). The manner of joinery and wood used (jackfruit wood and palmyra) are common for both type of houses in southern Kerala – for both the rich and the middle class. The practice of grooving lanks every 3" to 4" allows the carpenters to use varying sizes to achieve an aesthetically appealing look of uniformity. See: Dakshinachitra (20 August 2004) 'Hindu House – Trivandrum, Kerala', Kerala [website]. Retrieved from: http://dakshinachitra.net/scripts/keralalayout.asp (accessed 30 March 2012)

[20] Pondicherry Past and Present (10 February 2000) 'French Buildings', Domestic Architecture [website]. Retrieved from: http://www.ifpindia.org/ecrire/upload/digital_database/Site/Pondi/data/part_2_2.html#header (accessed 29 March 2012)

[21] Ghosh, S., et al. (2009) 'A study of Infiltration, Ventilation, Daylighting and Microclimate in Dakshinachitra buildings', ICAMB School of Mechanical and Building Sciences, VIT University, Vellore.

[22] Ghosh, S., et al. (2009) 'A Case study on building form suitability in traditional and modern south Indian buildings from Dakshinachitra', ICAMB School of Mechanical and Building Sciences, VIT University, Vellore.

[23] Auroville (30 September 1998) 'Auroville in brief', Auroville [website]. Retrieved from: http://www.auroville.org/av_brief.htm (accessed 3 April 2012)

[24] Ghosh, S., et al. (27 August 2008) 'Energy Efficiency in Indian Buildings: The Auroville Experience', *Paper Presented at ICAMB. School of Mechanical and Building Sciences, VIT University. January 2008.* Vellore, India.

[25] Ghosh, S., et al. (27 August 2008) 'Energy Efficiency in Indian Buildings: The Auroville Experience', *Paper Presented at ICAMB. School of Mechanical and Building Sciences, VIT University. January 2008.* Vellore, India.

[26] Autodesk (2000) 'Autodesk Ecotect Analysis', Products. Retrieved from: http://usa.autodesk.com/ecotect-analysis/ (accessed August 2011)

[27] Hensen, J. L. M. (1991) *On the thermal interaction of building structure and heating and ventilating system.* Doctoral Dissertation. J. A. Eindhoven: Eindhoven University of Technology (FAGO).

[28] Although a 2°C change is not relevant in lay terms, thermodynamically it has a significant impact. A 2°C drop in the mid-30s has a more profound effect than a 2°C drop in the mid-20s. This is because the saturation vapour pressure curve is exponential (Tetens, 1930). Hence the amount of humidity in ambient air is reduced with a drop in temperature, which effects the comfort level in the zone positively.

[29] India Mapped (2010) The Republic of India, All Indian States [website] Retrieved from: http://www.indiamapped.com/all-indian-states/ (accessed 26 April 2012)

[30] Exxon Mobile (2012) The Outlook for Energy: A View to 2040, Energy Outlook [website]. Retrieved from: http://www.exxonmobil.com/energyoutlook (accessed 15 May 2012)

[31] Evangelista, G. (2010) 'Poverty, Homelessness and Freedom: An Approach from the Capabilities Theory'. *European Journal of Homelessness*, Vol. 4, pp. 189–202.

[32] Council of Architecture (2002) Conditions of Engagement and Scale of Charges

Preamble, Professional Practices [website]. Retrieved from: http://www.coa.gov.in/ practice/practice.htm (accessed 6 April 2012)

[33] Council of Architecture (2002) 'Minimum Standard for Architectural Education' [website]. Retrieved from: http://www.coa.gov.in/Rev.%20Min.%20Std.pdf (accessed 27 April 2012)

[34] The USAID/ECO-III initiative Energy Conservation and Commercialization was itself an initiative of the (BEE).

[35] The BEE was itself a joint initiative by the Indian government and the United States, begun in January 2012 under the initial phase of ECO (the Energy Conservation and Commercialization) project agreement. ECO has helped many Indian states develop energy-conservation strategies and test new approaches through projects in different phases. It has helped the states of Punjab and Gujarat to develop Energy Conservation Building codes (ECBC) with an objective to improving energy efficiency in the building sector. The third phase of ECO reiterated the importance of developing a strong curriculum for educational training of architects and engineers involved in Sustainability and Architecture by including this aspect as one of the five major tasks in its collaboration with the BEE.

[36] INTACH is a non-profit, non-governmental organisation having major centres in Pondicherry, Hyderabad and Bangalore in South India.

Bibliography

Auroville (30 September 1998) 'Auroville in brief', Auroville [website]. Retrieved from: http://www.auroville.org/av_brief.htm (accessed 3 April 2012)

Autodesk (2000) 'Autodesk Ecotect Analysis', Products. Retrieved from: http://usa.autodesk.com/ecotect-analysis/ (accessed August 2011)

Borden, M. (2003) 'Living with Vastu Energy', Vastu Overview [website]. Retrieved from: http://www.vastu-design.com/overview.php (accessed 15 March 2012)

Council of Architecture (2002) Conditions of Engagement and Scale of Charges Preamble, Professional Practices [website]. Retrieved from: http://www.coa.gov.in/practice/practice.htm (accessed 6 April 2012)

Council of Architecture (2002) 'Minimum Standard for Architectural Education' [website]. Retrieved from: http://www.coa.gov.in/Rev.%20Min.%20Std.pdf (accessed 27 April 2012)

Dakshinachitra (20 August 2004) 'Hindu House – Trivandrum, Kerala', Kerala [website]. Retrieved from: http://dakshinachitra.net/scripts/keralalayout.asp (accessed 30 March 2012)

Dakshinachitra (20 August 2004) 'Merchant's House from Chettinad, Tamilnadu', Tamilnadu [website]. Retrieved from: http://dakshinachitra.net/scripts/tn-merchanthouse.asp (accessed 1 April 2012)

Danino, M. (2008) 'New Insights into Harappan Town Planning, Proportions and Units, With Special Reference to Dholavira'. Man and Environment, Vol. XXXIII, No. 1, 2008, pp. 66–79.

Das, K. S. (1944) The Economic History of India. Munshi Ram Manohar Lal, p. 143.

Evangelista, G. (2010) 'Poverty, Homelessness and Freedom: An Approach from the Capabilities Theory'. European Journal of Homelessness, Vol. 4, pp. 189–202.

Exxon Mobile (2012) The Outlook for Energy: A View to 2040, Energy Outlook [website]. Retrieved from: http://www.exxonmobil.com/energyoutlook (accessed 15 May 2012)

GardenVisit (9 November 1998) 'Kuccha and Pakka', Indian Garden and Buildings [website]. Retrieved from: http://www.gardenvisit.com/history_theory/garden_landscape_design_articles/west_asia/indian_garden_hindu_buddhist (accessed 28 March 2012)

Ghosh, S., et al. (2009) 'A Case study on building form suitability in traditional and modern south Indian buildings from Dakshinachitra', ICAMB School of Mechanical and Building Sciences, VIT University, Vellore.

Ghosh, S., et al. (2009) 'A study of Infiltration, Ventilation, Daylighting and Microclimate in Dakshinachitra buildings', ICAMB School of Mechanical and Building Sciences, VIT University, Vellore.

Ghosh, S., et al. (2009) 'Building fabric characteristics in traditional & modern architectural forms in DakshinaChitra', ICAMB School of Mechanical and Building Sciences, VIT University, Vellore.

Ghosh, S., et al. (27 August 2008) 'Energy Efficiency in Indian Buildings: The Auroville Experience', Paper Presented at ICAMB. School of Mechanical and Building Sciences, VIT University, January 2008. Vellore, India.

Hensen, J. L. M. (1991) *On the thermal interaction of building structure and heating and ventilating system.* Doctoral Dissertation. J. A. Eindhoven: Eindhoven University of Technology (FAGO).

India Mapped (2010) The Republic of India, All Indian States [website]. Retrieved from: http://www.indiamapped.com/all-indian-states/ (accessed 26 April 2012)

Khan, O. (1995) 'Indus Valley Civilization at Lothal', A Walk Through Lothal [Website]. Retrieved from: www.harappa.com (accessed 11 November 2011)

Mofidi, S. M. (2007) 'Passive Architectural Cooling Principles for Arid Climates'. Paper presented at the 2nd PALENC Conference and 28th AIVC Conference on Building Low Energy Cooling and Advanced Ventilation Technologies in the 21st Century, September 2007, Crete Island, Greece.

Gaur, N. A. (2002) *Sthapatya Ved-Vastu Sastra.* New Age Books.

Omved Lifestyle (2010) 'Vastu: Its ancient literature', Vastu [website]. Retrieved from: http://www.omved.com/our-products/vastu (accessed 17 March 2012)

Panambur, S., et al. (2012) 'Energy efficiency in architectural designs in the Indus Valley Civilization: Lessons learnt for new designing', Reinventing Architecture and Interiors: the past, the present and the future, IE International Conference.

Pondicherry Past and Present (10 February 2000) 'French Buildings', Domestic Architecture [website]. Retrieved from: http://www.ifpindia.org/ecrire/upload/digital_database/Site/Pondi/data/part_2_2.html#header (accessed 29 March 2012)

Prokerala (2005) 'Kerala Climate', Kerala [website]. Retrieved from: http://www.prokerala.com/kerala/climate.htm (accessed 19 March 2012)

Raymond, A. (2011) *Golconde.* Pondicherry: Sri Aurobindo Book Distribution Agency.

Steadman, P. (2006) 'Why are most buildings Rectangular?' *Architectural Research Quarterly*, Vol. 10, No. 2, pp. 119–130.

Des LAUBSCHER, Ingrid LEUJES

CHAPTER 10
DESIGN INTERVENTION FOR SOCIAL UPLIFTMENT

The Rebirth of Democracy and Freedom – A Role for Design

In 1994, the first democratic election was held in South Africa. The African National Congress (ANC) came into power and Nelson Mandela, an ANC activist who had spent 28 years incarcerated as a political prisoner, became the President of South Africa. South Africans of all races were euphoric at the prospect of equal quality of life for all citizens. In this regard, Chief Justice Pius Langa (2005) stated that:

> When the Constitution was adopted in 1994, a new order was established in South Africa that brought about an end to oppression and authoritarianism. The new Constitution was founded on the values of human rights, freedom, dignity, non-racism, non-sexism and the rule of law. An open society was created with government based on the will of the people and in which every citizen is equally protected by law.[1]

Political equality, however, does not equate to economic, cultural and social equality. Despite the many improvements made by the ANC government such as the reconstruction and development of housing and the growth of the black middle class, for example, there are those who have been left behind in the move to improve welfare for all: and as Roger Southall points out, 26 per cent of South Africans remain unemployed.[2] Even if this number is halved by 2014, as the ANC aims to achieve, 35 per cent will still be living under the breadline because many wage earners support an average of six people.[3] As Southall indicates, the vast majority of the very poor are

Black Africans and *Coloureds* who continue to live in townships – underlying this are issues of education.[4]

Southall discusses the 'division and dissent within the ruling party itself over the crisis in education' and highlights 'popular protests against perceived failures in "delivery" by provincial and local government.'[5] Such issues remain major causes for concern, to which Devan Pillay adds global concerns over the economy by underlining that South Africa is not isolated from the global crisis of capitalist growth and that, in fact, 'we are a microcosm of the world's crisis'.[6] All of this indicates that there is still much work to be done to improve the quality of life for many South Africans, particularly in creating a quality environment. That this was the initial intention of the ANC can be seen in the following selected excerpts from the Bill of Rights (1996):

1. The Bill of Rights is a cornerstone of democracy in South Africa. It enshrines the rights of people in our country and affirms the democratic values of human dignity, equality and freedom.

2. The state must respect, protect, promote and fulfil the rights in the Bill of Rights.[7]

3. Everyone has the right:

    (a) to an environment that is not harmful to their health and well-being; and

    (b) to have the environment protected, for the benefit of present and future generations, through reasonable legislative and other measures that

        i.   prevent pollution and ecological degradation;

        ii. promote conservation; and

        iii. secure ecologically sustainable development and the use of natural resources while promoting justifiable economic and social development.[8]

Developing the role of design in attaining these goals, John Jones views it as 'an organic process centred on, and defined by, the participation of the people intended to use it'.[9] Along similar lines, Arnold Wasserman describes design as 'the integration of art and technology… that serve human needs'.[10] Increasingly, international bodies are defining it in the same vein. The International Federation of Interior Architects/Designers (IFI), for example, calls for designs that enhance the quality of life by providing both dignity and pride, and that upgrade the standard of life for all.[11] However, in what is often termed our *commodity culture*, the poor are not usually included in the 'all of humanity' definition and are not of interest to designers – unless funded, for instance, by the government. Yet, as the IFI Declaration of 2011 suggests: 'it is for Humanity, our intimate client, that we design and shape the spaces that shape the human experience.'

According to these definitions and stated aims, design has to be viewed as a key component of any attempt at creating the healthy social and physical environments outlined in the new South African Constitution. It is thus logical to direct design interventions towards people in need of an improvement in the quality of their lives, even if they cannot afford the fees of a designer. These ideas underlie some of the arguments put forward at the ERA 05: World Design Congress in Copenhagen. In particular, they were central to the work of DOT (Designers of Today), a group of young Danish designers who spent five per cent of their working time designing for the needy without charging a fee.[12] These were ideas that would manifest themselves in the South African context at Greenside Design Center through its *10% Programme*.[13]

The *10% Programme* – Community and Education

Partly in response to the Government's call for higher education to have a greater impact on social transformation, Greenside Design Center's management took the decision to go ahead with this experimental educational community-engagement programme in 2005. In April 2004, the Council on Higher Education (CHE) had issued guidelines and instructions for a set of Criteria for Institutional Audits. This was organised through the Higher Education Quality Committee (HEQC) – a permanent committee of the CHE. Criterion 18 of this audit document lays down guidelines for community engagement in higher education in South Africa and it was specifically in response to this requirement that the *10% Programme* was formulated. It states:

Quality related arrangements for community engagement are formalised and integrated with those for teaching and learning, where appropriate, and are adequately resourced and monitored. The measures by which it is determined that the above criterion is met are:

- Policies and procedures for the quality management of community engagement

- Integration of policies and procedures for community engagement with those for teaching and learning and research, where appropriate

- Adequate resources allocated to facilitate quality delivery in community engagement

- Regular review of the effectiveness of quality related arrangements for community engagement.[14]

Although community engagement is specifically mentioned in the CHE documentation, no project of the size, complexity and ambition of the *10% Programme* has, to our knowledge, been undertaken by any other private education provider locally or internationally.[15] In 2009, it received the International Federation of Interior Architects/ Designers (IFI) 'Design For All Award' in recognition of its 'excellence in design in the service of humanity'. This award allowed us to spread the idea of *design intervention in the interest of the under privileged* and a dedicated *10%* section of our website now also facilitates the dissemination of the project and its principles. The website explains the intentions of the *10% Programme* and details all the projects done thus far which are available free to other institutions for downloading.[16]

10% involves students and lectures spending 10 per cent of the academic year, which equates to approximately four weeks, on community design projects. Projects to be tackled are agreed upon by lecturers but are often proposed in outline by students and members of different communities. Students sign up to the projects that interest them and, after some necessary reshuffling, cross-disciplinary groups are formed and assigned to available lecturers and projects.[17] Throughout, and upon completion of the project, each group presents its work to the community, the whole GDC student body and its academic staff. The intention is to ensure that it becomes a learning experience for all.[18]

Early on, students are warned to listen to and record community peoples' problems and their ideas for solutions, rather than being enticed into a 'we know better' attitude which often predominates in standard designer–client relationships. In this sense, our approach is intended to echo arguments put forward by Bruce Mau who states: 'When we use the term "we", we don't mean designers as separate from clients, or as some extraordinary class of powerful overseers. We mean "we" as citizens collectively imagining our futures. It is critical that the discussions go beyond the design fields themselves and reach out to the broadest audience, to the people directly affected by the work of designers'.[19]

The idea is that the design studio becomes a research laboratory for students and lecturers to address a specific community's needs. The projects contained within the programme vary enormously, from designing community centres in under-developed areas, to looking at how design can add value to children's games, to examining how the lives of animals at the Johannesburg Zoo can be improved through the development of toys and structures. The lecturers, as project leaders and participating designers, allow their groups to self-direct their research, employ their design processes and develop their own design solutions; and, in this sense, the projects become opportunities for students to develop their own research and design interests, and also to work in a team.

The teams consist of the clients (members of the community), students from different design disciplines, different levels of study and different cultural backgrounds.[20] The aim of this mixture is to keep students open minded by exposing them to different ideas and viewpoints. This not only assists students in the development of their projects but also in their relationships with their community. The premise is that the community-engagement programme will produce designers who are capable of testing their design solutions against concrete problems and, eventually, producing solutions for 'the real world' as it manifests itself in South Africa.

From a purely educational perspective, these projects instigate what is, in essence, action learning – a notion defined by Reg Revans.[21] It was developed for the teaching of managers but has subsequently attracted the interest of educators as well and is, in basic and general terms, a form of learning-by-doing.[22] Beyond that, however, this system is also premised on the argument that solving a problem or taking advantage of an opportunity should have important consequences, if deep learning is to take place. It is also premised on the idea that consultation amongst peers facing the same problems or opportunities is more likely to induce learning because the people involved bring different experiences to the table and thus provide a broader range of ideas and skills.[23]

Not only are students engaging in action learning in terms of design, but in most of the projects undertaken, they learn also how to realise their designs through building, making and finding sponsorship. The students, along with the clients, make elements, keep costs minimal and actually construct their design projects in ways that sometimes resemble Walter Segal's *self-build* houses.[24] Colin Ward, on the Walter Segal Trust website, describes house construction using the Segal method as requiring minimal expertise and, as a result, it enables people to build their own houses in an ecologically sound and financially affordable way.[25]

This is an important aspect of the *10% Programme* and, early on in the project-development stage, students and clients must determine what resources are available and how these resources might influence design decisions. Generally, with projects of this nature, groups need to remain cognisant of the fact that funding is very limited and that this influences the kinds of design interventions that can take place. The groups are encouraged to look for sustainable design solutions, which almost inevitably mean sourcing materials on site or in the near vicinity.

Another important factor that they must consider is the fine tuning of the brief to suit the specifics of the problem dealt with, once all the information available is gleaned from discussions with the community and the initial research is complete. Once finished, however, these projects do not come to an end. In line with GDC's interest in sustainable design, the projects are run over a few years to ensure enduring relationships with community partners and to ensure that the research our groups generate is archived in our library. The aim in this regard is to build up a resource for community-based design work for future generations of design students and lecturers at GDC, and other national or international institutions.

10% – A Case Study

One example of the *10%* design projects to be found in this resource is entitled *Street Hawkers* and was completed in 2011. The name reflects the fact that members of this enterprise were originally informal traders or, as we have come to know them in South Africa, hawkers. *Street Hawkers* were made aware of the *10%* project through Kagiso Mabele, a past GDC student who dropped out during his first year of study due to lack of funding, and Jabulani Ngwenya, a student sponsored by GDC who ultimately obtained a BA Degree in Interior Design. They approached GDC for help in developing their enterprise which they referred to as a *concept shop*. Des Laubscher, Onica Lekuntwane and Jennifer Kopping, lecturers at GDC, evaluated the proposal and a decision was taken to include it as one of the eight projects to be completed during the 2011 *10% Programme*.[26]

Figure 1: View of Dube from the station showing the back of the taxi rank to the right.
Photograph by Kagiso Mabele.

Figure 2: The Shop interior showing recycled movable shelving.
Photograph by Kagiso Mabele.

Street Hawkers is located in the suburb of Dube, in Soweto (an acronym for South Western Township). Soweto was created during the Apartheid era in conjunction with the Group Areas Act – a law that sought to segregate South Africa's various racial groups. Thanks to its close proximity to Johannesburg, the economic hub of South Africa, Soweto is also the most metropolitan township in the country and sets trends in politics, fashion, dance and music; most of the eleven official languages of South Africa can be heard on the streets. The actual shop is ideally located to catch passing trade as the Dube Railway Station entrance is diagonally opposite and there is a taxi rank on the opposite side of the street. Thus, there are plenty of potential clients passing by daily (Figure 1).

Initially, students were required to come up with design solutions that could be used by the *Street Hawkers* in their attempts to find appropriate sponsors for the realisation of the project. The design presentations thus needed to be put together in such a way as to show stakeholders and possible funders what was possible through good design. As it turned out, the students also found sponsorship, although this was not required by the brief. Most importantly, however, the mandate for the project required that the students took an empathic approach to their community.

Jennifer Kopping quotes the Harvard Business Design School as saying, 'empathy is the ability to imagine the feelings, attitudes and belief systems of others... "Empathic design" is a term that is used in the business context as a technique for developing ideas and collecting information for product development.' She goes on to quote the Harvard Business School as stating that:

> The techniques of empathic design – gathering, analysing, and applying information gleaned from observation in the field – they are familiar to top engineering/design companies and to a few forward thinking manufacturers, but they are not common practice. Nor are they taught in marketing courses as they are more akin to anthropology than marketing science. In fact, few companies are set up to employ empathic design: its techniques require unusual collaborative skills that many organisations have not developed. Market researchers generally use text or numbers to spark ideas for new products, but 'empathic designers' use visual information as well. Traditional researchers are generally trained to gather data in relative isolation from other disciplines whereas empathic design demands creative interactions among members of an interdisciplinary team.[27]

Kopping further quotes Dev Patnaik, founder and chief executive of the growth strategy firm Jump Associates and author of *Wired to Care: How Companies Prosper When They Create Widespread Empathy*:

> Companies prosper when they're able to create widespread empathy for the world around them... Every one of us understands empathy on an individual level: the ability to walk outside of ourselves and walk in someone else's shoes, to get where they are coming from, to feel what they feel. Widespread empathy is about getting every single

person in an organisation to have a gut-level intuition for the people who buy their products and services (the folks who really matter).[28]

Empathic design techniques used for business can also be applied by designers and, in every *10%* project, this is underlined. In this case, students were working with the Dube community and their client the *Street Hawkers*, and so using empathetic design techniques meant that they did not impose any of their design ideas and solutions on the client, but rather interacted, observed, analysed, listened, gathered data, felt and imagined what their client and the community wanted and needed. In a sense the students were thoroughly documenting what existed and then tasked themselves with the challenge of meeting the specific needs they found.

The first few days of the project were spent in brainstorming sessions with members of the community and their client. As a starting point, the group visited the site and took photographs of all aspects and details they could find, without necessarily prejudging their relevance. Upon further discussion and thought, however, eight issues that could be dealt with through design interventions were identified. These were translated into spaces and refined to six. Consequently, since its inception in 2010, the *Street Hawkers* concept shop has been divided into six very specific spaces that correlate to these issues. Some of these spaces were outdoors while others were indoors and were described by the students as follows:

- The Shop

This is the main building and the point of business which generates the most profit for the Street Hawkers. The shop uses shift crates as shelving and has boxed shelving along one wall (Figure 2).

- The Gallery

The Gallery is actually just one wall within the shop. It serves as an area used to exhibit artworks by various local artists. This is an initiative that was identified by the client as a means to create awareness about art in the community. It also gives artists in and around Dube a platform to display and sell their work.

- The Design Studio

This is a very small space, the size of a double couch placed behind the entrance door of the shop. It is used for brainstorming and coming up with design ideas. However, because of lack of equipment available for drawing, and the lack of a drawing board, it has not been a very functional space in practice.

- The Tattoo Parlour

The shop area leads into a small room, which is essentially a wide corridor, that is used as a Tattoo Parlour. Tattoos are popular and help promote the Hip Hop and street culture the Street Hawkers are trying to promote in and around Dube.

The outdoor spaces were described as follows:

• The Entertainment Area

The Entertainment Area is accessed from the street as well as from the store and the backdoor of the Tattoo Parlour. It is where Hip Hop and various other musical events take place. The *Street Hawkers* have their own band and host other bands that play various types of music. This is a major source of income for the Hawkers with an average of three hundred people converging on this space to attend weekend events. The entrance fee charged is 10 SA Rand (equivalent to approximately 1 Euro). They also sell food and drinks during these events and this too provides important income.

• The Art Studio

A section of the Entertainment Area is used as an Art Studio. Saturday-morning art classes, called the 'Build South Africa Initiative', are held for the children of the community and have an average of ten pupils per class. The Art Studio is a small space but is extremely popular among the children of the community and is part of the *Street Hawkers*' drive to promote art and design in the community. This is seen by the *Street Hawkers* as an opportunity to uplift the community and provide children with positive forms of expression.[29]

After having identified, through extensive conversations with the clients and community leaders, the concrete design requirements of the project, the students divided into groups to come up with proposals for each of these areas. Common to all the areas to be designed was the need to improve and upgrade space usage. The Shop Group deduced that the entire building was in need of renovation and improvements and this included renovations to the roof, flooring and walls. Furthermore, they identified that improvements to the electricity and plumbing systems were essential.

A more specific problem was the question of storage and display. In response to this, the Shop Group proposed using a simple wooden modular structure with cool drink crates attached to it. It could be conveniently used as storage or display depending on the given need at a given time. The structure could also have other uses such as, for example, housing the till or as a DJ booth when carried into the outdoor entertainment space. The use of moveable shelving and found objects such as paint tins for further storage also provided a solution to the same problem that was both ecologically sound and economically efficient.

Another good example of the use of found materials implemented by this group was the use of a large tree stump found on site that was 'converted' into a display sculpture. This allowed members of the community to carve both messages and voids into the trunk so as to communicate and create spaces for display and storage. In order to encourage passers-by to 'hang out', which is in keeping with the street culture that the store is promoting, the design team also proposed adding a balustrade at the edge of the pavement directly outside the shop front which people could sit or lean on, and converse.

The Shop Group also decided to work on the branding for the shop in terms of the logo and signage of the street façade. Because of the position of the store in relation to the train station and the taxi rank, the *Street Hawkers Concept Shop* could, if well branded, benefit from its visible location. The final solution for the logo was a combination of letters and a hawk image that were made into stencils for spray painting. The use of the logo and the overall branded image was repeated in the employment of rubber stamps for use on all stationary that also allowed individuals to write their names in the space provided.

The Gallery Group faced similar challenges with regard to space, storage, display and lighting. These were exacerbated, however, by the very small area that the Gallery occupied: one wall within the store. The proposed system was a combination of retractable shelves and brackets that could be easily made by the clients and, to this end, the students also produced a graphic instruction manual to explain how the bracket mechanism was to be constructed. The shelves fold out when they are needed to display objects and fold back against the wall when not in use.

This group was also faced by the problem of inadequate lighting. It responded by recommending the installation of track lighting for reasons of both flexibility and economy. Low-voltage spotlights were used to create an 'ambiance' that would complement, enhance and highlight the art work. The *Street Hawkers* also wanted to gain more recognition and awareness among the local community for the art space and the artists and, to achieve this, the students produced graphic designs for posters, business cards, T-shirts, price tags and letterheads. A consignment form was also designed which could be given by exhibiting artists to prospective buyers. The aim was to promote good business practice and professional relations.

The Design Studio Group was faced with a different issue. While the *Street Hawkers* are designers, and this is something they really wanted to promote, there was not enough space to allocate a separate area for design activities. Consequently, this group decided to design a fully mobile and multifunctional design desk that could be stored when not in use or, alternatively, be used for display purposes until needed. The desk included storage space, a light box and a flat surface to be used as a drawing and writing surface. Modular cubes for seating, product display and storage were also designed for this area and the prototypes were painted with iconic international figures that would appeal to the followers of Soweto street culture.

This group also designed stationary that could be employed by any designer who might want to use the space. It included business cards and letterhead with the corporate logo designed by the Shop Group. The students addressed the issue of creating public awareness of the *Street Hawkers Concept Store* by creating a Facebook page that is used as a platform to keep the community and the public at large informed about the store's events. The creation of the Facebook page was also a way of tapping into the tourist audience so as to expand regional, national and international awareness about Soweto street culture and the *Street Hawkers* in particular.[30]

The group charged with coming up with solutions for the Tattoo Parlour also had many

Figure 3: The Tattoo Parlour showing the screen and the skateboard shelves.
Photograph by Kagiso Mabele.

Figure 4: The Stage in the Entertainment Area.
Photograph by Kagiso Mabele.

issues to address. Serious renovations to the space were needed to repair the uneven floor, fix the ceiling and install running water – work which was carried out by students and members of the community. The space was also very confined and needed storage, shelving and display units. More importantly, there was no privacy and the space did not meet the hygiene and cleanliness standards needed for a tattoo parlour. Furthermore, the Tattoo Parlour would also be required to double up as a backstage facility for the Entertainment Area, as access to the outdoor entertainment area from the shop was through this space (Figure 3).

The group addressed the issue of space and privacy by designing screens to separate sections of the parlour for tattoos and body piercing. The flexible screens could also be folded away if necessary and placed in different positions to cordon off different areas. They could also be used as a backdrop for the stage in the Entertainment Area. The group was determined to create sustainable and cost-effective design solutions and, to this end, a prototype was made of the proposed screen using low-cost wooden frames covered in hessian. Patterns were woven into the hessian to enhance the *Street Hawkers*' promotion of community art and design and the frames were joined together with simple door hinges and screws.

The Tattoo Parlour Group also proposed an innovative shelving solution using old skateboards, which tied in with the overall image of the *Street Hawkers*. Should the space be needed for other functions, the products could be removed and the skateboards folded towards the wall to free up the wall and create a little more space in this very small room. Another important design consideration was to install a sink with running water in this area, along with sanitary bins which allowed for the disposal of waste products such as the needles used in the tattooing. This was of course essential to improve the hygiene standards of the parlour.

The Entertainment Area is the largest exterior space of the store and, as already mentioned, the monthly Hip Hop and other musical events are held here. It posed some of the most challenging problems to the designers as the outside floor was very uneven and the concrete was crumbling, allowing a live electrical conduit to be exposed. In places there was in fact no concrete at all, only sand. The first step was to level the floor and redirect the electrical conduit safely within a newly laid concrete floor; something done by a local construction team that donated their services to the project (Figure 4).[31]

This area includes the backstage zone, stage, barbeque, bar facilities, a changing room, toilet facilities and adequate storage – a challenge for all eight groups involved in this project. Furthermore, it includes a new canopy as the space is open to the elements and had to be designed in such a way as to ensure safety and adequate crowd control because of the large numbers that fill the space during events.[32]

The students decided to design a fixed stage adjoining the Tattoo Parlour (which doubles as the backstage area). It was designed to have lockable storage units below it where large equipment such as amplifiers and portable lighting units could be stored,

Figure 5: Bar area with painting behind.
Photograph by Kagiso Mabele.

Figure 6: Children painting their art-studio wall.
Photograph by Kagiso Mabele.

and has a permanent roof structure constructed from beams and corrugated iron. From a safety perspective, the design includes ropes and bollards to keep the crowd from invading the stage area and there is an entrance gate, constructed of sheet metal, that leads directly into the street. It was proposed that this be painted with blackboard paint to allow for the chalk-paint advertising and marketing of upcoming events. In addition to all this, there is also an under-cover bar area outside with under-counter drink storage, barbeque and other food-storage facilities which is placed next to this entrance so as to double up as the ticket sales point (Figure 5).

The main challenges facing the Art Studio Group overlapped with those of the Entertainment Area: to level the floor space, cast a new concrete slab and to design a roof structure so that the space could be used in all weather conditions. Furthermore, the group had to cater for the lack of electrical supply to the area and provide furniture for activities that took place on the floor. Furthermore, they also had to find ways of trying to get sponsorship for art materials. Their design outcomes included the use of recycled items such as buckets for chairs, as well as crates for storage and display. They also designed games made from recycled materials and constructed a magnetic board with magnets in bottle tops, each one of which had letters of the alphabet painted on them. The children could make all the games from recycled materials and take them home after classes. In line with all our sustainable goals, they could basically make their own toys (Figure 6).

The Street Hawkers Concept Store – A Summary

To sum up the project as a whole we need to take a backward step through time. At the end of each week, the six groups each had to demonstrate their progress through presentations made to all the other groups of students, the lecturing staff, members of the community and the *Street Hawker* clients themselves. Each of these groups gave critical feedback that helped in solving problems and redefining design solutions, and ensured that constant checks were made regarding the sustainability and cost-effectiveness of the proposals – something that was essential if the projects were to be later carried out by the community.

Part of the final brief presented to the students was the creation of digital presentations that the *Street Hawkers* could take to sponsors or interested investors. The success of this was evident by the end of the second week, by which time the students had already found a property developer who was willing to sponsor all the building materials and supply skilled workmen to assist in the implementation of the renovations required. There was also a 10,000 SA Rand (1,000 Euro) cash donation from the same project developer.

The electrical work and maintenance required were also sponsored by a prominent electrical contracting firm and the Gallery Group decided to donate 100 SA Rand each towards printing the business cards, tags, letterhead and posters. There were also initiatives aimed at collecting art supplies for the children's art classes with one of the lecturer's, Onica Lekuntwane, making a set of bottle-cap magnets with the letters of the alphabet on them for the children using the Art Studio.

By the beginning of the fourth week, all the construction areas had been laid out and the building materials had been delivered to site. Construction for all areas began with emphasis placed initially on the major renovations required to the actual store, the stage and bar area, the art studio and the tattoo parlour, including the installation of a sink with running water. In the short span of four weeks the majority of the objectives for the project had been achieved and, on top of this, all incomplete details were included in the digital presentations which were handed to the *Street Hawkers* so that they could be completed when time and money became available.

The client and the community were extremely grateful for the efforts of the students for whom it was also an amazing and gratifying experience. They saw design being used as a significant tool in the improvement of a community that, just four weeks earlier, did not believe that design could play a role in improving the quality of their lives. Furthermore, for many of these students, this was their first experience of working in a disadvantaged community and it therefore broadened their perspective of living conditions in South Africa. It also helped build a certain understanding and cement bonds between the diverse range of people involved.

The fact that the students and clients managed to find considerable sponsorship illustrates the idea of community engagement, even in a country which is now perceived 'to be following international neoliberal trends rather than the socially egalitarian ethos which was at the heart of the historical mission of the ANC.'[33] In this regard, it is also interesting to mention some of the institutional benefits that the *10%* community programme brings to the Greenside Design Center – a privately run institution. Firstly, it allows the institution to forge new partnerships within the broader community and exposes staff and students to situations that are both challenging and rewarding. It also helps remove the rigid staff–student hierarchy that can sometimes stifle creative thinking.

Furthermore, through the documenting and archiving of projects annually, it also creates a huge resource for future collaboration with particular communities and other institutions. Because of the nature of the *10% Programme* and the way it is structured, it has also made our institution a leader in community-development curriculum design in South Africa. It aids in the professional development of staff in the teaching and learning environment by testing our teaching methods against real problems and allows us to guide students towards an understanding of real and meaningful design. It obviously also brands GDC as a champion committed to using design as a decisive tool to uplift the quality of life for all.

Moreover, the nature of these projects means that the members of a group lose their 'titles' and become accountable members of 'society', each sharing a common problem. The skills, knowledge, values and attitudes of each individual become emphasised in this process and it is hoped that the *10% Programme* will inspire self-directed, life-long learners who will continue making contributions to community through design. In other words, we hope we are producing the socially responsible professional designers so desperately needed in South Africa today.

Notes

[1]   Langa, P. (2005) Foreword in R. Ranger, P. Thornley & S. Schoolman (eds), *The Making of Constitution Hill.* Rosebank (SA): Penguin.

[2]   Southall, R. (2010) From short-term success to long-term in decline. In: J. Daniel, P. Naidoo, D. Pillay & R. Southall (eds), *New South African Review 2010: Development or Decline?* Johannesburg, (SA): Wits University, p. 9.

[3]   Ibid., p. 13.

[4]   'Black African', 'Coloured', 'Indian' and 'White' are the terms used by the government to distinguish between racial groups, terms inherited from the Apartheid era but now referring to cultural groupings rather than biological similarities and differences. Townships were created by the Nationalist Government to ensure that Blacks and Whites lived separately from each other. Townships, occupied by Blacks, were significantly distant from cities and towns occupied by Whites and living conditions were considerably lower. For example, it was only after the student riots in 1976 that electricity started to become available in the townships.

[5]   Ethel Hazelhurst reports that according to Gill Marcus, the Reserve Bank governor, South African teachers are paid highly by international standards but that numeracy and literacy are amongst the lowest in the world. Hazelhurst, E. (2012, October 15) Teacher salaries and learner numeracy do not add up. *Star Business Report.*

[6]   Pillay, D. (2010) South Africa and the eco-logic of the global world. In R. Ranger, P. Thornley & S. Schoolman (eds), *Number Four: The Making of Constitutional Hill*, New York, NY: Penguin Global, p. 33.

[7]   Preliminaries of the Bill of Rights. *The Bill of Rights of the Constitution of the Republic of South Africa. Government Gazette* (No. 17678) 1996.

[8]   Section 24, Chapter 2, 'Environment', *The Bill of Rights of the Constitution of the Republic of South Africa*, Ibid.

[9]   Jones, C. (1992) *Design Methods.* New York, NY: John Wiley & Sons, p. xvi.

[10] Wasserman, A. (2005) The New Design. *INDEX MAGAZINE* [sn].

[11] Declaration (2011) *The International Federation of Interior Architects/Designers. Retrieved from:* www.ifiworld.org

[12] DOT, Designers of Today, a group of young professional Danish designers, aims to reassess the role of design by engaging in necessary charitable work. Dot presented their idea at a workshop linked to the ERA conference in Copenhagen in 2005. Their website (www.designersoftoday.org) has since become defunct.

[13] Greenside Design Center is a private education provider, which offers degrees and honours degrees in interior, graphic and multimedia design. Retrieved from: http://designcenter.co.za/

[14] Council on Higher Education, *Criteria for Institutional Audits* [sn]. Retrieved from: www.che.ac.za/documents/d00006/

[15] Cumulus International Association of Universities and Colleges of Art, Design and Media established working groups at its Projecting Design 2012 conference in Santiago. One of these groups was entitled *The Sustainability Group.* In this instance, social

sustainability was included in the understanding of the word. Retrieved from: www.cumulusassociation.org

[16]   This information is available at: http://designcenter.co.za/news-and-events/10-percent/

[17]   GDC usually runs eight projects for different communities within the four-week community engagement period. Any student can bring a proposal to the institution which is then brought before the Community Engagement Committee, consisting of various academic staff from all disciplines, who evaluate and decide which projects are most worthy of engaging with. This part of the process allows for any individual or group to bring proposals to the committee for approval provided that a community with needs has been identified. Once all eight projects are approved by the committee, general briefs are written for each group and these are refined as each group is tasked to further identify needs of the given community. This is done through an inclusive process that starts with interviewing specific members of the community, particularly community leaders and others who are actively involved, to determine how, through collaboration, changes can take place.

[18]   Similar projects on 'Design for Social Innovation' are run internationally and are showcased in DESIS (Design for Innovation and Sustainability) NETWORK showcase projects on Design for Social Innovation. The projects showcased were similar in nature to GDC projects and GDC showcased one of its *10%* projects at the 2012 event in Santiago, Chile. For more information, see: www.desis-showcase.org

[19]   Mau, B., Leonard, J., & The Institute without Boundaries (2004) *Massive Change*. London: Phaidon, p. 18.

[20]   In this sense, the *10%* projects echo Wasserman's comments that 'designers, together with practitioners from technical and scientific fields formerly associated with design, migrate freely across design disciplines.' Wasserman, A. (2005) The new design in *INDEX MAGAZINE* [sn].

[21]   Revans, R. (2011) *The ABC of Action Learning*. Farnham: Gower Publishing, pp. 4–19.

[22]   The nature of design education in general as a process of learning by doing is covered extensively in the work of Donald Schön which forms the template of much design teaching, including that at GDC, today. See: Schön, D. (1987) *Educating the Reflective Practitioner*. San Fransisco: Jossey-Bass.

[23]   Revans, R., op. cit.

[24]   Mackean, J. (1989) *Learning from Segal: Walter Segal's Life, Work, and Influence*. Michigan: Birhauser.

[25]   Ward, C., Walter Seal – Community Architect. Retrieved from: *http://www.segalselfbuild.co.uk/about.html*

[26]   Another project from this programme was presented by Corlia de Swart, a lecturer at GDC, at an interdisciplinary conference at Oxford University entitled *Animal Enrichment: A Playful Tool*, 2012. For this project the 'community' selected were animals at the Johannesburg Zoo whose health was deteriorating due to a lack of exercise.

[27]   Leonard, D., & Rayport, J. (1997 November–December) Spark Innovation Through Empathic Design. *Harvard Business Review*, 75 (6), pp. 102–113.

[28]   Patnaik, D., Innovation Starts with Empathy. Retrieved from: http//designmind.frogdesign.com

[29] It must be remembered that during the Apartheid era no art or design was taught to children in the townships and little has changed in this regard during the nineteen years of democracy in South Africa.

[30] www.Facebook.com/streethawker.conceptstore

[31] At this point, the father of one of the students donated a construction team and building materials thereby extending the notion of community interaction one stage further.

[32] The Entertainment Group also had to redesign the area used for the skate park, which adjoins this area.

[33] Southall, R., From short-term success to long-term decline, op. cit., pp. 18–19.

Bibliography

Council of Higher Education Publication (2004) *Criteria for Institutional Audits*. Retrieved from: www.che.ac.za/documents/doooo61

Daniel, J. (2010) South Africa and the eco-logic of the global capitalist crisis. In Daniel, J., Naidoo, P., Pillay, D., & Southall, R. (eds) *New South African Review 2010: Development or Decline?* Johannesburg SA: Wits University Press.

Hazelhurst, E. (2012, October 15) Teacher salaries and learner numeracy do not add up. *Star Business Report*.

Leonard, D., & Rayport, J. (1997 November–December) Spark Innovation Through Empathic Design. *Harvard Business Review*. 75 (6), pp. 102–113.

Mau, B., Leanord, J., & The Institute without Boundaries (2004) *Massive Change*. London: Phaidon.

Patnaik, D. [Sa] Innovation Starts with Empathy. Retrieved from: http//designmind.frogdesign.com

Ranger, R., Thornley, P., & Schoolman, S. (eds) (2006) *Number Four. The Making of Constitution Hill*. Rosebank, SA: Penguin.

Revans, R. (2011) *The ABC of Action Learning*. Farnham: Gower.

Schön, D. (1987) *Educating the Reflective Practitioner*. San Fransisco: Jossey-Bass.

Southall, R. (2010) From short-term success to long-term in decline. In J. Daniel, P. Naidoo, D. Pillay & R. Southall (eds), *New South African Review 2010: Development or Decline?* Johannesburg, SA: Wits University.

The Bill of Rights of the Constitution of the Republic of South Africa (1996) *Government Gazette* (No. 17678).

Georgios KARATZAS,
Nikos BELAVILAS

CHAPTER 11
ECONOMIC CRISIS AND REFORM – CONSEQUENCES IN PLANNING, ARCHITECTURAL PRACTICE AND EDUCATION

Economic Crisis and Reform

The first decade of the 2000s was an extremely interesting period for Athens, which repeatedly captured the world's attention for several reasons. The capital of Greece welcomed the mixed blessing of the Summer Olympic Games of 2004, was faced with major riots during December 2008 and became the focal point of the country's financial crisis; this latter event, igniting extensive protests and demonstrations culminating in the 'indignants' movement in the summer of 2011. Today, Athens is experiencing a severe deadlock: neglect and deterioration of the city centre; the establishment of immigrant ghettos; the severing of the social fabric; the decomposition of the middle class; the perceived breach of security; and increasing homelessness.

Over the past decade, the tradition established with the fall of the military dictatorship in 1974, of considering the city and its infrastructure as a 'public asset', has been overturned. This was most notable during the preparations for the Summer Olympics between 2000 and 2004, when a new emergency statutory framework for urban planning was introduced in the name of speed and efficiency. For the first time, public works, state property and enterprises of public interest were privatised. However, the end of the Games did not initiate a return to the former public status quo. On the contrary, the financial crisis that occurred a few years later promoted the 2004 'emergency' model to the position of permanent planning policy. More recently in 2010 and 2011, a series of new laws have been added to this which essentially abolish the state's position of primacy in urban planning decisions, eliminate public consultation at local-government level, and reduce environmental and archaeological controls. In short, the private sector has been allowed to establish land uses that have transgressed previous town-planning and environmental norms. At the same time, these laws transfer state land assets to the newly founded Asset Development Fund so as to contribute towards the reduction of the country's international debt. The consequences of this deregulation have been profound.

Politics, Economic Models, Law-making and the Evolution of Space Regulation Concepts

Urban space has always been inextricably linked to social, political and economic processes and phenomena. Planning as a 'science', for example, emerged as a way of addressing the variety of issues related to rapid and large-scale urbanisation. The complex system of institutions, processes and implementation tools it encompasses today is generally intended to produce policies and plans that serve the 'public interest'. On the other hand, however, planning can also be seen as a means to exercise power, as it has direct consequences on the economic, social, political and cultural life of the locality it concerns.

The history of planning as an exercise in control and power in Greece is different to that of other countries in the developed world. It is directly linked to the peculiarities of the Greek capitalist system and the resulting specifics of the urbanisation processes of Greek cities – which only really began after 1922[1] with the settlement of Greek refugees from Asia Minor. Until the end of the Second World War, most Greek cities did not possess large-scale manufacturing plants and were not subject to the pressures of industrial concentration. One consequence of this was that Modern Movement concepts concerning rational town planning had little impact on planning decision-making processes until quite late.

Up until the post-WWII period, there had been a number of proposals and regulatory plans for Athens which were deemed to be either fragmentary or not flexible enough to foresee demographic changes (as in the case of the settlement of the refugees resulting from the Greek–Turkish population exchange in the 1920s). Alternatively, they were simply seen as too unrealistic due to the meagre financial means available for their implementation. These plans for the city go back to the early nineteenth century but continued throughout the twentieth, with the last ones of note being the Spatial Plan and Program for the Capital City, by Doxiadis Associates, in 1976 (Figure 1) and the Athens Regulatory Plan of 1985.[2]

The post-war period, and especially the 1960s, marked the golden age of the Greek capitalist system and resulted in unprecedented economic growth and immense

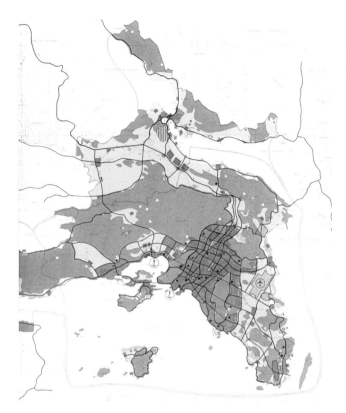

Figure 1: Spatial Plan
and Program for the
Capital City. Doxiadis
Associates (1976).

urbanisation. It was then that debates on the need for realistic planning were revived and several institutions were established to deal with the issue. The military junta (1967–1974) brought forward two laws that aimed to modernise the existing statutory framework,[3] both of which became active after the fall of the regime. Other laws were introduced a few years later, supplanting those of the junta and presenting the notion of 'regulatory plans that would be self-funded through their own implementation'.[4] Improper functioning of planning institutions and the non- or partial implementation of these plans, however, meant that it was not until 1985 that any real restrictions were imposed on land use or building construction.[5] The resulting chaotic framework was essentially one of *no control*, as it permitted a selective application of regulations.

The Athens Regulatory Plan (1985)

After the socialist party came to power in 1981, a new planning framework was introduced which was in tune with the new political agenda and prioritised processes of public participation and consultation.[6] It also promoted the concept of a more equitable distribution of the profit generated from the overvaluation of urban land after its inclusion into the city plan.[7] The Athens Regulatory Plan was made a state law in

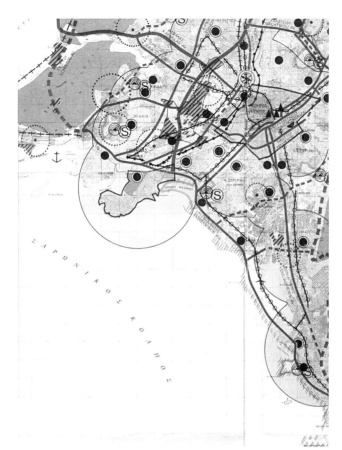

Figure 2: Aspect of the Athens Regulatory Plan. Ministry of Urban Planning, Ekistics and Environment (1985).

1985[8] and saw the introduction of the generalised application of local plans, both for cities and the rural areas surrounding them (Figure 2).[9] Some of the most important aims set out in the 1985 plan include:

a. The stabilisation of the urban population with a view to its gradual decrease

b. The control of the capital city's economic activity

c. The restraint of the territorial expansion of the city

d. The statutory protection of coastal areas and the prohibition of building activity along them

e. The implementation of effective land-use control

f. The organisation of a uniform transport system.[10]

Despite the introduction of this law, however, the 1985 domestic financial crisis brought the state to the brink of bankruptcy. This coincided with the European Economic

Community's shift towards neoliberal policies and the subsequent agreement of the member states on the liberalisation of markets, goods, services and capital. These two events led to the introduction of austerity measures and rendered any chance of obtaining the financial backing necessary for the regulatory plan practically impossible. In addition, prohibition of illicit building, as described in the regulatory plan, triggered a series of domestic reactions which further impacted negatively on the possibilities for its implementation.[11] Given this climate, it is no surprise that the 1985 plan was never fully implemented. It became a utopian goal for future planners and has become a standard pre-election pledge for politicians ever since.

Changes in Economic Principles: Towards a More Liberal Market Economy and the Olympics

The late 1980s and early 1990s saw the fall of the communist bloc and the failure of state-controlled capitalism. This led to the doctrine of the 'market economy' being seen as the only viable alternative and thus becoming the unquestionable context in which the Maastricht Treaty of 1992 was debated and passed. It represented a new stage in European integration and saw new limits placed on independent exchange and monetary policy at national levels. At the time, the Greek state made every effort to be incorporated into the core of this new European monetary system, despite the fact that major financial problems had already accumulated over the previous decades. As a result of these efforts, free-market economic practices and programs were implemented such as a reduction of the public deficit, general deregulation, privatisations of state-run corporations and the sale of state property.[12] All of this followed the widely propagated notion that the reason for the problems of the Greek economy was 'the wasteful and counterproductive expansion of the public sector'.[13]

The successful bid for the hosting of the 2004 Summer Olympics in 1997 was considered a rare opportunity for economic growth, on the one hand, and the incorporation of Greek cities into the global cities network on the other.[14] The recently adopted regulatory plan of 1985 did not, however, foresee the accommodation of activities and land uses associated with such a mega-event. Consequently, the already debilitated and weakened plan was unable to meet the new goals. However, since time was a critical factor for meeting the criteria of the 2004 candidacy file, the necessary interventions were realised without updating the existent regulatory framework. Furthermore, no attempt was made to compile a new plan that would meet the new demands but rather, an emergency law was adopted in 1999 for the planning of the Olympic facilities.[15] Its major objective was the reduction of the time and paperwork required for the realisation of infrastructure projects. Although it was referred to as an 'update' of the regulatory plan, in essence it was the quite opposite – it represented its abolition.

The hosting of the 2004 summer Olympics signified a new era in Greek planning history, and the emergency laws and statutes that followed marked a transition from *universal design* (which was until then considered to be the norm) to *strategic planning*. The implications, however, were more severe than just a shift in planning priorities, as the organisation of the summer Olympics deeply affected the overall structure of the

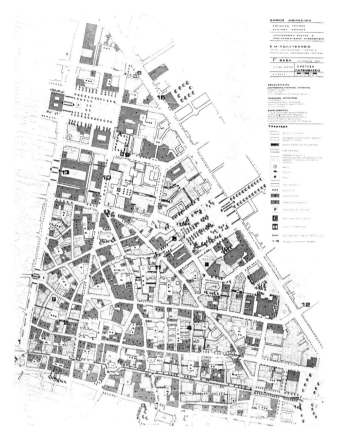

Figure 3: Aravantinos et al., Master Plan for the Historical Centre of Athens, Urban Research Laboratory, School of Architecture, NTUA (1996): Proposal.

state. Timely construction of the required infrastructure gave the necessary pretext for the adoption of (neoliberal) policies and, in that sense, the summer Olympics became a means to an end. That end was the adaptation to the neoliberal model and the gradual transformation of existing state structures. Greece, a small-scale and failing economy, already a core member of the European Union,[16] thus irreversibly changed its state structure so as to align with the established economic trends of the times.

Changes in State Structures and Priorities: From Protection from Private Misconduct to the Effective Development of State Property and the Olympic Legacy

During this period, several public organisations and institutions were forcibly incorporated into the private sphere and made into *sociétés anonymes* (S.A.). Such companies included the 'Public Properties Company S.A.'[17] which had a portfolio of 379 assets covering a total area of 7,000 hectares. These assets included hotels, marinas, beaches, mountain slopes and caves.[18] Another company was the 'Olympic Properties S.A.' which, prior to its 2011 merger, was responsible for the management, use and exploitation of many of the former Olympic venues at the end of the Games. Interestingly however, it was not subject to any parliamentary control and, at the end of the Games, the company proceeded to lease Olympic facilities to private entrepreneurial consortia that offered no benefit to the public whatsoever. Consequently, under the guise of turning Athens into a metropolitan tourist and investment centre, zones of uncontrollable private profit were gradually cemented throughout the city.[19]

In addition, several private or semi-private investment consortia claimed an unprecedented share in planning and decision-making processes during this period of 'reform', with Public and Private Partnerships (PPPs) being the most obvious.[20] Under the laws introduced to foment these partnerships, the project belongs exclusively to the private partner throughout the duration of the contract. The private partner is thus able either to rent it privately or to rent it back to the public sector, so that the latter can make it available to its citizens.[21]

Despite the tight schedule for construction, and the long-term consequences of the planning laws introduced in the build-up to the Games, a number of impressive buildings were constructed and important infrastructure projects realised.[22] However, after the Games many of these projects were simply put to use in private ventures such as the conversion of the Olympic Media Village into the *Athens Mall* – the first shopping centre of its kind in Athens.[23] The International Broadcasting Centre[24] was

Figure 4: N. Belavilas et al., Master Plan of Ellinikon Former Airport Metropolitan Park of Athens, Urban Environment Laboratory, School of Architecture, NTUA (2010): Proposal.

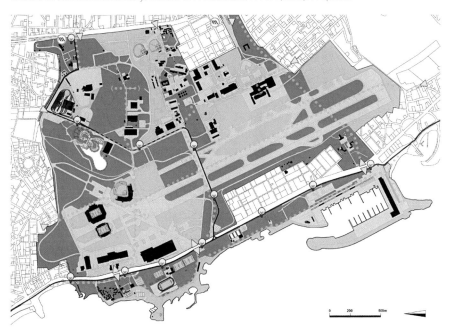

converted into another mall-type investment, *The Athens Golden Hall*, and is managed by the same company that controls the *Athens Mall*. The Agios Kosmas Sailing Centre became a marina for tourist and private yachts that restricted public access to the waterfront, while the disused 'Ellinikon', Athens' former airport, hosted a number of outdoor and indoor sporting events before becoming the subject of an international architectural competition for a public park in 2005.[25] This public project was never realised and, despite a local and national protest in favour of a public green scheme, Ellinikon is now up for full privatisation in an attempt to relieve the public debt (Figure 4).

Law No. 3894/2010 – The End of Planning

These attempts to move the Greek economy towards liberalism are underpinned by Law No. 3894/2010. This law on 'the acceleration and transparency of strategic investments' is more colloquially known as 'fast-track'. Its aim is to accelerate and simplify the necessary processes required for the realisation of large investment projects and is again premised on the idea that the existing bureaucratic system was responsible for limited investments in the Greek economy. In addition to reducing bureaucracy, 'fast-track' challenges existing planning practices previously hailed as successes in that, 'for reasons pertaining to the overriding public interest', it allows for exemptions from building controls and restrictions.[26,27] Furthermore, in order to make the investment climate as attractive as possible, all auxiliary works and services required to render the investment successful must be executed by the state (or the broader public sector) as a matter of priority. According to the (amended) civil servants' code, failure to do so even entails penalties and sanctions to individuals or relevant public bodies.[28,29]

All of this clearly loosened planning controls over a number of years. However, their effective abolition was ultimately achieved by the specification and implementation of the Special Integrated Development Plans of 2010.[30] This law unambiguously allows the government to overrule existing laws in favour of private development.[31] As with Law No. 3894/2010, these decisions are ratified by presidential decree following recommendations by the Ministry of Environment, Energy and Climate Change and by the Ministry of Infrastructure, Transport and Networks. Not only can they supersede older decisions, they can bypass parliamentary debate.[32] Recent legal provisions, then, enhance the possibilities of large-scale capital whilst virtually abolishing any planning controls or limitations on private developments. One may argue that planning, in traditional terms at least, is over. It certainly appears that urban transformation will not now follow the aspirations of parliament-controlled collective bodies but, rather, will be the result of the incidental flow of domestic and foreign capital.[33]

Changes in the Nature of the Architectural Profession in the Post-Olympic Period

Due to the almost exclusively touristic aims of the Olympic Games, the broader city centre and its 'everyday' neighbourhoods were neglected. The prioritisation of private interests over public needs, and the absence of public interventions with any social content, has resulted in the accumulation of structural social problems that are leading to the social disintegration of the city centre. Gradual population decline, the emergence of ghettos and an increase in vacant buildings all began to raise concern only three years after the Games. As a result, the dominant public discourse on downtown areas began to change. The formerly euphoric tone suddenly altered and fear and suspicion were propagated, primarily by the media, which described the effects of drug addiction, homelessness and illegal immigration in these areas in the grimmest of terms.[34]

Despite the clear contextual background to these issues, the dominant political discourse insists that the problems that exist are limited to specific building blocks and particular streets; and furthermore, that solutions are a matter of architectural and urban-regeneration projects. Three misconceptions are propagated by these arguments: that local issues are unrelated to broader ones, namely economic concerns; that law enforcement is a long-term solution; and of most interest in our context, that social problems demand physical and spatial solutions.[35] Although planning may have a role to play in solving these problems, these arguments divorce it from the deregulatory neoliberal policies that are causing the issues in the first place.

The Weakening of the Small Practice – and the Need to Adjust or to React

The recent changes to the dominant economic model and the planning system in Greece have not only resulted in the emergence of these social issues: they have also induced significant change in the nature and structure of commercial practices in recent years. Sole practitioners and small-scale offices have traditionally comprised the backbone of the local practising architectural community; and it is this scale of architectural practice that has been most directly affected by the changing situation. [36] While access to public projects has always been limited and difficult, in the current neoliberal climate it is practically non-existent; recent amendments to design and construction legislation clearly favour 'flexible' large architectural studios over 'unproductive' and 'cumbersome' small practices. Indeed, the terminology used in government policy documents demonstrates this in its description of a preference for the 'establishment of groups and companies that will have permanent staff and will be able to undertake the complete study of a technical project'.[37]

In this context, in which the establishment of a minimum-fee structure has also been abolished, a large portion of the work currently carried out by sole practitioners is not related to architectural design at all. Many sole architects are now regulating and implementing the documentation of illicit buildings and undeclared flat spaces. It is an activity that has fallen to the small practices due to the small profit margins it offers and, in addition to reducing the income of architects, it also turns them into bureaucrats specialised in the implementation of the state's emergency tax measures. As such, it renders them 'ethically complicit' with private, semi-legal developments that, in many cases, contribute to the further deterioration of urban, rural and natural landscapes.

The entry of real-estate and land speculation into the reality of architectural practice at this level has undeniably induced ideological confusion – intentionally or not. Sole practitioners and small practices that wish to break free from the limits of this restricted professional activity are left with only one alternative: to align themselves with the aims of large-scale capital. The partnership between small professional formations and big businesses is particularly beneficial to the latter, as it provides the necessary moral and social legitimisation of their larger investment schemes – projects that are besieging mid-sized plots, or even whole areas, both inside and outside city limits. Whilst these projects are on a smaller scale than the aforementioned Olympic and strategic projects, they are equally motivated, in the long run, by private gain.

Of course, in this environment of limited professional potential, young architects and small practices may accept the opportunities offered by large investment schemes to develop their ideas, often in the context of particularly interesting projects involving neglected historic areas whose regeneration can have a profound community impact. One example of this is the project to regenerate the historical downtown areas of Keramikos and Metaxourgeio, led by the private consortium Oliaros. This privately led project has already restored several ageing properties and has acquired a large proportion of the derelict heritage stock. In addition, it claims it will develop more of its properties when the state has completed its part of the regeneration initiative, namely alterations to land-use definitions and the introduction of laws to limit traffic and allow for the pedestrianisation of walkways.

The aim of Oliaros is to redefine the existing character of the area by introducing a new cultural and urban identity model and, to this end, it has established an NGO that aims to attract community support.[38] Its communication strategy includes the organisation of artistic events, architectural competitions and urban-design studies, and has participated in research programmes with foreign universities. It also exerts pressure on local and central government institutions to include their independent proposals into various European programmes and broader planning strategies.

Noteworthy small practices have already joined forces with this group and have produced remarkable projects and studies. However, the tactics employed raise questions that relate to the broader role of both architecture and architects nowadays, as well as the necessity of such initiatives. The architectural community in Greece stands divided on this issue. Large-scale capital may be able to promote high-quality architecture, but such projects inevitably lose any claim to genuine grassroot origin and control, despite their alleged social aims, as in the case of Oliaros. Criticisms from architects opposing projects such as these focus on their gentrifying architecture, contemporary art and alternative lifestyle formula – a formula that often pushes poorer people out of the developed area as property values increase.

Whilst this type of project involves the adaptation of architects to their new conditions, there are examples of outright resistance to the advance of market economy practices as well. One such example is the case of a refugee housing complex in Alexandras Avenue – a group of eight functionalist buildings of great architectural and cultural significance which currently accommodate low-income dwellers and squatters. During the 1990s, the Ministry of Public Works and the Public Real Estate Corporation began expropriating individual apartments, gradually, so as eventually to gain ownership of four of the buildings in question.

Their ultimate aim was to demolish the whole complex and open the cleared plot to private development. However, a huge campaign began to save these buildings under the umbrella of conservation, as they are unique examples of modernism in the heart of Athens. Pro-preservation groups included local residents, various public bodies, the Association of Architects and the Athens School of Architecture. Pro-demolition groups included local and central government, and private investment companies that had already compiled development strategies for the broader area. Controversy over the future of the complex took many forms, including both court appeals and violent street clashes.

In 2003, the Central Council of Modern Monuments of the Ministry of Culture, in line with the local- and central-government views on the facilitation of private investment initiatives, proposed statutory protection for only two of the eight buildings of the complex. It was only due to the pro-preservation parties' appeal to the Council of State, and its subsequent decision to annul the Ministry of Culture's partial listing, that the totality of the complex remained intact. Immediately after the Council of State's decision, the Central Council of Modern Monuments re-examined the case and, in 2008, decided on the final and irreversible statutory protection of all eight buildings of the complex. Of course, the preservation and promotion of the complex is not yet certain but, as a listed monument, it is at least safe from demolition. This is an example of how the architectural profession and citizens themselves are standing directly against the neoliberal changes affecting planning and development in Athens through direct resistance and collective protest.

Dilemmas for Architectural Education in a Changing Reality

The question for architects is whether to oppose the demands of the new economic conditions or not. It is a question that divides the architectural community down the middle. One of the reasons for this split is perhaps the educational tradition in Greece and the emphasis it places on the social roles and social responsibilities of architects. This educational tradition, that has nurtured generations of students, is currently challenged from both within and without. The reasons for the challenge are the same as those affecting practice-deregulation and a neoliberal economy.

The door to neoliberalism in education has been opened by the government's attempts to remove article 16 from the Greek Constitution on the public and free-of-charge character of all levels of education – something that would almost certainly result in the establishment of private universities.[39] The establishment of private universities is a taboo in Greece as the possible introduction of tuition fees raises the question of the right of access to education. Furthermore, the models of private education that are being discussed promote a market-oriented education that links learning with 'useful knowledge' – a template that is considered as a diversion from the broader academic ideals that have traditionally underpinned the Greek education system.

Those ideals are, in general, an open-ended view of education as the endeavour to foment critical individuals with broad-based knowledge, skills and sensibilities. In architecture, this has meant the establishment of a broad and interdisciplinary curriculum that encompasses and reconciles elements of the humanities, the social and natural sciences, technology and the arts. It is the general view inside the academy that architectural education should have a holistic approach and be diverse. It should aim to develop the aesthetic and compositional ability of its students and ensure their acquisition of solid technical and design knowledge while, at the same time, facilitating their understanding of external fields such as sociology and psychology. Consequently, programs of study have been developed to cover areas such as architectural and urban design, landscape and environmental design, construction and building technology, town and regional planning, as well as the arts and the humanities.[40]

While the emphasis on the arts, humanities, construction and architectural design has long formed part of design education in Greece, the emergence of urban design, town and regional planning as subjects has been a more recent phenomenon. In particular, the gradual decline of post-war construction and building in the 1970s and 1980s induced reflection and critical thinking on the abrupt and uncontrolled transformation of the image, shape and functions of the city. This resulted in the introduction of wider aims for the architectural profession and education, and the curricula that evolved as a result moved along the following axes: the growing significance of humanities; the growing importance of technology and the evolution of fine arts; and the shift of the architectural focus from the object to the landscape – including the city.[41]

This interdisciplinarity and broad-based view of education are today being called into question as 'vocational teaching' is being given more priority as a way of meeting the alleged 'needs' of industry. Neoliberal ideological demands in architectural education, then, are not only questioning the financial model of education but also its curriculum. They seek to fragment the architectural discipline into separate fields of knowledge, with the parallel depreciation of some and promotion of others. As a result of this, for example, planning, building preservation, landscape architecture and interior design have been established as independent disciplines run in separate academic departments within universities, technological educational institutes and in private educational institutions.

The motives behind this are to be found in industry's desire to have specialist workers rather than broader critical thinkers. It results in the fragmentation of knowledge and a limited understanding of the range of issues related to architecture, planning and design in general – issues that often require an in-depth knowledge of disciplines such as economics, the arts and the social sciences. Specialised programs may provide qualified professionals in their particular science, but they fail to promote either integrated knowledge or the social responsibilities that were once at the heart of Greek architectural, planning and design education. These specialised programs could neutralise the ideological, political and social contents of education as an integrated whole.

Just at the moment when Greece needs its academics to be able to examine the problems created by the deregulation of the planning system, and by the economy at large, and the implications for the built environment, they are subject to the same forces that lead to short-term thinking and isolated, profit-orientated actions. It is a situation that limits the ability of the academy to respond, as it is busy defending itself and its model of learning. Despite this, universities are still responding. Debates are held, conferences are organised, papers are published and books are still written. More specifically, design projects are still set that encourage students to deal with social issues and think more broadly about what factors are at play.

Urban Design Student Projects at the National Technical University of Athens

If we consider student design projects in planning, for example, they still tend to place great importance on promoting the qualities of existing urban environments, detailed urban living analysis and the creation of infrastructures that may help a given region or area economically and socially. What is sought is the complete understanding of the relationship between parts and the whole; an understanding of built form and un-built voids; of the function, development and future prospects of existing building blocks and axes of communication; of the interrelationship between private and public domains; of the urban green and much more.

Projects are often directed to interventions of varying scales with the aim of linking the specific with the general both physically and more conceptually. In this context, students are encouraged to propose new forms of dwelling, commerce, recreation and workspaces, as well as to develop a deep understanding of local and metropolitan centres. Covering this range of factors foments cross-disciplinary thinking by addressing issues of architecture, planning and economics and is reinforced by working at different scales. In the context of projects set by the School of Architecture of the National Technical University of Athens, for example, the areas studied can range between 2 to 5 hectares in size and proposals are designed at various scales. As a result, students consider a whole range of issues and factors that influence the specifics of living. One example is a project for the former industrial zone of Agios Dionysios, Piraeus.

Ideas for the Regeneration of Agios Dionysios

Agios Dionysios is one of the fastest, most dramatically changing zones of the Piraeus port area. The area's contemporary identity was determined by two critical factors: the deindustrialisation that occurred during the 1980s and 1990s; and the re-adaptation of the port's industrial character to passenger-only use that began in the 1980s and was completed in 2003 with the relocation of commercial and customs activity to a new port to the west. As industrial plants closed down one after the other, Agios Dionysios gradually became a huge derelict brown-field area. Attempts to redefine its role were included in the Athens Regulatory Plan (1985), the Piraeus General Urban Plan (1988) and three specially compiled urban studies between 1992 and 1994.[42]

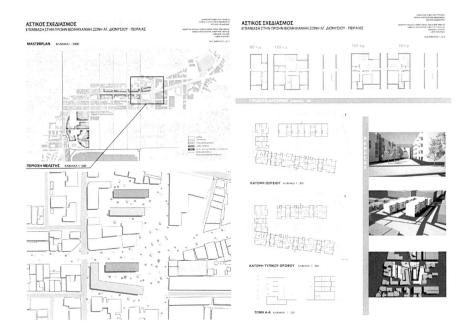

Figure 5: Interim presentation. Proposal in progress by students: D. Gkotsis, A. Pliakos and L. Zabensky, February 2012, School of Architecture, NTUA.

In the 1990s, shipping companies began to use the vacant buildings and plots on the water side of the port while other companies began to use vacant industrial buildings and plots further inland. This resulted in an informal mono-functional zone along the waterfront that became a 'barrier' with peculiar urban qualities and an uncertain future. A disused railway line also runs through the area and further separates the former industrial area, adding to the sense of urban fragmentation and exclusion that now characterises it (Figure 5).

The projects set for students were aimed at achieving both a functional and morphological regeneration of the area and, as a result, students were encouraged to introduce new uses and building forms so as to re-articulate the character and image of the area. They engaged with the site on two distinct but related levels: functional, economic and social restructuring; and formal and structural alterations to the particular built environment. The project aimed to focus on the axis along the disused railway tracks at a depth of one-to-two urban blocks with a chain of selected local interventions on four or five plots neighbouring the railway corridor. It aimed at incorporating new uses compatible to dwelling and reintegrating the railway corridor back into the urban fabric (by using it as a basis for a sustainable green strategy). Furthermore, it sought to devise measures that would relieve heavy traffic from and to the port, and to promote means of permeability through the area so as to reconnect the surrounding residential areas with the seafront.

Clearly then, a project like this is not divorced from the social and economic conditions currently faced by Athens or the country in general. It responds directly to them and does so in a way that reveals the importance placed on a global education – an education that allows students to think across scales and disciplines and to see questions of architecture and planning as integrated into a more complex socio-economic and cultural web. However, it is also premised on an awareness of the need for planning to exist as an organised and coherently controlled system that permits isolated problems to be tackled as part of a broader range of policies and plans.

Conclusions

This integration of education into a broader tapestry of socio-political issues is, in many ways, a microcosm of practice. Indeed, education in Greece is subject to many of the same pressures as the architecture and planning professions today. These pressures have led to the conversion of the emergency measures, implemented after the announcement of the successful 2004 Olympic bid, into a permanent model. They are also evident in the proposed measures intended to create a favourable climate for foreign investments – measures that essentially annul planning policy in order to prioritise investment aims. This change of focus has resulted in the degradation and abandonment of downtown areas and the creation of a form of unprecedented humanitarian crisis.

Furthermore, these pressures are seen in the depreciation of the traditional role of the architect, the favouritism shown towards large-scale professional groupings and the division of the architectural community regarding how to respond to the changing conditions. In education, they have led to the challenging of the roots of the existing educational tradition and its association of architecture with the arts, humanities and the social sciences. They even threaten the free-tuition model that lies at the bedrock of the Greek system. Whether these pressures will prevent architecture and planning from influencing the social and the political, and whether, as a result, these disciplines are doomed merely to reproduce the dominant neoliberal ideology, is yet to be seen.

Notes

[1]   The Convention Concerning the Exchange of Greek and Turkish Populations (1923) was signed in the aftermath of the Greek–Turkish war of 1919–1922 and provided for the simultaneous expulsion of Christians from Turkey to Greece and of Moslems from Greece to Turkey.

[2]   Briefly, we can mention the most notable plans concerning Athens, named after the institutional bodies or people who compiled them: i. the Kleanthis–Schaubert (1832) and its revision by ii. L. von Klenze (1834) which formed the basis for future plans to come; iii. the Stavridis committee (1860); iv. the S. Leloudas proposal (1919); v. the Kalligas committee (1924); vi. the Planning Service of the Municipality of Athens (1945); vii. the Ministry of Reconstruction proposals (1947); viii. the Athens-Ecumenopolis plan (1960); and ix. the Doxiadis Associates spatial plan (1976).

[3]   These were the decrees: 1003/1971 'On Active Urban Planning' and 1262/1972 'On Regulatory Plans'.

[4]   These were Law No. 947/1979 and Law No. 341B/2.4.1980.

[5]   In essence, from 1832 to 1985, land was practically free of land-use regulations and the construction industry operated on it virtually with no restrictions. A similar regime was the norm for building, as myriads of changing legal provisions provided loopholes according to market demands.

[6]   The key law in this respect was Law No. 1337/1983.

[7]   Sarigiannis, G. (2010, October 11) Τα ρυθμιστικά σχέδια Αθηνών και οι μεταβολές των πλαισίων τους (Regulatory plans for Athens and the transformation of their frameworks). Retrieved from: http://www.greekarchitects.gr/gr/αρχιτεκτονικες-ματιες/τα-ρυθμιστικά-σχέδια-αθηνών-και-οι-μεταβολές-των-πλαισίων-τους-id346

[8]   Law No. 1515/1985, 'On the Athens regulatory plan'.

[9]   General Urban Plans specialise in the organisation and development of space within cities; Urban Control Zones specialise in the constraint of residential zones and space regulation around and in close proximity to cities. In contrast to existing historical plans, the economic feasibility of this particular one (and future plans to follow for other cities) was already consolidated in the adopted legislation (Law No. 947/79 and Law No. 1337/1983).

[10]   Totsikas, P. (1996) Αθήνα και ανατολική Αττική: Πραγματικότητες και προοπτικές (Athens and east Attica: Realities and perspectives). In Technical Chamber of Greece (ed.), Ένα όραμα για την Αθήνα: η συνέχεια, ο καταστατικός χάρτης, Συνέδριο του ΤΕΕ (A vision for Athens: the follow up, the Charter, TCG Conference) (pp. 120–127). Athens: Technical Chamber of Greece.

[11]   Tolerance of illegal building constituted an established practice of the state as it substituted for the lack of a comprehensive housing policy and allowed the development of a 'clientelist' relationship with the electoral body. Maloutas, T. (2003) La vivienda autopromovida: soluciones de post-guerra en Atenas (The self-promoted housing solutions in post-war Athens). Ciudad y Territorio, Tome XXXV, No. 136–137, pp. 335–345.

[12]   Typical in this sense were the program of economic stabilisation (1991–1993), the program of economic convergence (1993–1998) and the program of economic stability (2000–2004).

[13]   Mantouvalou, M., & Balla, E. (2004) Μεταλλαγές στο σύστημα γης και οικοδομής και διακυβεύματα του σχεδιασμού στην Ελλάδα σήμερα (Changes in real estate and building and the planning challenges in Greece). In Πόλη και χώρος από τον 20ο στον 21ο αιώνα (City and urban space from the twentieth to the twenty-first century), honorary volume for Emeritus professor A. Aravantinos (pp. 313–330). Athens: NTUA, University of Thessaly, The Greek Association of Urban and Regional Planners.

[14]   Gospodini, A. (2007) Χωρικές πολιτικές για τον σχεδιασμό, την ανταγωνιστικότητα και την βιώσιμη ανάπτυξη των ελληνικών πόλεων (Policies for spatial planning, competitiveness and sustainable development of Greek cities). Aeihoros, Vol. 6 (1), pp.100–145.

[15]   Law No. 2730/1999.

[16]   In that sense, it is not strange that most of the infrastructure projects were financed

from funds coming from outside Greece, mainly from the second and third Community Support Framework.

[17] Founded in 1998. The original name was 'Company for the Development of the Greek National Tourism Organisation's Property'.

[18] Public Properties Company (2012) Assets List. Retrieved from: http://www.etasa.gr/versions/eng/page.aspx?itemID=SPG183

[19] Portaliou, E. (2007) Αστικός ανασχεδιασμός στην Αθήνα και την ευρύτερη περιφέρεια της Αττικής (Urban redesign for Athens and the Attica prefecture). Retrieved from: http://www.monumenta.org/article.php?IssueID=2&lang=gr&CategoryID=3&ArticleID=75

[20] Law No. 3389/2005 on Public and Private Partnerships promotes unprecedented forms of synergy between public authorities and private enterprises concerning the construction, financing, and management of public infrastructure and services.

[21] It is important to mention that contracts following Public and Private Partnerships can be characterised by their potential lack of transparency, since there is no provision for parliamentary control. PPPs thus become the means for deeper and more aggressive privatisation of public infrastructure and services.

[22] New gigantic building projects were constructed overnight on green-field and brown-field sites. The Olympic Village, a new residential area that accommodated the 18,000 athletes and their families, and the Main Press Centre, a building covering a floor area of 52,000sqm, are just two specific examples. New infrastructure projects, such as the new international airport, port extensions, the metro and tram systems, the ring road and new highways, and the suburban railway (to name a few), were given priority and were constructed with a specific timeframe in mind. Large- and small-scale urban interventions transformed the image of the city. The unification of the archaeological spaces transformed the historical core into one of the largest open-air museums and produced high-quality urban spaces. Athens was made into a proper European metropolis and found its way into the global cities network; an object of pride to its residents, of awe to its visitors and of envy to its competitors.

[23] The mall covers a rentable surface of 58,500sqm above ground and offers 90,000sqm below ground in auxiliary and parking space.

[24] This project consists of 83,000sqm above ground and 66,500sqm below ground.

[25] Ellinikon International Airport was Athens' international airport for sixty years up until 2001. During the Olympics it accommodated several sporting events in brand-new, purpose-made buildings that included: two baseball fields, a Canoe–Kayak Slalom centre and two separate indoor courts. The 2005 competition was intended to turn the whole of the former airport into a metropolitan park, by keeping the newly built sports infrastructure. The competition was organised by the Greek Ministry of Environment, the International Union of Architects and the Organisation for the Planning and Environmental Protection of Athens.

[26] Law No. 3894/2010, Chapter II, 'Special Conditions', article 7, paragraph 1.

[27] These particular deviations are approved by presidential decree and concern as per Law No. 3894/2010, Chapter II, 'Special Conditions', article 7, paragraph 2. It states: a. Distances between buildings and plot boundaries, as well as distances between buildings and other facilities; b. Floor-to-area ratio; c. Volume-to-area ratio; d. Building

coverage; e. Permissible heights. It is important to mention that, in all of the above, no particular thresholds are set. Deviations are related to each investment proposal and are accepted, or rejected, according to national interest. In addition, for investments located in areas outside approved urban plans or outside building boundaries of settlements of less than 2,000 residents, or settlements built before 1923 (a date that marks the mass arrival of refugees due to the Greek–Turkish exchange of populations), a mere presidential decree is required. This follows a proposal by the Ministry of Environment, Energy and Climate Change and the issuance of opinion by one of directorates, the Central Urban Planning and Dispute Council (founded in 2011). As per Law No. 3894/2010, Chapter II, 'Special Conditions', article 7, paragraph 3.
In addition, and contrary to existing laws in effect, Law No. 3894/2010 also allows the exclusive allocation of use over the foreshore, the backshore, the adjacent or adjoining coastal space, or even the seabed. As per Law No. 3894/2010, Chapter II, 'Special Conditions', article 8.

[28] Ibid. 26, article 9.
[29] It should be noted that elements favourable to the investor also include the compulsory expropriation of properties or the establishment of rights on real estate in order to serve the investment. As per Law No. 3894/2010, Chapter II, 'Special Conditions', article 10, paragraph 1. The expropriation may even take place prior to the tender. A presidential decree is not required in this case and its pronouncement is ratified by the joint decision by the ministries of Finance, of Culture and Tourism, of Environment, Energy and Climate Change and of Infrastructure, Transport and Networks, acting in favour of the public interest. Expropriations are deemed to be of 'urgent and major significance. For their declaration, a simple general plan/diagram on the horizontal plan shall suffice, its scale thereof not exceeding 1:2000, depicting the area to be expropriated'. As per Law No. 3894/2010, Chapter II, 'Special Conditions', article 10, paragraph 7. It is important to mention that the law states that, in order to ensure the construction, expansion, modernisation or service of the investments, expropriations can include wider zones than just the required area necessary for the realisation of the projects described. For that, again, a presidential decree is not required, just a joint decision of the above ministries. As per Law No. 3894/2010, Chapter II, 'Special Conditions', article 10, paragraph 9.
[30] Law No. 3894/2010, Chapter VIII, article 24.
[31] The Special Integrated Development Plans become the means to: a. Delineate the areas that will accommodate the investment; b. Specify and approve, 'without prejudice' of existing plans and laws already in effect regulating spatial development and organisation of the areas in question; c. Enforce special conditions and restrictions to the areas surrounding the strategic investments, in favour of the latter; d. Define the environmental and building conditions for each individual investment.
[32] It is important to highlight the fact that not only do they 'prevail over any contrary or different regulation' described in the existing local plans (General Urban Plans, Urban Control Zones, city plans, urban studies, land-use plans), but they are given the power to initiate presidential decrees to amend the latter, as well.
[33] Ibid. 13, p. 314.

[34] Chatzimichalis, K. (2011, December 19) Το δημόσιο έλλειμμα σχεδιασμού για την πόλη (The absence of planning for the city). Η εποχή *online newspaper*. Retrieved from: http://www.epohi.gr/portal/politiki/10856

[35] Ibid. 34.

[36] 'Sole practitioner' is defined here as permanent collaborations between individuals, or practices with a limited number of employees. In recent published data (Technical Chamber of Greece, 2009), self-employed sole practitioners comprise 63% of the overall practising registered architects, while 17% work in firms. A large proportion of the rest are employed in the public sector and a minimal percentage in large practices. As for the nature and size of firms, a similar survey of the Engineers' Pension Fund (ETAA-TSMEDE) has shown that 5,000 out of the 6,500 active firms engaged in engineering (including architecture) employ up to three engineers (Aggelis et al., 2011).

[37] Access of sole practitioners and small offices to public works is nowadays constantly diminishing. One reason for this is the gradual dominance of the design-and-build system, which is argued either to disregard quality architecture or to confront architecture as a 'necessary evil', and compel architects to comply with the desires of the construction company. See: Aggelis et al. (2011) Μικρά Αρχιτεκτονικά Γραφεία: Η σημασία τους σήμερα (Small architectural practices: their importance today). In Network of Small Architectural Practices (ed.), Μικρά αρχιτεκτονικά γραφεία: κοινωνικός ρόλος και επαγγελματική πρακτική (*Small architectural practices: social role and professional practice*) (pp. 7–16). Athens: Network of Small Architectural Practices.
Another reason is the lack of national competitions which, in the past, were the means for meritocratic project assignment of public works.

[38] Oliaros Blog, 'About'. Retrieved from: http://www.oliarosblog.com/?lang=en&p=about

[39] Hellenic Parliament (2008) The Constitution of Greece. Retrieved from: http://www.hellenicparliament.gr/UserFiles/f3c70a23-7696-49db-9148-f24dce6a27c8/001-156%20aggliko.pdf

[40] The growing importance of humanities in the traditional architectural curriculum has strengthened the social role of the architect, on the one hand, and has broadened its role in academia on the other, by opening up new fields of questioning. Apart from the need of new academics for the new knowledge domains, the diversification of the curriculum has contributed in the birth of a new professional identity, that of the architect–educator. This refers to practising architects with close relations to, or within, academia, who combine theory and practice in new innovative directions. In order to serve this professional identity, architecture curricula needed, and still needs, to cultivate architecture further as a body of knowledge, through theory, history, critique and independent thinking.

[41] Kotionis, Z. (2002) Η εκπαίδευση ως επινόηση του επαγγέλματος του αρχιτέκτονα (Education as an invention of the profession of the architect). In Simaioforidis, G. (ed.), Αρχιτεκτονική Εκπαίδευση και Επαγγελματική Πρακτική (*Architectural Education and Professional Practice*) pp. 98–104. Athens: SADAS-PEA and Untimely books.

[42] These different urban studies were compiled independently by: a. the Ministry of Environment Spatial Planning and Public Works; b. the Municipality of Piraeus; and c. the Piraeus Traders Association.

Bibliography

Aggelis, G., Koutsoumpos, L., Kosma, A., & Champaloglou, M. (2011) Μικρά Αρχιτεκτονικά Γραφεία: Η σημασία τους σήμερα (Small architectural practices: their importance today). In Network of Small Architectural Practices (ed.), Μικρά αρχιτεκτονικά γραφεία: κοινωνικός ρόλος και επαγγελματική πρακτική (*Small architectural practices: social role and professional practice*) Athens: Network of Small Architectural Practices, pp. 7–16.

Chatzimichalis, K. (2011, December 19) Το δημόσιο έλλειμμα σχεδιασμού για την πόλη (The absence of planning for the city). Η εποχή *online newspaper*. Retrieved from: http://www.epohi.gr/portal/politiki/10856

Gospodini, A. (2007) Χωρικές πολιτικές για τον σχεδιασμό, την ανταγωνιστικότητα και την βιώσιμη ανάπτυξη των ελληνικών πόλεων (Policies for spatial planning, competitiveness and sustainable development of Greek cities). *Aeihoros*, Vol. 6 (1), pp. 100–145.

Hellenic Parliament (2008) The Constitution of Greece. Retrieved from: http://www.hellenicparliament.gr/UserFiles/f3c70a23-7696-49db-9148-f24dce6a27c8/001-156%20aggliko.pdf

Kotionis, Z. (2002) Η εκπαίδευση ως επινόηση του επαγγέλματος του αρχιτέκτονα (Education as an invention of the profession of the architect). In Simaioforidis, G. (ed.), Αρχιτεκτονική Εκπαίδευση και Επαγγελματική Πρακτική (Architectural Education and Professional Practice, Athens: SADAS-PEA and Untimely books, pp. 98–104.

Maloutas, T. (2003) La vivienda autopromovida: soluciones de post-guerra en Atenas (The self-promoted housing solutions in post-war Athens). *Ciudad y Territorio*, Tome XXXV, No. 136–137, pp. 335–345.

Mantouvalou, M., & Balla, E. (2004) Μεταλλαγές στο σύστημα γης και οικοδομής και διακυβεύματα του σχεδιασμού στην Ελλάδα σήμερα (Changes in real estate and building and the planning challenges in Greece). In Πόλη και χώρος από τον 20ο στον 21ο αιώνα (*City and urban space from 20th to 21st century*), honorary volume for Emeritus professor A. Aravantinos, Athens: NTUA, University of Thessaly, The Greek Association of Urban and Regional Planners, pp. 313–330.

Portaliou, E. (2007) Αστικός ανασχεδιασμός στην Αθήνα και την ευρύτερη περιφέρεια της Αττικής (Urban redesign for Athens and the Attica prefecture). Retrieved from: http://www.monumenta.org/article.php?IssueID=2&lang=gr&CategoryID=3&ArticleID=75

Public Properties Company (2012) Assets List. Retrieved from: http://www.etasa.gr/versions/eng/page.aspx?itemID=SPG183

Sarigiannis, G. (2010, October 11) Τα ρυθμιστικά σχέδια Αθηνών και οι μεταβολές των πλαισίων τους (Regulatory plans for Athens and the transformation of their frameworks). Retrieved from: http://www.greekarchitects.gr/gr/αρχιτεκτονικες-ματιες/τα-ρυθμιστικά-σχέδια-αθηνών-και-οι-μεταβολές-των-πλαισίων-τους-id346

Totsikas, P. (1996) Αθήνα και ανατολική Αττική: Πραγματικότητες και προοπτικές (Athens and east Attica: Realities and perspectives). In Technical Chamber of Greece (ed.), Ένα όραμα για την Αθήνα: η συνέχεια, ο καταστατικός χάρτης, Συνέδριο του ΤΕΕ (*A vision for Athens: the follow up, the Charter, TCG Conference*), Athens: Technical Chamber of Greece, pp. 120–127.

BIOGRAPHIES

Dr Nikos Belavilas, Assistant Professor, School of Architecture NTUA, architect TCG, is a practising architect, registered in Greece. He studied architecture at the Technical University of Athens (1985) and completed a PhD thesis at the same university (1991). He has won prizes in Greek and European urban design competitions. His academic work includes numerous research programs, books and articles on issues that relate to industrial heritage, the rehabilitation of historical urban centres and the environment. He has served as president of the board of TICCIH Greece (2004–2009) and ICOMOS scientific evaluator for the UNESCO World Heritage List (2007, 2009, 2011).

Dr Graham Cairns BA. B(Arch). MA. PhD. IE. RIBA.

Dr Graham Cairns, UK, 1971; author and academic. He has taught at Universities in Spain, the UK, Mexico, South Africa and the United States and has worked in architectural studios in London and Hong Kong. In the 1990s he ran a performing arts company, Hybrid Artworks, with a specialism in video installation and performance writing. He has presented papers at numerous international conferences and has published articles on architecture, film, advertising and interiors.

He is the author and editor of five books: *The Architect Behind the Camera*, Abada Editores, Madrid, 2007; *Deciphering Advertising, Art and Architecture*, Libri, Publishing, Oxfordshire, 2010; *The Architecture of the Screen – Essays in Cinematographic Space*, Intellect Books, London, 2013; *Reinventing Architecture and Interiors – the past the present and the future*, Libri, Publishing, Oxfordshire, 2013, and this current publication. He is currently conducting research on his latest project at Columbia University, New York and is editor of the scholarly journal Architecture_MPS (ARCHITECTURE_MEDIA_POLITICS_SOCIETY).

Dr des. Mary Dellenbaugh graduated in 2006 with a BSc with honours in Forest Science from the University of New Hampshire. Funded in part by a two-year German Academic Exchange Service (DAAD) scholarship, she relocated in 2007 to Germany to pursue her master of arts in landscape architecture at the Hochschule Anhalt in Bernburg. In November 2013, she successfully defended her dissertation in geography at the Humboldt-Universität zu Berlin, and currently specialises in post-socialist urban dynamics, European real estate markets and the relationship between space, place and power.

Professor Sat Ghosh is currently Senior Professor at the School of Mechanical and Building Sciences, VIT University, India. He is also a member of the School of Earth and Environment, University of Leeds, UK. Previously, he has worked at the University of Cambridge on Environmental Fluid Mechanics. He teaches and researches on the generic theme of 'Energy in the Built Environment'. His papers have been published by the Royal Society of Great Britain and other leading scientific journals across the world. CNN International and the BBC also covered stories on his research. His team at VIT has worked on numerous innovative applications such as the development of rain simulators for rain-starved districts of India and adjustable agricultural sprays to minimise spray drift. He was recognised with the prestigious Atmospheric Science Letters Editor's Award by the Royal Meteorological Society of Great Britain in 2012.

Jefa Greenaway is an architect, speaker and emerging academic. Jefa is a descendant of the Wailwan/Kamilaroi peoples of north-west New South Wales and is also of German descent. Jefa graduated with a Bachelor of Architecture [Hons] (2000) and Bachelor of Planning & Design (1996) from the University of Melbourne and an Associate Diploma of Applied Science (1994) from Box Hill TAFE. He is a director of Greenaway Architects, a design-driven practice undertaking residential, commercial and cultural projects. In addition, he is a co-founder of Indigenous Architecture Victoria, a not-for-profit organisation providing support and advice regarding all aspects of architecture related to Aboriginal people in Victoria. His work has been exhibited, published and awarded in numerous forums. He continues to lecture, tutor and lead design studios at the University of Melbourne and seeks to raise awareness of the value of Indigenous culture to the profession of architecture.

Professor Dr Ing. Andrea Haase is registered as an architect and urban planner in the FRG and UK. She is the Director of the Dessau Institute of Architecture and Facility Management (DAF), Anhalt University, Dessau, Germany. Previously she taught at the Technical University in Aachen, Germany, where she was a member of the working group Land Use, Built Form and the Environment in the international and multi-disciplinary research project URBINNO. Her PhD was titled 'The Influence of

Innovations on Spaces and Functions – the Case of the Agglomeration of Duisburg'. She combines the three fields of research, teaching and consultancy and focuses on both international and regional aspects of urban and landscape transformation. In Dessau, in 2006, she founded the office WERTESTRUKTUREN – Office for Cross-disciplinary Working and, in 2011, moved the office to Munich, where she cooperates with Rainer Schmidt Landscape Architects and Urban Planners GmbH, Munich, Berlin.

Puay-peng Ho is Professor of Architecture and former Director of the School of Architecture at the Chinese University of Hong Kong (2007–2013). He received architectural training at the University of Edinburgh and a doctorate from the School of Oriental and African Studies, University of London. His research and publications are primarily on Chinese architectural history and Buddhist art. He also directs the Centre for Architectural Heritage Research (CAHR) in academic and research work – including conservation and consultancy services for historic buildings in various districts of Hong Kong.

Professor Dr (Architect SAFA) Helka-Liisa Hentilä is Dean of Education at the Faculty of Technology, Head of the Department of Architecture and Professor in Urban Design and Planning at the Department of Architecture, University of Oulu. She is in charge of teaching urban-planning courses with a focus on sustainable, strategic urban and rural planning. Her previous research has focused on sustainable land use for northern settlements and she has acted as a leader of several cross-disciplinary research projects. She has extensive experience of teaching architecture and urban planning in different schools of architecture, including the Royal Institute of Technology in Stockholm and the University of Art and Design in Helsinki. She is also a registered architect and planner with a solid experience of architectural and urban planning practices. She is an author of 15 prize-winning national and international architecture competition entries, mainly in the field of urban design and planning.

Georgios Karatzas, PhD Candidate, school of architecture NTUA, architect TCG ARIAS, is a practising architect, registered in Greece and the United Kingdom. He studied architecture at the University of Dundee and the Glasgow School of Art (2004). He has completed postgraduate programs in architectural conservation at the Edinburgh College of Art (2005) and in town and regional planning at the Technical University of Athens (2009). He is currently completing a PhD thesis at the Technical University of Athens. His research focuses on issues that relate to conservation and built heritage management with particular emphasis on identity, ideology, history and nation building.

Professor Des Laubscher is a Past President of the International Federation of Interior Architects/Designers, a federation representing the interests of over 100,000 designers in 43 countries worldwide. He is also a fellow of Design for the World, a multi-disciplinary organisation concerned with humanitarian aspects of design based in Barcelona, Spain. In 2001 he was appointed a Visiting Professor of Design at Nottingham Trent University because of his achievements in promoting socially responsible design on an international level. He has presented papers related to design issues in many countries around the world, including Korea, Japan, Australia, Bali, China, Spain, Denmark, England, Brazil, Mexico and the USA, to mention a few. He has also been a juror for many design competitions internationally and is a Director of the Greenside Design Center, College of Design, South Africa.

Ingrid Leujes has an MA in Visual Studies and a postgraduate diploma in Higher Education. She is a co-founder and Director of the Greenside Design Center. She has structured the course and lectured in both the interior- and graphic-design programmes at the Design Center. She freelances as a designer in both fields. She has a broad range of interests including New Media Art, Psychology, Phenomenology and, more recently, Social Sustainability. Her main interest, however, is Education, in which she has been involved for thirty-five years. She has presented papers and facilitated workshops, pertaining mostly to design education and South African design, both locally and abroad. Her latest paper, presented in Brisbane and published in *The International Journal of the Inclusive Museum*, was awarded best paper published in that journal for 2010. The title was 'New Media Interactivity in the Museum – Democratization or Dumbing Down?'

Dr Jeffrey Logsdon is a scholar and practitioner in landscape architecture and landscape theory. He is a Loeb Fellow (1996) at the Harvard University Graduate School of Design and a former Head of Writtle School of Design, Chelmsford, England. Dr Logsdon has developed, led and accredited (by Landscape Institute) professional graduate landscape architecture programmes and taught landscape architecture in the United States, France, the United Kingdom, and Germany. In landscape-architecture practice his primary work specialises in applied landscape theory, systems, urban design, protected landscape, landscape ecology and collaboration in the collective disciplines of art, architecture, and landscape. Dr Logsdon's current work and research in landscape theory embraces the realm of form making, perception and dynamics in landscape and music, and systems thinking in socio-cultural and biophysical frameworks. His thesis and work in progress embrace the pedagogy of landscape-architecture theory applied to expanding landscape meaning, progressing landscape theory, thinking in terms of functional aesthetics, and phasing and abstracting form in the design process as part of the concept of intimate theory.

Dr Robert G. MacDonald, RIBA, PFRSA, is Reader in Architecture at Liverpool John Moores University and Emeritus President of Liverpool Architectural Society.

Dr Janet McGaw is an award-winning architect and a senior lecturer in architectural design at the University of Melbourne, where she completed her PhD by Creative Works in 2008. Since then, her work has been published in a range of international journals including: the *Journal of Architectural Education*, the *Journal of Architecture*, *Emotion, Space and Society* and *Architectural Theory Review*. Her current work includes a linkage project with Reconciliation Victoria, the Victorian Traditional Owners Land Justice Group and Melbourne City Council, funded by the Australian Research Council, which is investigating Indigenous Placemaking in Melbourne. She has developed a new interdisciplinary subject in the Melbourne School of Design that teaches creative research methods to students of architecture, landscape architecture and urban design. As the faculty nominee on the University-wide Indigenous Strategy Development Group, she is a strong advocate for inclusion of indigenous ways of knowing in the University curriculum.

Yelena McLane, Ph.D. is a practicing museum and exhibition designer and an adjunct lecturer in the Florida State University Department of Interior Design. Her research focuses on the design of educational spaces, space syntax theory, and the function of architecture in fostering free movement, literal and figural accessibility, and serendipitous encounters, leading to more transformative learning experiences. She holds a Doctorate in Art Education and a Master's degree in Interior Design from the Florida State University, and a Specialist degree in Russian Philology from the Moscow Lomonosov State University, Russia.

Siddhartha Mukherjee is a graduate student at TU Delft, the Netherlands. He is studying Fluid Mechanics and has been awarded the 'TU Delft Climate Research Institute excellence scholarship'. He did his BTech in Mechanical Engineering at VIT University, India. His main field of interest is atmospheric physics, chaos and turbulence in fluid motion, and its application to various fields including architectural design and scientific modelling. He aspires to contribute actively in these areas of research and to strike a communion between science and art in education. He is an avid reader who loves to travel and is also a professional photographer whose works have been exhibited in various public forums.

Joel Olivares Ruiz studied architecture and psychology in Xalapa, Veracruz. As an architect he worked on over 20 building projects with Enrique Murillo in his early career before moving to Italy where he studied Industrial Design with Oscar Cogoj at the International University of Art in Venice. Subsequently, he studied a master's in Industrial Design at the Polytechnic University of Milan under the constructivist painter Nino di Salvatori, the Concrete Art artist Bruno Munari and the Italian theorist Attilia Marcolli. There he developed his interest in visual perception. Upon returning to Mexico, he taught architectural design, architectural theory and aesthetics in the Department of Fine Arts at the Universidad Veracruzana. It was there that he developed the Iconographic Method as a way of teaching creativity. In 1988 he participated in the foundation of the Gestalt University of Design where he still works today, conducting research into creativity, design methodology and phenomenology. His doctoral thesis, *The Graphic Language of Architecture*, was completed at the Polytechnic University of Madrid, Spain.

Shreyas Panambur is a graduate student at Texas A&M, USA. He is studying Industrial Engineering and is interested in studying Supply Chains, Operation Research and Optimization. He did his BTech in Mechanical Engineering at VIT University, India. He wants to involve himself with real-time industrial problem solving at multiple scales. He loves to travel and is a professional photographer whose works have been publicly exhibited. He is also a trained classical Indian musician and plays the Tabla drums.

Manuel Shvartzberg studied at the Bartlett School of Architecture, University College London. He has worked for, among others, OMA/Rem Koolhaas and was project architect for David Chipperfield Architects in London, where he led a number of international arts/cultural projects. In 2008 he co-founded the award-winning experimental practice Hunter & Gatherer, with which he has lectured and made projects for various institutions on questions of art, architecture and critical theory. Since 2011 he has been teaching in Los Angeles, California, at CalArts, Woodbury University and University of Southern California. He is currently based in New York City where he is completing the PhD in Architecture program at Columbia University.

Dr Jillian Walliss teaches landscape architecture at the University of Melbourne. She has an expertise in design studio pedagogy and has played a major role in developing the new Master of Landscape Architecture program at the Melbourne School of Design. She has taught previously at the University of Tasmania, the University of Adelaide and Victoria University of Wellington (New Zealand). In 2009 she completed her PhD at the Australian National University. This work focused on the post-colonial transformation of national parks and national museums in Australia and New Zealand and has been published in prominent international journals including *Space and Culture*, *Environment and History* and *Museum and Society* and the edited book *The Right to Landscape: Contesting Landscape and Human Rights*. Her current research explores how civic space is conceived in an increasingly global design practice.

Lisa Kinch Waxman, PhD, FIDEC, IIDA, ASID, LEED-AP IC+C, is a professor in the Interior Design department at Florida State University. She has a BS in Interior Design from Florida State University, an MS in Interior Design from Oregon State University and a PhD in Art Education from Florida State University. Her current research includes the design of third places and spaces that foster community, as well as housing for people with special needs. She is a NCIDQ certificate holder and a licensed interior designer in Florida. She was the 2011–2012 president of the Interior Design Educators Council (IDEC). She teaches research methods, computer-aided design, environment and behaviour, sustainability and graduate studio.